Managing Editor's Note

Beginning with the proofreading of this issue, I am taking over the managing editor's duties. Robert Valine will remain as publisher and editor in chief. This means that I will be supervising the play selection, the copy editing, and layout. Robert will worry about distribution, finances, and me.

Hereafter we want to print a little more material about some of our scripts, especially those that seem technically innovative. Thus, after Adele Edling Shank's *SUNSET/SUNRISE* you'll find an interview which we requested Adele to grant her husbant Ted, the play's first director, about the hyperrealistic style which she evolved in order to write this play.

Our proudest news is that West Coast Plays has been awarded a grant of $4850 from the National Endowment for the Arts. This will buy enough caulking to keep our brave vessel afloat on the inflated seas for some issues to come.

—Rick Foster

Contents

The Playwrights

ADELE EDLING SHANK (*SUNSET/SUNRISE*)

Her plays and translations have been produced in Los Angeles, Sacramento, San Francisco, and New York as well as at the University of California, Davis, where she received her M.A. in playwriting. Her translation with Everard d'Harnoncourt of Arrabal's *The Architect and the Emperor of Assyria* is published by Grove Press and has been produced by A.C.T. and directed by Tom O'Horgan at La Mama in New York. Her articles on theatre have been published by *The Drama Review* and several European journals. Her recent plays include *Fox & Co.*, a contemporary version of Ben Jonson's *Volpone.* She lives in Davis and San Francisco.

TED PEZZULO (*Skaters*)

Ted Pezzulo began his theater training as an actor at the Yale University School of Drama and Catholic University Department of Speech and Drama. It was while acting on Broadway in *Rosencrantz and Guildenstern Are Dead* that Mr. Pezzulo wrote his first play, *A Song for the First of May.* He received the New American Playwright Award in 1971 for *Where Did Mr. Foster Go?* and *Toccata.* His next play, *The Wooing of Lady Sunday,* was published in *Best Short Plays 1974* and was later published together with *April Fish* in the acting edition by Dramatists Play Service.

Mr. Pezzulo is one of the founding members of the Joseph Jefferson Theater Company's Playwrights Unit, where *Skaters* was developed and first produced in 1977.

MADELINE PUCCIONI (*Two O'Clock Feeding*)

She lives in Rodeo, California, with her husband and four-year-old daughter, Allison. She grew up in Salinas, California, moving to the Bay Area in 1964. She holds B.A. and M.A. degrees from San Francisco State University. Her first play, *Laundramat,* was performed at Berkeley Stage Co. and at the Julian Theatre. She has taught playwriting and California history and is currently working on a play about mothers and daughters.

ALBERT INNAURATO (*Earth Worms*)

Albert Innaurato was born in 1948 of first-generation Italian-American parents. He received an M.F.A. degree from the Yale School of Drama in 1974. His plays include *Gemini, The Transfiguration of Benno Blimpie, Earth Worms, Ulysses in Traction, Urlicht, Lytton Strachey Lucubrates de Rerum Sexualis,* and *Aggy. Gemini* is currently the longest-running straight play on Broadway, where it has been at the Little Theatre since May 1977. *The Transfiguration of Benno Blimpie* was performed off-Broadway and ran in Los Angeles and Philadelphia, as well as in London. *Earth Worms* has been presented off-off-Broadway, and ran at the Berkeley Stage in 1978. *Ulysses in Traction* was given its New York première at the Circle Repertory Company. Mr. Innaurato has won two Obies, for *Benno Blimpie* and *Gemini,* and a Drama Desk Citation.

AVAILABLE

West Coast Plays 2 (Spring 1978)

Robert Gordon's *And*
Michael McClure's *Goethe: Ein Fragment*
Louis Phillips' *The Last of the Marx Brothers' Wri*
John Robinson's *Wolves*

West Coast Plays 3 (Fall 1978)

Robert Eisele's *Animals Are Passing from Our Liv*
Nicholas Kazan's *Safe House*
J. Paul Porter's *St. George*
Susan Rivers' *Maud Gonne Says No to the Poet*
William Whitehead's *And If That Mockingbird Don't Sing*

Order from:
West Coast Plays
P.O. Box 7206
Berkeley, CA 94707

$4.95 each (add 6% sales tax in California)

SUNSET/SUNRISE:
A Hyperreal Comedy

Adele Edling Shank

Produced by the Dramatic Art Department, University of California, Davis, in February 1979. Directed by Theodore Shank.

CHRISTINA	Rachel LePell
SARAH	Terri Hensley
JOSH	Eli Simon
DIANE	Pamela Downs
JAMES	Kevin McKeon
LOUISE	Mary Seward-McKeon
ANNE	Jude Lemons
CHARLES	Robert Kriley
LINNEA	Jean Conway
GEM	Susan Murphy
DANNY	Blair Tatton
GIDEON	Joe Sutton
COLLEEN	Kelley McLaughlin
TRIPLE A MAN	Rik Myslewski

Photos by Stan Shank.

CHARACTERS

LOUISE: Wife of James, mother of Anne and Josh. A forty-seven-year-old housewife.

JAMES: Husband of Louise, father of Anne and Josh, brother of Gem. A forty-eight-year-old lawyer.

JOSH: Son of Louise and James, brother of Anne, boyfriend of Christina. A twenty-two-year-old unemployed ex-student with no vocation.

ANNE: Daughter of Louise and James, sister of Josh. An eighteen-year-old student.

GEM: Sister of James, bride of Danny. A forty-eight-year-old businesswoman.

DANNY: Husband of Gem. A thirty-two-year-old unemployed teacher.

GIDEON: Son of Gem by her first marriage, housemate of Colleen and father of her baby. A thirty-two-year-old professional organizer.

COLLEEN: Housemate of Gideon and mother of his baby. A twenty-six-year-old secretary.

DIANE: Neighbor of James and Louise, ex-wife of Charles, mother of Christina. A forty-two-year-old professional woman.

CHARLES: Ex-husband of Diane, father of Christina, escort of Linnea. A fifty-two-year-old doctor.

CHRISTINA: Daughter of Diane and Charles. A twenty-year-old student.

LINNEA: Charles's date. A twenty-five-year-old heiress.

SARAH: Friend of Christina. A nineteen-year-old student.

TRIPLE A MAN: A middle-aged mechanic.

SETTING

The play is set in the back yard of a suburban California home. The curtain line is the back property line and the audience sees the landscaped back yard and the back of the house. There are fences right and left extending from the curtain line out of sight past the house on both sides. Forced perspective should not be used. There is a gate in the left fence near the house. There is a car parked in a driveway to the right of the house. An electrical cable runs from the car to a patio outlet. There are areas of concrete and wood patio and shrubbery. There is a swimming pool with a diving board. With minor rewriting the script can be staged without the pool, with it offstage, or without it being functional, but one can be made on any stage that has a trapped floor.

The house, like other things on the stage, should be realistic, made of real building materials, with functional glass windows, a roof, etc. Three pairs of sliding glass doors lead from the patio into the house; one to the master bedroom (right), another to the family room (center), and a third to the kitchen (left). Whatever parts of the rooms inside can be seen should be furnished appropriately.

Downstage left is a functional barbecue with a picnic table and benches near it. There are several chaise-longues and chairs around the pool. Upstage center there is a TV monitor on a rolling cart. A video camera and a microphone are mounted on top of the monitor and plugged into an electrical outlet. Upstage left against the outside kitchen wall is a well-stocked bar and two bar stools. There is a kitchen window above the bar. Upstage right is a ping-pong table. There are benches built in front of planters along both fences.

The house has been the home of Louise and James and their two children for about ten years.

TIME

Next summer.

SUNSET/SUNRISE:
A Hyperreal Comedy
Adele Edling Shank

ACT ONE

At curtain CHRISTINA *and her friend* SARAH *are lying motionless on chaise-longues near the swimming pool. They are sunbathing. The young women are pretty and healthy and look very good in their bikinis. Inside the kitchen we see* LOUISE *cutting parsley to add to a rice pilaff casserole.* JAMES *is sitting in the family room reading a newspaper. We hear neighborhood ambiance sounds—a lawnmower, a dog barking, a bird singing. It is hot. For two minutes there is no movement at all, then* SARAH *changes suntanning positions.* CHRISTINA *is almost asleep; her always present book lies open beside her. She raises her head and after a pause calls to her boyfriend* JOSH *who is out of sight inside his car.*

CHRISTINA: Josh?
JOSH: Yeah?
CHRISTINA: When's your aunt coming over?
JOSH: I don't know. Later. (*Silence.*) Why?

CHRISTINA *does not reply, puts her head down and closes her eyes.* JAMES *laughs and says something which we do not hear to* LOUISE. *She replies. A telephone rings in* DIANE*'s house next door (left). We hear* DIANE*'s very indistinct voice talking on the phone. After a long pause* DIANE *calls to her daughter from the other side of the left fence.*

DIANE: Christina!
CHRISTINA: Yes.
DIANE: Telephone.
CHRISTINA: Who is it?
DIANE: Your father.
CHRISTINA: I'll call him later.
JOSH: (*His head appears inside the car. He watches* CHRISTINA *and* SARAH.) Hey!

CHRISTINA *looks up, gets up and crosses right to the car.* JOSH *rolls down the window, leans out and kisses her.* DIANE *calls from the other side of the left fence.*

DIANE: He says never mind, he'll see you later.

JAMES *comes out of the kitchen wearing swimming trunks and carrying a glass. He watches* CHRISTINA *and his son* JOSH *kissing, then crosses to* SARAH *and sits down beside her.* CHRISTINA *says something to* JOSH *and we hear him say no. He tickles her and half pulls her through the window. She laughs and escapes.* CHRISTINA *returns to her chaise-longue and lies down.* JOSH *rolls up the window and disappears. A radio starts playing inside the car.*

JAMES: How about it, girls, would you like a drink?
SARAH: Yes, please.

CHRISTINA *nods. She is reading.*

JAMES: (*Calls in the direction of the kitchen.*) Louise?
LOUISE: Yes?
JAMES: The girls'll have drinks. What'll it be, ladies, gin and tonic?
SARAH: Umhum.
CHRISTINA: Fine.
JAMES: Gin and tonics.
LOUISE: All right. (*We hear the refrigerator opening, ice cubes rattling as she fills an ice bucket.*)
JAMES: (*Runs his finger along a line on* SARAH*'s back. When she looks up at him he smiles.*) Strap mark.

LOUISE *comes out carrying a tray.* JAMES *gets up and goes to her. He watches as she makes two drinks at the portable bar.* CHRISTINA *speaks in an undertone to* SARAH.

CHRISTINA: Cut it out OK!
SARAH: Me! What did I do? (CHRISTINA *turns her back to* SARAH *and resumes reading.*) Christina? (*Getting no response she shrugs and lies down.*)
JAMES: (*Brings* SARAH *and* CHRISTINA *their drinks.*) Here we are, ladies.
SARAH: Thanks.
JAMES: Welcome.

CHRISTINA *comes forward and takes her drink.* JAMES *sits down next to* SARAH. CHRISTINA *gives* SARAH *a disgusted look and crosses to* LOUISE *who is looking at the pile of charcoal briquettes.*

JAMES: Not getting too red are you?
CHRISTINA: (*To* LOUISE.) Can I help?
SARAH: Gosh, I sure hope not.

LOUISE: Oh, no, dear. I don't really think so. Thanks anyway. I don't know whether to light it now or wait. (*Looks without emotion at* JAMES *who is testing the temperature of* SARAH'*s skin.*)

JAMES: Does that hurt?

LOUISE: I think I'll light it now. (*Squirts charcoal lighter fluid on the pile of briquettes and lights it. The briquettes will have to be presoaked with fluid in order to get them ready in the time necessary.*)

CHRISTINA: Hey, Sarah. Ping-pong?

SARAH: OK.

JAMES: I'll play the winner.

SARAH: That'll be me. (CHRISTINA *says something we don't hear to* SARAH, *who reacts defensively.*) I didn't start it!

JAMES: (*Sits staring into his drink.* SARAH *and* CHRISTINA *make normal ping-pong-playing sounds and comments throughout. He lies back balancing his drink on his paunch.*) I am not looking forward to this afternoon.

LOUISE: It'll be all right. But I wish Gem and Danny would get here. I've got to talk to her.

JAMES: It's not going to work, Louise. (LOUISE *looks at him without comment and turns to go into the kitchen. He holds up his empty glass.*) Louise?

LOUISE: (*Comes and takes the glass and makes him another drink.*) Have you talked to Josh yet?

JAMES: (*Sighs, then speaks facetiously.*) No. Is he "in"?

LOUISE: (*Looks at the car.*) Of course he's in. When you talk to him try to use a little tact. Don't push him. If he wants to make a change, fine, if not, that's fine too.

JAMES: You talk to him.

LOUISE: I will if you want me to. (*She brings him his drink.*)

JAMES: No. No, I'd better. (LOUISE *goes into the kitchen.*)

SARAH: (*Puts down her ping-pong paddle.*) It's too hot.

CHRISTINA: Cards?

SARAH: Sure.

The girls go into the kitchen and ask LOUISE where the cards are. JAMES *crosses to the car, taking his drink with him. He knocks on the car window.* JOSH *appears and rolls down the window.*

JAMES: Hey, Josh. How's it going.

JOSH: (*Rubbing an automobile coil with a rag.*) Hiya, Dad. I think I got the carburetor cleaned yesterday and I'm working on this . . . uh . . . this thing now. That should do it.

JAMES: You want me to call Triple A?

JOSH: No need. I'll get her going.

JAMES: (*Ill at ease, as if he were talking with a stranger.*) Say look, Josh, I wonder if I could talk to you a minute.

JOSH: (*Shuts off the radio and leans out the window.*) Sure thing, Dad.

JAMES: Your mother and I have given this situation our attention and . . .

JOSH: Do you have to talk like a lawyer?

JAMES: Sorry. (*Chuckles.*) Well, yes, I guess I do. (*Pause.*) Well, we've had an idea that I think just might appeal to you.

JOSH *looks at him, saying nothing.* CHRISTINA *and* SARAH *come out of the family room. They play cards quietly at the picnic table.*

JAMES: Let me say first, we understand that you wanted to leave home, that in fact you have left home, and we respect your decision. Of course, if you ever change your mind, you're always welcome. But we're not pressing you about it. The thing is, your mother worries that you may not be as comfortable out here as you should be.

JOSH: I'm fine, Dad. I've got everything I need.

JAMES: Well good, good. But we thought maybe there was a better solution. This car is . . . well, it's no great beauty.

JOSH: I like this car.

JAMES: We thought we would buy you a house trailer and move it in here. Your mother says you'd have more room and it would certainly look a lot nicer.

JOSH: You don't understand, Dad. I want to keep it simple. A mobile home, well . . . it just isn't for me. But look, if you want me to get the car out of here just say so.

JAMES: No, no, certainly not. We want you to stay.

JOSH: If you don't like the looks of it, I could move it out to the street.

JAMES: No! No, you stay right where you are. It was just an idea. Your mother wanted me to talk to you about it, that's all.

JOSH: Right. (*There is an awkward pause.*) Was there something else, Dad?

JAMES: (*Starts to say something else then changes his mind.*) No. No, I guess not.

JOSH: OK. I'll see you later then.

JAMES: You're coming to the party, aren't you?

JOSH: Sure thing. Wouldn't miss it. (*He rolls up the car window and disappears.* JAMES *turns toward the pool with a sigh.*)

LOUISE: (*Coming out of the kitchen carrying a plate. She crosses to* JAMES.) A little something to get you through till dinner.

JAMES: Ummm. What are these?

LOUISE: *Bouchées parmentier au fromage.*

JAMES: Huh?

LOUISE: Potato cheese sticks.

JAMES: Well, they're great, whatever you call them.

LOUISE: Thank Julia. (*Turns and starts to go toward the kitchen.*)

JAMES: Hey! (LOUISE *turns back. He takes her hand and squeezes it.*) Thanks.

LOUISE: (*Smiles down at him.*) You're welcome. How'd it go with Josh?

JAMES: No dice. He's happy where he is.

LOUISE: (*Sighs, goes to the barbecue and checks the progress of the charcoal.*) You know the house next to the Reeds? (JAMES *grunts, his mouth full.*) Marian was telling me someone tried to burn it down last night.

JAMES: What!

LOUISE: Apparently the people were away and someone squirted charcoal lighter fluid on the outside walls and tried to light it. Scorched the siding.

JAMES: I'll be damned.

LOUISE: They think it was just kids.

LOUISE *goes into the kitchen and we hear the sounds of food preparation. A red light comes on on the video camera on top of the* TV *monitor and* ANNE*'s face appears on the monitor. Her head completely fills the screen. She is* 18, *pretty in a simple fresh way, and very vulnerable.*

ANNE: Mom?

JAMES: (*Shouts in the direction of the microphone.*) She's in the kitchen, Annie. (*Calls.*) Louise!

LOUISE: (*Appears at the kitchen door.*) Yes?

JAMES: Annie. (*He lies back and eats.*)

LOUISE: (*Comes out of the kitchen and goes to the monitor.*) Yes, dear?

ANNE: I've finished *Northanger Abbey.*

LOUISE: Good.

ANNE: Put another book on OK?

LOUISE: You did finish it?

ANNE: Yessss. Can I have some history now please?

LOUISE: Oh, all right. I'll be right there.

The red light goes out and the monitor goes dark. A car is heard stopping in front of the house and doors open and close. LOUISE *goes into the family room and disappears into the front of the house.* JAMES *turns on a radio which plays an actual radio station broadcasting in the present time. He finds some soft music.* CHRISTINA*'s tolerance for such shlock is low and she puts down her cards and crosses to the radio.*

CHRISTINA: Do you mind?

She changes the station to rock music and takes the radio back to the picnic table. CHARLES *and* LINNEA *enter from the driveway right.* CHARLES *is a good-natured, very nice pipe-smoking* 52*-year-old doctor. He lived next door with his wife and daughter until he and* DIANE *were divorced three years ago. He has little in common with his fashionably dressed date,* LINNEA, *but her beauty and wealth are good for his ego. They do not know each other well.*

As CHARLES *passes the car he thumps the top of it with his hand.*

CHARLES: Hiya, Josh. (JOSH*'s head appears.*)

JAMES: (*Gets up to greet them.*) Charlie! Glad you could make it. (SARAH *shuts off the radio.*)

CHRISTINA: Hi, Daddy.

CHARLES: Hi, sweetie. Linnea, this not-so-little beauty is, believe it or not, my daughter Christina.

CHRISTINA: Sorry, Daddy, it isn't all that hard to believe.

CHARLES: She thinks it's her job to keep my ego deflated. She's very good at her job. (LINNEA *laughs.*) And this is my old friend, Jimmy.

JAMES: It's a pleasure to meet you.

LINNEA: Thank you. What a wonderful afternoon, isn't it?

JAMES: It's getting better and better. Oh, yes. This is Christina's friend Sarah.

JOSH *gets out of his car, waves when introduced, then opens the hood and leans over the engine. He installs the coil.*

JAMES: And that's my son Josh.

LINNEA: Hello, Josh.

JAMES: How about it, Linnea, would you like a drink?

LINNEA: Thanks, I'd love one. The water looks tempting.

JAMES: Why not have a swim? You can change in the guest room.

LINNEA: Ummm. Sounds lovely.

SARAH: I'll show you. It's through here.

SARAH *and* LINNEA *go into the family room.* LOUISE *comes into the family room from the front of the house and we partially hear* SARAH *introducing* LINNEA *and* LOUISE. CHRISTINA *goes to her lounge, rearranges her towel, lies down and reads.* JOSH *gets behind the wheel of his car.* JAMES *looks helplessly at the bar.*

JAMES: I'll just call Louise. What will you have, Charlie?
CHARLES: Don't bother Louise. I'll do it.

JOSH *tries to start the car. The engine turns over but the car doesn't start. He gets out and looks under the hood again.*

JAMES: She's a nice-looking woman, Charlie.
CHARLES: Yes.
JAMES: Known her long?
CHARLES: Not really. A few weeks. Refill?
JAMES: (*Hands him the glass.*) Thanks. Vodka tonic. Is she . . . uh . . . as young as she looks?
CHARLES: (*Chuckles.*) Probably. I haven't asked. (JAMES *laughs.*)
LOUISE: (*Comes out from the family room and greets* CHARLES *with a hug and a kiss.*) Charles, how nice to see you.
CHARLES: It's good to be here. How are things with you?
LOUISE: Oh, I'm just fine, Charles. As always. Look, I hope it's all right—Diane's coming over.
CHARLES: I thought she might be here. No problem. It will be good to see her.

JOSH *again tries to start the car and again fails.*

LOUISE: And Gem and her new husband. And Gideon and his girl friend and their baby.

JOSH *looks again under the hood, comparing his repair manual with the engine.*

CHARLES: I thought Gem and Gideon weren't speaking.
JAMES: They aren't. But Louise thinks they ought to be. Why I don't know. They've got nothing to say to each other.
LOUISE: The baby makes a difference. I don't even know what her name is.
CHARLES: Who?
LOUISE: This woman Gideon's been living with. (*She goes into the kitchen.*)
JAMES: Damn nonsense. Should have left them all alone. (*Perplexed.*) You know, she's a surprisingly stubborn woman some-

times. (*They take their drinks to the picnic table and sit down. A pause.* JAMES *stares into his drink.*) We miss you around here, Charlie. Things aren't the same.

CHARLES: (*Also staring into his drink.*) That's good to hear. I . . . uh . . . in a whollllle lot of ways I wish I still lived next door. (JOSH *again tries to start the car and again fails.* CHARLES *is staring at the left fence, then shakes off the sentimentality with an effort.*) But I try not to think about that. It isn't healthy to live in the past—a definite sign of encroaching old age.

JAMES: I don't think so. The Jacobs kid was telling me how much fun it used to be when his aunt lived in Sacramento. He lives in the past and he's only eight. (*They laugh together. Pause.*)

CHARLES: (*Gently.*) How's Anne?

JAMES: (*Sighs.*) Oh, the same.

JOSH: (*He has locked the car and closed the hood, and now crosses toward* JAMES.) OK if I use the phone?

JAMES: Of course you can use the god damned telephone! (JOSH *goes into the family room.*) Why does he talk like that? For Christ sake, he's lived here all his life!

CHARLES: I'm a dermatologist, not a psychiatrist.

JAMES: (*His words are a protracted sigh.*) Yeah . . . well . . . oh, hell. You know, sometimes . . .

Silence. A car is heard stopping in front of the house and car doors opening and closing. LINNEA, *now wearing a bikini and beach jacket, enters with* SARAH *from the family room.*

JAMES: Well! That was worth waiting for.

SARAH *crosses to the diving board where she sits and blows up a pool toy.* LINNEA *crosses to* CHARLES *at the bar.*

CHARLES: Very nice. Wine?

LINNEA: Please. (*He hands her a glass of white wine. She raises her glass in a toast.*) Thank you. To sunny summer afternoons.

CHARLES: And beautiful women to decorate them.

JAMES *has joined* SARAH *at the diving board. They take turns blowing up the pool toy and talk quietly.* LOUISE *has come out of the kitchen.*

CHARLES: Can I fix you a drink, Louise?

LOUISE: Not now, thanks, Charles.

JOSH: (*Comes out of the family room and crosses toward* CHRISTINA *as the doorbell rings. He stops.*) You want me to get it, Mom?

LOUISE: Thanks, Josh, I'll go.

As LOUISE *goes to the front door* JOSH *crosses to* CHRISTINA *and pounces on her.* LINNEA *and* CHARLES *seem to have nothing to say to each other.* LINNEA *turns away from him and wanders idly over to the center chairs and sits down.* CHARLES *joins her.* JOSH *is tickling* CHRISTINA.

JAMES: Take it easy there, Josh.
JOSH: Aw, Dad, I'm having fun.

GEM, DANNY, *and* LOUISE *enter from the family room.* GEM *is a stylish, handsome, funny and ironic, 47-year-old, highly competent and successful businesswoman whose personal life has been less successful.* DANNY, 32, *is her fourth husband. He is stable and thoroughly nice, and although a little shy he relates well to everyone he meets. A modern man, he has no stereotypical ideas of what man-woman relationships and duties should be. When they enter they are continuing an ongoing conversation.* GEM *colors the words first with romance, then with boredom.*

GEM: Yes, it was wonderful. Sun and sand and blue sky! But after a week of that it becomes sun and sand and blue sky.
JAMES: (*Comes forward and hugs* GEM, *who kisses him on the cheek.*) Welcome home, Gem.
GEM: Thank you, Jimmy. We're glad to be back.
JAMES: (*Shaking hands with* DANNY.) And you must be my new brother-in-law.
JOSH: Hi, Aunt Gem. (GEM *waves at him.*)
DANNY: (*Laughs nervously.*) Yes, yes, I am. I'm glad to meet you. I suppose I must . . . uh, be a surprise to all of you.
JAMES: No, no. Nothing Gem does surprises us anymore. But she keeps trying. Well, let's see. Linnea, this is my sister Gem and her new husband, uh . . .
DANNY: Danny.
JAMES: Danny. This is my son Josh, Sarah, Christina, and Charles. (*They exchange appropriate greetings.*)
GEM: (*Moves to* CHARLES.) Charles, how good to see you.
CHARLES: You look terrific, Gem.
GEM: Honeymoons agree with me. Danny, come and say hello to a very nice man.
DANNY: (*Shakes hands with* CHARLES.) How do you do.
GEM: Charles is a doctor. He specializes in pimples.

GEM laughs. DANNY is embarrassed. JAMES crosses to LINNEA and they talk out-of-focus and upstage. SARAH spreads a towel out near the edge of the pool and lies down. She puts one hand in the water and moves it back and forth slowly. CHRISTINA continues reading and JOSH sits silently near her. LOUISE brings GEM a scotch on the rocks.

GEM: Thank you, Louise.
LOUISE: What would you like, Danny?
DANNY: Let me help. (*He and* LOUISE *cross to the bar.*)
GEM: (*Looking regretfully after* DANNY.) I did it again.
CHARLES: What?
GEM: Embarrassed him. I don't mean to, damn it.
CHARLES: (*Laughs gently.*) Don't worry. He'll get used to you.
GEM: Thanks! Excuse me, Charles, I should say hello to the kids.

GEM crosses to JOSH and CHRISTINA. CHARLES crosses to LINNEA and JAMES center and joins their out-of-focus conversation. When a conversation is indicated as being out-of-focus the audience should be able to hear a realistic murmur of sound without being able actually to hear what is being said. Stage whispering or other "cheating" should not be used, but the out-of-focus conversations should be controlled by volume and positioning. The content should be improvised in rehearsal but precisely set before performance.

GEM: How goes it, Josh?

We do not hear JOSH's response because the focus shifts to DIANE who enters from the kitchen. DIANE is an energetic 42, happy in her professional life, and if she feels a want in her personal life she disguises it well. Her mind moves faster than her tongue and she speaks in spurts. As DIANE enters she sees CHARLES, her ex-husband, who has his back to her. She stops, calls to LOUISE.

DIANE: I put the salad in the refrigerator.
LOUISE: Thanks, Diane.
DIANE: Hello, Charles.
CHARLES: Well, hello there.
GEM: Diane!

DIANE and GEM hug and exclaim greetings. DANNY is introduced to DIANE and they have an out-of-focus conversation. The focus moves to LINNEA as CHARLES turns back to her.

LINNEA: Oh, do you think so? I think stability is the proper foundation for a life of tedium. (JAMES *looks at her blankly. She laughs.*)

That's my personal motto this week. I'm big on personal mottos. Gives me something to do while I sit in waiting rooms.

JAMES: What do you do, Linnea?

LINNEA: That's what I do. I sit in waiting rooms. I spend my days waiting for and talking to lawyers, tax attorneys, accountants, bankers, real estate people, investment brokers, etcetera after boring etcetera. After a hard day's conferences I go home and I talk to the housekeeper, the gardener, the decorator, etcetera after frustrating etcetera. Being rich is a damn boring way to earn a living.

JAMES: (*Skeptically.*) Oh, I don't know about that. How about a refill, Linnea? (JOSH *crosses left and is about to join* JAMES *and* LINNEA *just as they stand up. They pause briefly to acknowledge* JOSH*'s existence.*) You've met my son Josh?

LINNEA: Oh yes, sure. Hi.

JAMES: Charles? How about it?

CHARLES: You know, James, I think it's your turn.

JAMES: Oh. (*He is startled, then looks around for help. He takes his glass and* LINNEA*'s to the group at the bar.*)

CHARLES: You are witnessing an historic event, Linnea. No one has ever before seen James make a drink.

JAMES: How about some refills, Diane?

DIANE: (*Hands him her glass, knowing he meant she should make them, and plays with him.*) Why thank you, Jimmy, I'd love one.

JAMES: (*He now has three glasses and looks helpless. He turns hopefully to* GEM.) Gem?

GEM: (*She also plays with him and hands him her glass.*) Yes, please.

JAMES: (*Looks with amazement at his load; tries to bluff through his ineptitude which embarrasses him a little.*) Well, let's see. Two white wine, one vodka tonic, and what are you drinking, Gem?

GEM: Scotch. You put the ice cubes in the glass, then pour from the scotch bottle into the glass.

JAMES: Yes, yes. Very funny. (*With great relief he discovers that the ice bucket is empty.*) By gosh, we seem to be out of ice. Hey, Josh, how about filling it up, eh?

JOSH: Sure, Dad.

Everyone laughs at JAMES*'s narrow escape.* JOSH *takes the ice bucket and starts into the kitchen, standing aside to let* LOUISE *out before he goes in.* LOUISE *is carrying a tray of shish-kebab skewers. She crosses to* JAMES.

LOUISE: Excuse me, I need you.

JAMES: You do?
LOUISE: Diane. Explain to Gem before they get here.

LOUISE and JAMES move downstage to the barbecue. DIANE pulls GEM center where they sit. LINNEA and DANNY talk quietly and out-of-focus near the ping-pong table. CHARLES crosses to CHRISTINA and sits down beside her. She looks up, then continues to read.

The following conversations take place simultaneously with the focus shifting from one in-focus conversation to another as the others continue out-of-focus.

GEM: What's going on?
DIANE: Patch up time. Family reunion.
GEM: What are you talking about?
DIANE: Gideon.
GEM: He's coming here!
DIANE: Yes, he and his girl friend.
GEM: Does he know I'll be here?
DIANE: Yes.
GEM: Does he know I'm married again?
DIANE: Yes.

JAMES: What is it?
LOUISE: It's Danny.
JAMES: He seems like a nice enough kid to me . . .
LOUISE: Yes. I like him. And I wondered, perhaps Anne should meet him.
JAMES: Of course she should . . .

GEM: They have a baby!
DIANE: Yes.

JOSH has come out of the kitchen with the full ice bucket.

JAMES: Josh! Fix those drinks for me will you?
JOSH: Sure.
JAMES: Make mine a vodka martini, with a twist.
JOSH: OK.

DIANE: Nobody's met this girl friend. Louise has kept in touch with Gideon. But he's resentful.

LOUISE: They've got a lot in common.

GEM: I know. They aren't married.
DIANE: No.

CHARLES *has been sitting silently by* CHRISTINA *and looking at* DIANE. *Now he speaks as the other conversations continue out-of-focus.*

CHARLES: It looks like she's getting along fine without me.
CHRISTINA: Oh, Daddy, really! What am I supposed to say?
CHARLES: Nothing. I didn't mean to put you on the spot. (CHRISTINA *returns to her book.*)

JAMES: Don't worry about it. I'll just introduce them and we'll see what happens. (JAMES *calls to* DANNY *and moves upstage to meet him. He puts his arm around his shoulder.*) Danny! Danny, there's someone else we'd like you to meet. I don't know if Gem has told you about our Annie. She's a special girl. (*Their conversation goes out-of-focus.*)

CHARLES: Does she, uh, have much of a social life?
CHRISTINE: That's none of your business you know.
CHARLES: I was just wondering. I want her to be happy.
CHRISTINA: She's happy, or she seems to be.
CHARLES: What do you mean by that?
CHRISTINA: Well, you know, it's hard to tell. I think she needs you. Well, not exactly you. A man. I keep telling her she needs a good screw.
CHARLES: Christina!
CHRISTINA: Well, she lives like a monk, for heaven's sake. It isn't natural. Look at you, you're getting along, you're making it, right?
CHARLES: I am not going to discuss my sex life with my daughter!
CHRISTINA: Oh, Daddy, you're so old-fashioned.

CHARLES *crosses to* LINNEA *and they talk quietly upstage.* CHRISTINA *returns to her book.* DANNY *nods his head in agreement and understanding and* JAMES *crosses to the microphone on top of the* TV *monitor. He calls into the microphone. Everyone stops talking and watches.*

JAMES: Annie! (*The light comes on on the video camera and* ANNE*'s face appears on the monitor.*)
ANNE: Yes, Daddy?
JAMES: We've got a surprise for you, honey. Some old friends are here, and a new friend too.

ANNE: Has Aunt Gem come?

GEM: (*Moves to within range of the camera.*) Yes, dear, I'm here. Hello there, Anne, how are you?

ANNE: OK. Mom said you just came back from St. Thomas.

GEM: Yes.

ANNE: Could you understand the language? That combination of seventeenth-century English and Danish must be weird.

GEM: Yes, dear, it's quite puzzling.

ANNE: They have a handicrafts cooperative which controls . . .

JAMES: (*Interrupts.*) Annie, there's someone else here who'd like to meet you. (*He draws* DANNY *toward the video camera.*) This is Danny. He's, well, actually he's your new uncle.

DANNY: (*Sits down in front of the monitor.*) Hello, Anne.

ANNE: You're Aunt Gem's new husband?

DANNY: Yes. Very new.

JAMES: (*Gestures to* GEM *to move away with him and speaks heartily.*) Well, we'll leave you two to get acquainted. (DANNY *looks panic-stricken but has no choice so turns to talk to* ANNE.) Louise! Let's get that food on, I'm starved. And we need some drinks here, how about it, Josh? Charles, how about you?

CHARLES: Why not. Linnea?

CHARLES *crosses to the bar and he and* JOSH *make drinks and pass them around.* LOUISE *puts the grill on the barbecue and prepares to cook.* JOSH *brings her a glass of white wine. Everyone makes appropriate conversation out-of-focus.* JAMES *explains to* GEM *that* LOUISE *thinks* DANNY *can help* ANNE *because of their common intellectual interests. Meanwhile* DIANE *offers to help* LOUISE, *goes into the kitchen and returns with plates, napkins, and forks which she sets on the picnic table.* CHARLES *brings* LINNEA *her drink and they talk.* DANNY *feels awkward and uncomfortable but tries to talk with* ANNE *in a natural and friendly way.*

ANNE: Do you feel insecure?

DANNY: How do you mean?

ANNE: Being her fourth husband, doesn't that result in serious feelings of insecurity?

DANNY: (*Laughing.*) No. I don't intend to let there be a number five.

ANNE: I see.

LOUISE: (*Comes forward trying to help their conversation along.*) Anne, dear, Danny is a teacher. He teaches German.

ANNE: *Wirklich? Ich studiere Deutsch. Es ist eines meiner Lieblingsfächer.*

DANNY: *Ihre Aussprache ist sehr gut.* (LOUISE *returns to the barbecue and puts the shish-kebab skewers on the grill to cook.* DANNY is still *ill at ease.*)

ANNE: Do you teach in a regular school, with lots of students?

DANNY: Actually I don't teach at all. I want to, but there aren't any jobs. I guess I'll have to recycle myself.

ANNE: Walter Cronkite says that the unemployment rate . . . (*Insert current statistic or news relating to unemployment.*)

DANNY *makes an appropriate response.* JOSH *crosses near the monitor and waves to* ANNE *as he passes in range of the camera. She waves back.* JOSH *unlocks the door and gets into the car, shuts the door and disappears.*

ANNE: I've never been to school.

DANNY: You father said you study at home.

ANNE: Yes. I've never had a real teacher. Just video people.

DANNY: Why don't you come out, it's a lovely evening.

ANNE: I can't do that. I'm allergic.

DANNY: Your father said . . .

ANNE: I can't come out without the special equipment and that's so awkward it isn't worth it.

DANNY *and* ANNE*'s conversation goes out-of-focus and there are long pauses between* DANNY*'s questions about her studies and* ANNE*'s questions about what a regular school is like.* JAMES *has joined* LINNEA *and* CHARLES. GEM *is sitting with* DIANE *at the picnic table.* LOUISE *goes into the kitchen.*

GEM: My egghead seems to be cracking her shell.

DIANE: Yes.

GEM: Diane? Is Louise all right?

DIANE: Ask your brother.

GEM: Oh, no. Not again.

DIANE: Afraid so.

GEM: You'd think she'd be used to it.

DIANE: She's not.

SARAH: (*Sits up suddenly.*) I'm hot.

GEM: She should have divorced him long ago.

DIANE: Maybe. She didn't want to.

GEM: What can we do?

DIANE: Nothing. When she finds out who the new woman is she'll be able to cope.

GEM: Personally I'd rather not know.

SARAH *is climbing onto the diving board.* JOSH'*s head appears inside the car. He stops* SARAH *before she dives into the pool.*

JOSH: Hey, Sarah!

SARAH: Yeah?

JOSH: Come here.

SARAH *gets off the diving board, crosses to the car.* CHARLES *crosses to the barbecue leaving* JAMES *and* LINNEA *alone.*

JAMES: Charlie, see if you can hurry up that food. I'm hungry.

LINNEA: Me too.

SARAH: (*She has her head almost inside the car.*) But how does it work?

We cannot hear JOSH'*s answer.* DANNY *gives a short nervous laugh at something* ANNE *has said.* LOUISE *comes out of the kitchen and crosses to the barbecue.*

GEM: How about you? How are you?

DIANE: Never better.

LOUISE: (*To* CHARLES.) Are they doing OK?

CHARLES: Looks like it.

GEM: God, I envy you.

DIANE: Don't do that. You look wonderful.

GEM: My bikini days are over. (*She indicates* SARAH *or* CHRISTINA.) I can't risk comparisons with that.

DIANE: Danny's very nice.

GEM: Yup. He's a real sweetie. You know, when Danny first asked me to marry him at first I thought it was preposterous, but then I just thought, oh, what the hell, why not! I'm crawling up to fifty and I deserve a treat.

DIANE: (*Laughs.*) Why not.

GEM: It can't last I'm afraid. But I hope we can make it through to the new year. I do so *hate* spending Christmas alone.

JOSH *gets out of the car, locks the door, and he and* SARAH *go into the kitchen to get beers.*

LOUISE: If they don't come soon we'll have to eat without them.

CHARLES: Maybe Gideon changed his mind?

LOUISE: Gideon has never changed his mind in his life. Or been late either for that matter.

DIANE: Danny looks uncomfortable. Let's go and rescue him.

GEM: I'm glad you said that!

GEM *and* DIANE *join* DANNY *at the* TV *monitor.* LOUISE *and* CHARLES *start toward the kitchen.* JAMES *and* LINNEA *move center toward the barbecue.*

LOUISE: Charles, I want to talk to you about triglycerides. I read this article yesterday and if I understand correctly they may be one of the major causes of heart attacks. But tell me, do the same foods contain both . . . (*Their conversation becomes indistinct as they go into the kitchen. An occasional word is heard—"animal fat, polyunsaturated, unusually high," etc.*)

DIANE: Hello, Anne. Do you feel like finishing the game we started yesterday?

ANNE: Yes, let's.

DIANE: Louise? Where's the chessboard?

LOUISE: On the tray in the family room. (DIANE *goes into the family room.*)

GEM: (*She feels ill at ease with* ANNE *and, as usual, speaks brashly as a result.*) Well Anne, what do you think of my latest?

DANNY: (*Gently.*) Gem.

DIANE *returns with a chessboard on a* TV *tray which she sets in front of the* TV *monitor. There is a game in progress on the board. It is set at move* 18 *of Game* III *illustrative of Philidor's defense (Staunton's* Chess Praxis, *pp.* 76–77*).* DIANE *sits down opposite the monitor with the chess game between herself and the monitor and they play.* ANNE *calls out her moves and* DIANE *moves the pieces on the board.* ANNE *apparently has a board in her room on which she also moves pieces. The first move (number* 19*) is scripted; subsequent moves should be called out at appropriate times.* GEM *and* DANNY *watch the game, make an occasional comment, then get up and move off together.* JAMES *and* LINNEA *sit at the picnic table.* JOSH *and* SARAH *come out of the kitchen with bottles of beer.*

JAMES: (*Joke flirting.*) Alone at last.

LINNEA: Not for long.

JOSH: (*Crosses to* JAMES *and gives his father a teasing poke.*) How's it going, Dad? (LINNEA *laughs.* JOSH *and* SARAH *go to the car and sit on the hood drinking beer and listening to the radio.*)

LINNEA: Tell me about your work. It must be exciting.

JAMES: Not really.

LINNEA: Don't you do trial work?

JAMES: Good god no! Trial lawyers either die young or become alcoholics. I did know one who managed to get by with a nervous breakdown.

LINNEA: What do you do?

JAMES: Oh, real estate mostly. (*Brightly.*) Some tax work.

LINNEA: Oh.

JAMES: It's not very interesting.

LINNEA: (*She has indeed lost interest and looks around at the other men.*) I see.

JAMES: (*Tries to recapture her attention.*) You are a very beautiful woman.

LINNEA: Yes.

ANNE: King's rook takes pawn.

JAMES: But not a modest one.

LINNEA: Modesty wastes time.

JAMES: Look, are you and Charlie, are you . . . involved?

LINNEA: Charles is the perfect escort. He takes me to a party and then leaves me alone.

JAMES: I just didn't want to . . .

LINNEA: Move in on your friend's territory? I'm no one's territory.

JAMES: Oh?

LINNEA: Interested?

JAMES: (*Backs off.*) Oh, well, sure. Of course. Uh . . . how about a refill, eh?

DIANE *calls her chess move.* CHARLES *and* LOUISE *come out from the kitchen.* LOUISE *is carrying salt and pepper.*

CHARLES: Meat for example. He eats altogether too much red meat.

JAMES: How about it, Charlie? I think we've got time for a short one.

CHARLES: (*Takes* JAMES*'s glass and fixes him a short drink.* LOUISE *turns the shish-kebab skewers on the grill.*) I'll pass.

JAMES: Linnea?

LINNEA: No, thanks. (*She crosses toward the bar, wandering aimlessly.*)

JAMES: (*Crosses to* CHARLES *at the bar.*) We lawyers have got it all over your doctors. We don't have to stay sober.

CHARLES: I don't know about that. We have very few emergencies in dermatology.

LINNEA *shows an interest in* JOSH*'s car. He shows off his living accommodations to her, the tape deck, stereo speakers, etc.* SARAH, *being ignored, leaves and joins* DIANE *and watches the chess game.*

CHARLES: Booze goes straight to the waist, Jimmy. And you're putting on a little weight aren't you?

JAMES: Huh? Me! No, no. Haven't gained five pounds in five years. I never touch potatoes you know, that's the secret.

LINNEA: Is it comfortable?

CHARLES: When's the last time you had a physical?

JOSH: What?

JAMES: Don't know. Louise keeps track of those things. (*Their conversation goes out-of-focus.*)

LINNEA: The bed.

JOSH: Oh, ah, yeah, sure. I . . . uh, you and Charlie, are you . . . I mean . . .

LINNEA: (*Amused at the duplicate conversation.*) No. We're not.

JOSH: I just didn't want to, uh . . .

LINNEA: I know. I know.

LINNEA *laughs and moves around the car.* JOSH *follows her giving a guided tour.* LOUISE *is salting the shish kebabs.* JAMES *crosses to her.*

JAMES: Louise?

LOUISE: Hum?

JAMES: Am I getting fat?

LOUISE: (*Looking only at the kebabs.*) Of course not, dear.

JAMES: You think I look OK?

LOUISE: (*Looks at him and smiles. She pats his stomach.*) You look fine.

JAMES: Maybe I should put on a shirt. (*He goes into the bedroom.*)

CHARLES: (*Brings the white wine bottle and refills* LOUISE*'s glass.*) He is, you know.

LOUISE: Thanks. What?

CHARLES: Putting on weight.

LOUISE: (*Turns back to the kebabs.*) I know.

CHARLES: I was just asking him when he last had a physical.

LOUISE: He doesn't need one. I'm very careful about what he eats, how much he sleeps, what exercise he gets.

CHARLES: He doesn't get any exercise! He doesn't even make his own drinks!

LOUISE: I know.

CHARLES *insists that* LOUISE *sit with him on the bar stools.* JAMES *comes out of the bedroom wearing a sport shirt. He looks around and crosses to* CHRISTINA. *He sits down beside her and aimlessly picks up her bottle of skin lotion. He squirts some out on her back and rubs it in.* LOUISE *watches him carefully as she listens to* CHARLES. DIANE, *waiting for* ANNE*'s next chess move, notices* LOUISE *watching* JAMES *and* CHRISTINA.

CHARLES: I want to give you some medical advice. I know you mean well, but you must realize that the way you are treating Jimmy isn't good for him. Louise?

LOUISE: Yes. Yes, I'm listening.

CHARLES: You feed him all the wrong things—too much booze, too little natural carbohydrate, too much meat, too little fiber. Protein is a good thing, but you're giving him an overdose. Louise, I know you want to keep your husband happy, but to put it bluntly, you are buttering him to death.

LOUISE: (*Stares at* JAMES, *then turns slowly to* CHARLES, *looks at him hard and speaks coldly.*) So what.

ANNE: Diane, it's your move.

CHARLES *stares at* LOUISE *open-mouthed as she gets up and addresses the entire group in a voice louder than necessary.*

LOUISE: We'll eat in a minute. Who wants beer, who wants wine? (*They raise their hands and call out their preferences.* LOUISE *keeps count of each.*) Charles, will you open the red wine?

DIANE *gets up abruptly and crosses to* LOUISE. CHARLES *pulls himself together.*

CHARLES: Yes, yes, of course.

ANNE: Hey, Diane? What happened?

DIANE: (*To* LOUISE.) It's not Christina, you know that.

LOUISE: It isn't?

DIANE: Remember? She was home with me that time when Jimmy lied about the dentist.

LOUISE: Yes, that's right. It's not Christina. I'm glad. And Linnea may be next, but she isn't now. Then who is it!

DIANE: Does it matter?

LOUISE: Yes! (*She is close to tears as she inspects the shish kebabs.*) Damn it, they're ready. Get the garlic bread!

DIANE: Yes, all right.

LOUISE: (*Goes into the kitchen.*) Get the beer, will you, Charles?

CHARLES: Yes, of course.

DIANE *and* CHARLES *exchange a concerned look.* DIANE *shrugs helplessly and she and* CHARLES *go into the kitchen.* CHRISTINA *goes to the diving board with the intention of diving into the pool.*

DANNY: I don't think it's that simple.

GEM: Perhaps not. But we always manage somehow to get at each other. We always have.

DANNY: Gem. Don't worry. It will be fine. Anyway, it doesn't really matter now, does it?

GEM: No, I suppose not.

LOUISE: (*Comes out of the kitchen with the pilaff casserole which she sets on the picnic table. She calls to* CHRISTINA *with annoyance.*) Not now, Christina. We're going to eat. Josh, bring Anne to the table, will you please? OK, everyone, dinner's ready. Just come and help yourselves.

CHARLES *and* DIANE *come out of the kitchen.* DIANE *brings out the salad,* CHARLES *the garlic bread and beer.* CHRISTINA *comes off the diving board.* JOSH *rolls the* TV *monitor to the picnic table as the others come forward to eat. A car has stopped in front of the house; doors open and close. People take plates and help themselves to pilaff and garlic bread and* DIANE *serves the salad.* LOUISE *serves the shigh kebabs from the barbecue, giving each person a small individual skewer. The sun has gone down by now, but it is still light.*

JAMES: This looks great, Lo'.

SARAH: It smells terrific. (*Others make appropriate comments about the food. The doorbell rings.*)

LOUISE: Damn, that's them. What timing! (*She gives the tongs with which she has been serving to whomever is nearest and goes into the family room.*) Just help yourselves please. (*People continue getting their food and beer or wine.*)

JAMES: Josh, how about a glass of wine?

JOSH: Sure, Dad.

CHARLES: Do I recognize your salad, Diane?

DIANE: Yes. I guess it hasn't changed much.

They laugh. When they have their food SARAH *and* CHRISTINA *take their plates and sit on the grass downstage of the picnic table.* JOSH *joins them.* LINNEA *and* JAMES *sit on the bar stools upstage of the picnic table.* CHARLES *and* DIANE *will sit at the table where they will later be joined by* JAMES *and* LOUISE. DANNY *and* GEM, *who is nervous, remain center.*

LOUISE *enters from the family room with* GIDEON *and* COLLEEN. GIDEON *is* GEM'*s only child. They have not spoken for several years, not since she married her previous husband.* GIDEON *is very conservative, a reaction against his mother's extravagant behavior, but he dresses fashionably. He tries hard to control his strong emotions. Above all else he values the continuity of his relationship with* COLLEEN, *his vivacious, fun-loving housemate.* COLLEEN *always does precisely what she wants to do.*

COLLEEN *leaves a portable baby bed in the family room.* GIDEON *carries the baby bundle very carefully.*

GIDEON: . . . we're late. The baby was napping and we never allow her naps to be disturbed.

LOUISE: Gem?

GEM *crosses to* GIDEON *and* COLLEEN, *and* LOUISE *returns to the barbecue. The others ignore the reconciliation scene, giving them privacy.* JAMES *is sitting at the bar with his back to* GIDEON *and* COLLEEN.

GEM: Hello, Gideon.

GIDEON: Mother.

GEM: The baby?

GIDEON: Yes. Your granddaughter.

GEM: A girl. (COLLEEN *takes a step forward, calling attention to her presence.*)

GIDEON: This is Colleen.

COLLEEN: (*She and* GEM *shake hands.*) I'm awfully glad to meet you.

GEM: Yes. Me too. And what is her name?

GIDEON: Oh, we haven't named her yet. We're waiting until she has a personality manifestation.

GEM: It must be awkward.

GIDEON: What?

GEM: Not having a name to call her.

GIDEON: No. It isn't.

GEM: Oh. Danny? Come and meet your stepson. (DANNY *crosses to join them.*)

GIDEON: Mother, really!

GEM: Sorry. Danny, this is Gideon and his . . . and Colleen.

DANNY: How do you do.

COLLEEN: Hello, Danny.

LOUISE: (*She has decided that since the reunion has taken place without disaster it is time for general introductions. She crosses to* GIDEON

Anne is "brought" to the table as dinner is served in the U.C. Davis production.

who comes forward. COLLEEN *stays back.*) Let's see, you know most of these people, Gideon, but it's been so long you may not recognize them. Colleen, Gideon, this is Christina, Sarah, and our Josh. You remember Diane and Charles? And this is Linnea, and of course James.

JAMES: Hum?

LOUISE: Gideon.

JAMES: (*Gets up and crosses to* GIDEON.) Oh, well, hello there, Gideon, glad you could make it.

COLLEEN: (*Sees* JAMES *for the first time. She goes to him and greets him with a hug.*) Jimmy, what a nice surprise! I didn't know you were going to be here. (*There is a surprised and embarrassed silence as everyone stares.*

LOUISE: I think they have already met.

JAMES *is stunned;* GIDEON *shows no reaction at all. A man suddenly appears near* JOSH'S *car. He is middle-aged and wears a work shirt and pants with a Triple A badge on the shirt. He is a completely competent mechanic, the only man present who can actually do anything physical. He carries a tool box.*

TRIPLE A MAN: Excuse me, folks. Did somebody here call Triple A?

JOSH: Yeah. Yeah, I did.

TRIPLE A MAN: What's the trouble?

LOUISE *laughs loudly and hollowly.* GIDEON *hands the baby to* GEM, *crosses to* COLLEEN *and* JAMES *with his hand outstretched.*

GIDEON: How are you, Uncle James?

COLLEEN: Uncle James!

JAMES: Yes. Gideon is my nephew. This is my house, my wife, my children.

COLLEEN: Oh, my gosh! I didn't know that! You mean . . .

JAMES: Colleen here works in my office building. I had no idea she was Gideon's . . . um . . . er . . . that she knew Gideon.

CHARLES: (*Tries to ease things along.*) Quite a coincidence.

LOUISE: (*Calm, smiling.*) Yes, isn't it.

TRIPLE A MAN: Life is full of surprises. (*To* JOSH.) Look, you want help or not?

JOSH: Yeah, sure. (*Crosses to the car, reaches inside and pulls the hood release.*)

LOUISE: Gideon, Colleen, come and have some food. (DIANE *hands* COLLEEN *and* GIDEON *plates of food and they move to the barbecue for shish kebabs.*)

TRIPLE A MAN: What seems to be the trouble?

JOSH: It won't start.

ANNE: Mom? Mom, what's going on?

LOUISE: Nothing, Anne. Gideon and Colleen have arrived. That's all.

SARAH: I don't understand. (CHRISTINA *shushes her.*)

TRIPLE A MAN: (*Lifts the hood.*) Battery OK?

JOSH: It should be. It's got a lifetime guarantee.

JOSH *and* TRIPLE A MAN *stick their heads under the hood.* GEM *can't decide what to do with the baby.* DANNY *takes it off her hands and handles it with complete assurance. He takes it into the bedroom and puts it on the bed.*

COLLEEN: Isn't it something. I met Jimmy in the elevator. I work in the office next to his law firm. We're always meeting in the elevator. (*Laughs, then eats. An awkward silence.*)

SARAH: Can I have the salt and pepper please?

TRIPLE A MAN: It's the coil.

JAMES: Well, Gideon, how are things going for you? Louise tells me you're doing well with that business of yours.

GIDEON: I enjoy it. It's very stimulating work.

GEM: Humph! You're an amoral bureaucrat!

DIANE: Gem!

GEM: Sorry. Sometimes my mouth is bigger than my brain.

LINNEA: (*Crosses to join* GIDEON, JAMES *and* COLLEEN.) What do you do, Gideon?

GIDEON: I organize campaigns.

LINNEA: Oh, politics.

GIDEON: No. Causes. I'm hired by various groups to organize campaigns to put over a certain course of action, a certain piece of legislation, or simply to shape public opinion.

LINNEA: It sounds fascinating.

GEM: It's unprincipled. He doesn't care who he works for as long as they pay him well.

GIDEON: (*To* COLLEEN.) My mother has very high principles. I should say high-priced principles. (*Everyone is uncomfortable but tries to ignore the friction.* GIDEON *notices that the baby is missing.*) What have you done with my baby?

DANNY: I put her down in the bedroom. She's sleeping. (GIDEON *goes into the bedroom.*)

TRIPLE A MAN: (*Comes forward wiping his hands on a cloth.*) Well, that ought to do it.

JAMES: What was the trouble?

TRIPLE A MAN: Some idiot hooked the coil up wrong. (JOSH *is humiliated.*)

CHRISTINA: I wonder which idiot that was.

TRIPLE A MAN: Want me to start it up?

JOSH: I'll do it. (*Gets into the car.*)

LOUISE: Can I offer you something to drink?

TRIPLE A MAN: Thanks very much, a beer would taste good. (LOUISE *gets up to get him a bottle of beer.* GIDEON *has taken the baby from the bedroom and put her in her carry-bed in the family room. He comes out and joins* COLLEEN. *The* TRIPLE A MAN *looks around.*) Sure is a nice place you folks have here.

LOUISE: Thank you.

TRIPLE A MAN: My wife and me, we were thinking of putting in a pool. But then we thought we'd better buy a house first. (*He laughs enthusiastically at his joke.* LOUISE *smiles as she hands him the beer. Others laugh with this visitor from outside.*) Thanks, this is real nice of you, ma'am.

LOUISE: You're welcome. (JOSH *starts the engine.* LOUISE *returns to the table.*)

TRIPLE A MAN: Sounds good. You mind if I give you a little advice, son?

JOSH: What's that?

TRIPLE A MAN: If you're gonna work on your own car you need a little training. They've got real good courses in that adult education program over at the high school. You could go nights, it wouldn't interfere with your job.

JOSH: (*Defensively.*) I've got a manual and I'm learning it as I go along.

TRIPLE A MAN: Sorry, but you know I don't think that'll do it. Doctors don't study brain surgery by correspondence course. (*He laughs enthusiastically, and then is embarrassed that others don't find it funny.*) No, I don't care what machine you open up, it's no place for amateurs. Well, so long. I'd better get going. Saturday night's always busy. (*He waves to* LOUISE *and sets down the beer bottle. He picks up his tool box.*) Thanks a lot for the beer, ma'am. Well, so long, folks, have a nice party. Take it easy, son. (*Exits past the car.* JOSH *sits on the hood and finishes his food. Conversation is not going well; most people feel ill at ease. There are long pauses and awkward silences.*)

LOUISE: More wine, James?

JAMES: Thanks.

CHARLES: Good food, Louise.

JAMES: Terrific. (*Others affirm the compliment. Silence.*) Well, Josh, you got her going.

JOSH: Yeah.

JAMES: Planning on going somewhere?

JOSH: No.

JAMES: Oh. I figured you must be thinking of taking off.

JOSH: No.

JAMES: Just want to keep the option open, heh?

LOUISE: James. (*Silence.*)

GIDEON: (*Looks at the others and chuckles superiorly.*) You know, I'm the only person here over thirty who's never been divorced.

LOUISE: You don't count, Gideon. It's easy not to get divorced if you don't get married.

DANNY: Besides, it isn't true.

GIDEON: Well, in your case it's just a matter of time. (DANNY *starts to reply but changes his mind.*)

SARAH: I don't think it's right to have a baby without being married.

CHRISTINA: Sarah!

SARAH: Well I don't.

GIDEON: Colleen and I have a commitment to each other and our child and it is based on mutual respect and trust, not on a legal document. Right, Colleen?

COLLEEN: Yeah.

SARAH: Do you have an open relationship?

CHRISTINA: Sarah!

GIDEON: Yes, certainly. We are bound to each other with ties of affection, not chains of bureaucracy. Right, Colleen?

COLLEEN: Sure.

GIDEON: Now my mother has quite a collection of legal documents. Her lawyer keeps a set of divorce papers all filled out and waiting. When she gets tired of her current husband all she has to do is call her lawyer and he fills in the blank with the name of the latest reject . . .

DANNY: (*Tries to remain good-natured, but it is an effort.*) Hey, hey! Easy there.

GEM: Gideon, you are a self-righteous little prig and a genuine bore.

CHRISTINA *puts down her plate and crosses to her refuge, her book. She lies down and reads.* JOSH *gets into his car.* LOUISE *rests her head on her hand as if she had a headache.* GIDEON *sets down his plate very precisely.*

GIDEON: I'm sorry, Aunt Louise, but it won't work. My mother never cared about me when I was a child, why would she be interested enough in her granddaughter to make peace with me now!

GEM: You're impossible! If I hadn't cared about you you never would have been born. I could have had an abortion, you know!

LOUISE: Anne, turn yourself off!

ANNE: Illegal abortions were very dangerous in those days. It's quite likely that not only . . .

LOUISE: Anne! (*The* TV *monitor goes dark.*)

GIDEON: Colleen, I'd like to leave as soon as you're finished.

COLLEEN: All right.

GIDEON: I'll wait for you inside. (*Goes into the family room. Silence.*)

JAMES: Gem, you went a little too far there.

GEM: I know. I'm sorry.

LOUISE: Does anyone want more pilaff?

CHARLES: No, thanks, Louise.

Others shake their heads or murmur "no." LOUISE *gets up and takes dishes into the kitchen.* DIANE *wheels the monitor back to its former position.* CHARLES *and* DANNY *help with the clean-up.* SARAH *is fascinated by* COLLEEN.

SARAH: I never knew anybody who had an open relationship before.

COLLEEN *smiles at her tolerantly.* GEM *gets up from the table, moves off to find her cigarettes, lights one.* GIDEON *comes to the family room door holding the baby.* COLLEEN *has finished eating.*

GIDEON: Colleen? About ready?

COLLEEN: I'll be right there.

GIDEON *goes back out of sight and* COLLEEN *pours herself another glass of wine.* DIANE, LINNEA, *and* CHARLES *take a load of dishes into the kitchen.* JOSH *calls from his car.*

JOSH: Sarah?

SARAH: Yes?

JOSH: How about a beer?

SARAH: Sure. (*Takes a bottle of beer to* JOSH *and remains outside the car talking to him.*)

COLLEEN: (*Alone with* JAMES *near the picnic table.*) I guess I sort of blew it, huh? Maybe Gideon and I should leave?

JAMES: (*Looks uneasily toward the kitchen.*) Well . . .

COLLEEN: Do you want me to go?

JAMES: No, no, of course not, but perhaps under the circumstances . . .

COLLEEN: To hell with the circumstances. I make my own rules.

JAMES: And I really admire that about you, but still, this is . . . well, a little awkward.

COLLEEN: Poor Jimmy. OK, we'll go if that's what you want. (*She refills her wine glass and sits down at the picnic table.*)

GIDEON: (*Appears at the family room door and calls.*) Colleen!

COLLEEN: Coming.

GIDEON *disappears and* COLLEEN *sips her wine. The video camera light has come on, but the monitor stays dark.* DANNY *has joined* GEM *center.*

GEM: I meant it you know. About the abortion. When I found out I was pregnant I wanted to get rid of it, but in those days it wasn't that easy. Jimmy had a friend who knew someone who could do it, but I was scared and we didn't have the money. So I had to have the baby and if you had to have a baby you had to get married. So I got married. Gideon has a right to be angry with me. I wasn't very good at mothering.

ANNE: (*Her face appears on the monitor.*) It might have been better if you'd put the baby up for adoption. Statistically . . .

GEM: (*Jumps with surprise, then anger.*) God damn it. Can't a person have a private conversation around here!

ANNE: I'm sorry.

GEM: You're not supposed to eavesdrop with that thing, you know! It isn't polite.

ANNE: All right, all right. I'm sorry. (*The light goes out on the video camera and the screen goes dark.*)

DANNY: Easy, honey. Don't take it out on Anne.

GEM: God damn it, I'm not doing anything right today.

GEM *goes to the bar and makes herself a drink. It is getting dark.* LOUISE *comes out of the kitchen with a brandy snifter. She gives it to* JAMES. CHARLES *is watching them.*

JAMES: What's this?

LOUISE: Something special. To celebrate.

JAMES: Celebrate what?

LOUISE: It's a special occasion. (*Pause. She goes to the kitchen door.*)
LINNEA: What's special?

LOUISE *has stopped outside the kitchen door and stands very still looking at* JAMES. CHARLES *stares at her. He stands as a shock of understanding runs through him.*

JAMES: Search me. Sometimes she just announces a special occasion. I never know why they're special, but it gives me an excuse to celebrate.

CHARLES: (*Moves quickly to* JAMES *and without hesitation takes the glass out of his hand.* LOUISE *goes into the kitchen.*) Haven't you had about enough, old boy?

JAMES: (*Looks at* CHARLES *with astonishment.*) Hey, what's the big idea?

CHARLES: (*Smells the drink.*) Hey, what is this stuff anyway?

JAMES: I don't know, I haven't had a chance to taste it!

CHARLES: Smells funny.

JAMES: It's probably old brandy. How about letting me have it, huh?

CHARLES: (*Smells the liquid again, then because he can't think what else to do, pretends to drop the glass, which breaks on the patio. People stare.*) Now look what I've done. Clumsy of me. Sorry, Jimmy. I'll get you a refill. (*Pours* JAMES *a drink from a brandy bottle on the bar.* GEM *and* DIANE *pick up the broken glass, whispering together.*)

LOUISE: (*Appears at the kitchen window.*) Everything all right?

CHARLES: Yes, yes, sorry, Louise. I just dropped a glass, clumsy me.

GEM: (*Sotto voce.*) Charles, what on earth is going on?

CHARLES *gestures to her to be quiet. He gives* JAMES *the new drink and* JAMES *and* LINNEA *move off to talk out-of-focus.* LINNEA*'s occasional low laugh punctuates the following conversation.* JOSH *has gotten out of the car and locked it.*

JOSH: Hey, Christina, want to play heartbeat?

CHRISTINA: Sure.

JOSH *and* SARAH *go into the family room and through to the front of the house to get part of the game.* CHRISTINA *arranges the chairs.* GEM, DIANE, *and* CHARLES *have been talking urgently in undertones.*

GEM: But that's crazy. You really can't believe this! Louise wouldn't (*Lowers her voice and laughs at the absurdity.*) poison anyone.

CHARLES: No, she wouldn't (*Lowers his voice.*) poison anyone. But she might (*Lowers voice.*) poison Jimmy. I must say, he gives her plenty of reason.

DIANE: People don't get (*Lowers voice.*) poisoned because they deserve it.

GEM: It's absolutely absurd. People don't do things like that.

DIANE: Look, what are you going to do? You can't move in and watch everything he eats and drinks!

CHARLES: I'll have to warn him.

DIANE: Terrific.

GEM: He'll never believe you.

CHARLES: I know that.

GEM: Charles, you are nuts. Absolutely bonkers. (*Starts for the kitchen.*)

CHARLES: Where are you going?

GEM: I'm going to talk to *my friend* Louise.

CHARLES: Don't let on that you suspect.

GEM: I *don't* suspect. (*Giggles. She goes into the kitchen.*)

DIANE: Charles, this doesn't make sense. What makes you think she . . . what you think?

CHARLES: It was just . . . there was something . . . we had this very strange conversation earlier which I didn't understand. And then there was this terrible sort of hard look on her face just after Colleen arrived, and then she had that same look just now when she handed Jimmy that glass. It just came into my head—my god, she's going to kill him! I couldn't just sit there and let him drink the stuff. I know it's hard to believe, but really you know she's unstable.

DIANE: Look, before you do anything stupid like telling Jimmy you'd better think this through.

CHARLES: You think I'm bonkers too. Around the bend.

DIANE: Not exactly. But don't say anything you can't take back.

CHARLES: I suppose you're right. I'm beginning to feel like a fool already.

They move off together. JOSH *and* SARAH *come out of the family room carrying a box containing the apparatus for Heartbeat.* JOSH *and* DANNY *fold up the ping-pong table to make more room.* JOSH *hooks things up to the speaker in the* TV *monitor. It is now almost dark. The lights are on inside the house.* LINNEA *stands up and moves away from* JAMES *with a laugh.*

LINNEA: Maybe. Let's just wait and see what happens.

LINNEA *joins* SARAH, CHRISTINA, JOSH, *and* DANNY *at the monitor.* LOUISE *and* GEM *come out of the kitchen,* LOUISE *carrying the special cognac bottle which she sets on the bar.* GEM *carries candles which she puts on the picnic table and on a small table near the monitor.* GEM *joins* DANNY *with an affectionate gesture.*

GIDEON *and* COLLEEN *come out from the family room without the baby.* GIDEON *walks past* GEM *without indicating having seen her and goes straight to* LOUISE.

GIDEON: Aunt Louise, I would like to apologize for the unpleasantness. You've been very kind and understanding always. I'm sorry that the emotional situation got away from me.

LOUISE: Don't worry about it, Gideon. I'm glad you've decided to stay. (*She and* GIDEON *sit on the bar stools.* COLLEEN *joins* JAMES.)

JAMES: How did you pull that off?

COLLEEN: (*Laughs and sits down beside him.*) I told him that if he left it would look like he was running away from you.

JAMES: What!

COLLEEN: Well, he jumped to the conclusion that we've been seeing each other.

JAMES: But we haven't done anything!

COLLEEN: I didn't say we had. But we have been out a couple of times.

JAMES: Yes, but he thinks . . .

COLLEEN: If he wants to make assumptions that's his problem not mine. My evenings out are part of our bargain.

JAMES: Oh boy. I don't like it. You're going to get me in trouble.

COLLEEN: You'll be all right.

JAMES: I don't get it. Does he have his evenings out too?

COLLEEN: No, but he could have.

JAMES: Amazing. I wonder if Louise would go for this open marriage business.

COLLEEN: Don't be silly. You've got things worked out just about the way you want them, haven't you.

JAMES: I'll say I have. I've got the best of everything. (*He sips his drink and sighs with contentment.*) You know, Colleen, sometimes I get this really good feeling. Like now, you know, this time of the evening, there's a special way things look. I look at my son over there, and Louise, and I lay back and digest my excellent dinner and drink my excellent brandy and I think, by God, Jimmy, you have got it made, haven't you. It's a good life, and I'm a lucky man.

JOSH: (*Turns on the video camera and speaks into the microphone.*) Annie?

ANNE: Yes?

JOSH: We're going to use your monitor for heartbeat, OK?

ANNE: Hey, Josh. That's not fair.

JOSH: Well, you're not using it.

ANNE: If you use it, I can't use it.

JOSH: If you want to come on, just signal and we'll quit and you can have it back, OK?

ANNE: Oh, I suppose so.

DANNY: I've got a better idea. Why don't you come out and join us? (*The monitor goes dark and the light goes out on the video camera.*)

JOSH: She hasn't been out since last Christmas.

DANNY: I see.

JOSH *plugs a Pong game into the monitor and puts it on automatic so that the "ball" moves back and forth in an even horizontal pattern across the screen.*

JOSH: Who's going to judge?

JAMES: Be glad to.

JOSH: Nope, sorry, Pop, your timing's off. Charlie? How about you?

CHARLES: All right.

JOSH: Mom? Will you judge with Charles?

LOUISE: Of course.

LOUISE *and* CHARLES *sit together facing* JOSH *and the monitor.* GIDEON *stays on the outskirts of the group.* CHRISTINA *holds a pile of small cards and moves around as each player takes one. The players are* CHRISTINA, JOSH, SARAH, DANNY, *and* COLLEEN. DIANE, GEM, GIDEON, *and* JAMES *are spectators.*

CHRISTINA: Do you want to play, Gideon?

GIDEON: No, thank you very much. I'll watch if I may.

CHRISTINA: Linnea?

LINNEA: It's not my kind of game.

LINNEA *crosses to the bar and pours herself a drink as the game begins. Later* JAMES *inconspicuously crosses to her, blowing out the candle on the picnic table on his way. They move off to the left bench where they stay together.*

Each player has a card with a number on it which determines the order of competition.

JOSH: OK, who's got number one?

CHRISTINA: That's me. (*She goes to the* TV *monitor. The pong ball is moving on the screen.*)

JOSH: Ready?

CHRISTINA: Sure.

JOSH: (*Hands her the chest microphone, and explains the game to those who haven't played, using* CHRISTINA *to demonstrate.*) Now you see the pong ball, right?

COLLEEN: Right.

JOSH: She puts this microphone on her heart and there we are, that's Christina's heartbeat. You hear, it's slower than the pong ball. So she has to speed it up, try to make it match the speed of the pong ball.

DANNY: That's the object of the game?

JOSH: Right. The one who matches it closest wins.

GEM: How do you do that?

JOSH: Any way you can. Go to it, Christina! (*She hands him the microphone and the heartbeat sound stops.* CHRISTINA *runs in a large circle without much speed. They cheer her on. She stops in front of the monitor ready to quit.*) That'll never do it, get going! (*He gives her a push and she does another lap amid calls of encouragement.*)

DIANE: Come on, Christina!

GEM: Go, girl!

SARAH: Do some jumping jacks! (CHRISTINA *obliges with a couple of jumping jacks and then presents herself for re-testing.* JOSH *hands her the microphone and she puts it over her heart. The beat is faster, but does not quite match the speed of the pong ball.*)

COLLEEN: Is that good or bad?

DANNY: It's better, isn't it?

SARAH: Oh, no way!

JOSH: What do the judges say? (LOUISE *holds up a "6" and* CHARLES *a "7." Applause and positive reactions.*) A six and a seven. Thirteen points.

GEM: Not bad!

JOSH: You're getting better. OK, who's got number two?

COLLEEN: I do.

JOSH: You know how to play now?

COLLEEN: Sure.

JOSH: (*Hands her the heart microphone and she puts it over her heart. We hear her fast heartbeat.*) That's very fast.

COLLEEN: High metabolism.

JOSH: Well, you have to slow it down.

SARAH: Meditate. (*Laughter.*)

COLLEEN: (*Goes to* DANNY *and speaks to* GEM.) Do you mind if I borrow your husband?

GEM: Be my guest.

COLLEEN: Would you massage my shoulders please? (DANNY *obliges as the others hum a lullaby.* GEM *jokes about being jealous.*) Ummmm. That's nice.

GEM: I don't think I like this game.

JOSH: Just let me know when you feel ready.

COLLEEN: Ummmm. Ahhhhhh. OK, I'm ready. (*She moves in slow motion to the monitor, trying not to disturb her tranquillity.*)

JOSH: And what does the machine say? (COLLEEN *puts the microphone over her heart and her heartbeat has increased. There are whoops of laughter.* COLLEEN *laughs with the others.*) It's faster!

GEM: (*Reclaims her husband.*) You've got great hands, my friend.

JOSH: Scores please. (LOUISE *and* CHARLES *both hold up "5"s.*) A five and a five. Ten points. Who's number three?

SARAH: That's me. (*She enthusiastically moves forward and holds the microphone to her chest. Her heartbeat is slower than the pong ball.*)

JOSH: You have to speed yourself up.

GEM: Hey, Charles, how about a little side bet?

CHARLES: Wouldn't be proper. I'm an official.

DANNY: Fourteen will put you in the lead. (SARAH *dives into the swimming pool and swims back and forth as the crowd cheers her on. She comes out of the pool, goes to the monitor and holds the microphone to her chest. The pong ball and her heartbeat are almost synchronized. There is loud cheering.*)

JOSH: Scores! (LOUISE *holds up a "9" and* CHARLES *a "0."*) Nine and ten. Nineteen. Almost perfect.

ANNE *has entered from the family room and stands on the patio with the lighted room behind her. She is wearing a gas mask and wet suit. She watches unobserved, then takes a tentative step toward the players.* COLLEEN, *who is the first to see* ANNE, *screams. The heartbeat sound continues.*

LOUISE: It's all right, it's only Anne.

JOSH: (*Turns on the patio and shrubbery lights.* ANNE *is frightened. Everyone is staring at her. She turns and runs back into the house.*) Annie, Annie, it's OK.

DANNY: Anne, wait! (ANNE *has disappeared.*)

Blackout. The heartbeat sound continues for several beats, then stops. House lights come up.

ACT TWO

As the house lights go out the heartbeat sound begins, but with a normal rhythm. When the stage lights come up the performers are in exactly the same positions as at the end of Act One, and the lights return to the same setting. The performers remain frozen for a beat or two, then begin to move, continuing the same action impulse they had at the end of Act One. LOUISE *starts to move toward the house after* ANNE *who has exited. She goes into the house. There is a period of astonished silence.* JOSH *turns off the Pong game and the heartbeat sound stops.*

COLLEEN: Oh, my god, she scared me to death!
GEM: Josh, for Christ's sake, is all this light necessary?

> JOSH *goes and turns off the patio lights. The stage is lit by the lights which spill from inside the house, the candle near the* TV *monitor, and the shrubbery lights along both fences.* LINNEA *and* JAMES *whisper to each other, planning how to rejoin the others inconspicuously.*

JOSH: OK, Aunt Gem?
GEM: Thanks.
CHRISTINA: Why do you suppose she ran back like that?
DIANE: Colleen's scream must have frightened her.
COLLEEN: Sorry. But she scared the hell out of me.
SARAH: She scared me too. I didn't know who it was. Why does she wear that thing?
CHARLES: She thinks she can't come out of her special room without it because she's allergic to everything.
SARAH: Is she?
CHARLES: What difference does it make? She thinks she is, so she is.
SARAH: That doesn't sound very scientific to me.
CHARLES: That's because you don't know much about science.
GIDEON: Colleen, I really think it's time we were off. It's getting late.
COLLEEN: All right. I'll just say good night to Jimmy. Where is he?
SARAH: I'm cold.

> SARAH *goes into the house to change into pants and T-shirt as* COLLEEN *looks around for* JAMES. JAMES *gives* LINNEA *a push and she indignantly exits through the gate left of the house.* JAMES *pretends to be waking up after a sleep. He stretches and yawns.*

JAMES: Ahhhh. Well, hello there. Gee, I must have dozed off.

COLLEEN: (*She has seen* LINNEA *scuttle out the gate. She laughs.*) You missed all the excitement, Jimmy. Or maybe you didn't.

JAMES: Don't know why I conked out like that, just couldn't keep my eyes open.

COLLEEN: Your daughter made a surprise appearance.

JAMES: Did she really!

GIDEON: (*Crosses to* JAMES, *his hand outstretched.*) Sorry to wake you, Uncle Jimmy. We're going to be on our way and just wanted to say good night.

COLLEEN: I think we should stay, Gideon.

GIDEON: Colleen . . .

COLLEEN: We can't leave without saying good night to Louise. We'll have to wait until she comes back.

GIDEON: Yes. Of course. All right. (*A baby cries fussily inside the house.*) Excuse me. (*Goes into the family room and picks up the baby. He changes its diaper. The group around the* TV *monitor is putting the game away, picking up empty glasses, and discussing* ANNE *out-of-focus.*)

COLLEEN: Well, well, a little hanky-panky behind the rhododendrons, eh, Jimmy?

JAMES: Shhhhhh! It's, well, she's a very forward woman. I didn't want to hurt her feelings.

COLLEEN: (*Laughs.*) Sure. I understand. I figure we have an open relationship too.

JAMES: What's that supposed to mean?

COLLEEN: You're free to mess around and so am I.

JAMES: Now wait a minute, I don't . . .

COLLEEN: (*Moves toward the others, turns back to him.*) The spice of life, eh, Jimmy?

LINNEA *comes out of the house through the family room as if she were returning from using the bathroom.* COLLEEN *looks at her and laughs, then turns to join the group.* LINNEA *stares icily at both* COLLEEN *and* JAMES *and sits by herself near the pool.* COLLEEN *and* JOSH *sit on the ground on the opposite side of the pool.* CHARLES *has gone into the house to use the bathroom.* CHRISTINA, DIANE, *and* DANNY *talk near the car.* GEM *crosses to the bar.*

JAMES: (*To* GEM.) Where's Louise?

GEM: With Anne. Drink?

JAMES: Why not.

GEM: (*Pours* JAMES *brandy and scotch for herself. They are both rather drunk.*) We seem to be the only real drinkers in this sissy crowd.

JAMES: Yup. Hummm. That reminds me of something.

GEM: What?

JAMES: Can't remember. (*He is hit by a wave of sentimentality. They move downstage.*) Little sister?

GEM: Yes?

JAMES: You happy?

GEM: Irrelevant.

JAMES: Why's 'at?

GEM: It's presumptuous to expect to be happy. It's not a birthright, you know.

JAMES: (*Surprised.*) 'S not?

GEM: Nope. And since I don't expect to be happy I am not unhappy.

JAMES: (*Puts his arm around her shoulder.*) Hey, you know what?

GEM: What?

JAMES: I think you're terrific.

GEM: You're drunk. (*They giggle.*)

JAMES: So are you. (*They find this extremely funny and share affectionate laughter. Silence.*)

GEM: (*Sighs with tiredness.*) Maybe we'd all better go home. Before it gets too late.

JAMES: Naw. Stick 'round. Party's just starting. (LOUISE *comes out from the family room.*) 'Lo, Lo'. (*Giggles.*) How's our Annie?

LOUISE: She'll be all right.

JAMES: Maybe Charlie should take a look at 'er?

LOUISE: It isn't necessary. I gave her a tranquilizer.

JAMES: Hey Lo'. Whass this stuff?

LOUISE: Do you like it?

JAMES: 'S real good stuff.

LOUISE: I thought you'd like it.

JAMES: But it's making me drunk.

LOUISE: Never mind. Enjoy yourself.

JAMES: Whateya say we send all this nice folks home an' have a little party just ourselves?

LOUISE: (*Withdraws firmly from his embrace.*) I've got to talk to Danny. (*She crosses to* DANNY. SARAH *comes out of the family room and joins* COLLEEN *and* JOSH.) Danny?

DANNY: Yes, Louise?

LOUISE: I need your help.

DANNY: What can I do? (*They move aside for an out-of-focus conversation.* CHARLES *has come out of the family room and crosses to* LINNEA.)

LINNEA: But I'm bored. Really bored.

CHARLES: What's the matter, my friends not important enough for you?

LINNEA: Those are your words, not mine.

CHARLES: You said we were boring.

LINNEA: I didn't say that! But I will. You are boring. None of you *do* anything.

CHARLES: That isn't true.

LINNEA: You earn money. That doesn't count.

CHARLES: Not with you, you never had to earn any.

LINNEA: That's not the point. I like more action in my friends, more energy. You're all quitters. You hide in your back yards with your tails between your legs. Well, you may have quit but I haven't even started.

CHARLES: I wish you luck. How about taking Christina there with you when you go? She's been bored since the day she was born.

LINNEA: And she's perfectly happy. I'm leaving. Are you taking me home or not?

CHARLES: Not. Call a taxi.

LINNEA: Goodbye, Charles. (*Crosses to* LOUISE.) May I telephone for a taxi?

LOUISE: Of course. The number's by the phone in the kitchen.

LINNEA: Thank you. (*Starts toward the kitchen.*)

SARAH: (*Runs after her.*) I'd better go too, can you drop me off?

LINNEA: Why not? (*Goes into the kitchen.*)

SARAH: (*Waves a general good night.*) Good night, everyone. Thanks a lot, it's really been a lot of fun. I'll call you, huh, Christina?

CHRISTINA: Sure. (*Being absorbed with various preoccupations no one else responds to* SARAH. CHRISTINA *joins* JOSH *and they sit in companionable silence.* GEM *crosses to* DANNY.)

SARAH: Well, good night, thanks again. (*Goes into the kitchen and waits while* LINNEA *finishes calling for a taxi. They then disappear together into the front part of the house.*

GEM: (*Takes* DANNY*'s arm.*) Hey, husband mio. Let's go home, huh?

DANNY: Sure. But it'll be a little while. Louise wants me to talk to Anne.

GEM: Ouffff. I'm tired.

DANNY: Why don't you go in and lie down? I'll come and get you as soon as I can.

GEM: OK. But hurry. I don't like lying alone.

GEM *goes into the family room and out into the hall.* LOUISE *and* DANNY *resume their conversation about* ANNE. CHARLES *sits staring into the swimming pool.* DIANE *crosses to him and puts her hand on his shoulder. She has heard the argument with* LINNEA. *They feel emotional but try to keep it light.*

DIANE: I'm sorry.

CHARLES: Don't be. It was becoming a problem.

DIANE: What was?

CHARLES: Sustaining my sexy-older-man-attractive-to-gorgeous-younger-women image. It's a relief to have it over actually.

DIANE: But you are attractive, you know.

CHARLES: Am I? Thank you. But somehow it seems less important to prove it than it used to be.

DIANE: You have changed!

CHARLES: (*Laughs. Pause.*) You've changed too.

DIANE: Yes.

CHARLES: Your energy used to frighten me. Now it doesn't.

DIANE: It's focused now. It took me a while to figure out what was wrong. I used to go around with a scream just below the surface. But that's gone. I seem to know what I'm doing now. (*Small laugh.*) At least most of the time.

CHARLES: Perhaps time heals more than wounds. Diane?

DIANE: What? (*Pause.*)

CHARLES: I'd like to go home with you.

DIANE: (*Tries to return to banter.*) Your place or mine?

CHARLES: (*Refuses to let it turn light.*) Our old bedroom, our old bed. (*Silence.*)

DIANE: All right.

CHARLES: Shall we leave separately? We don't want to shock Christina.

DIANE: There's no shocking Christina. But Charles, I want you to understand. I'm not sorry you left.

CHARLES: I am.

DIANE: So let's go, shall we?

CHARLES: Yes. (*They leave through the up left gate holding hands and giggling. Others watch them leave and smile.*)

JAMES: Hey, Lo,! How about that?

LOUISE: Yes. I'm glad. (JAMES *chuckles happily.*)

JOSH: (*Upstage right with* CHRISTINA.) Looks like your folks are going to get it together.

CHRISTINA: Humph! It's amazing how stupid people can be.

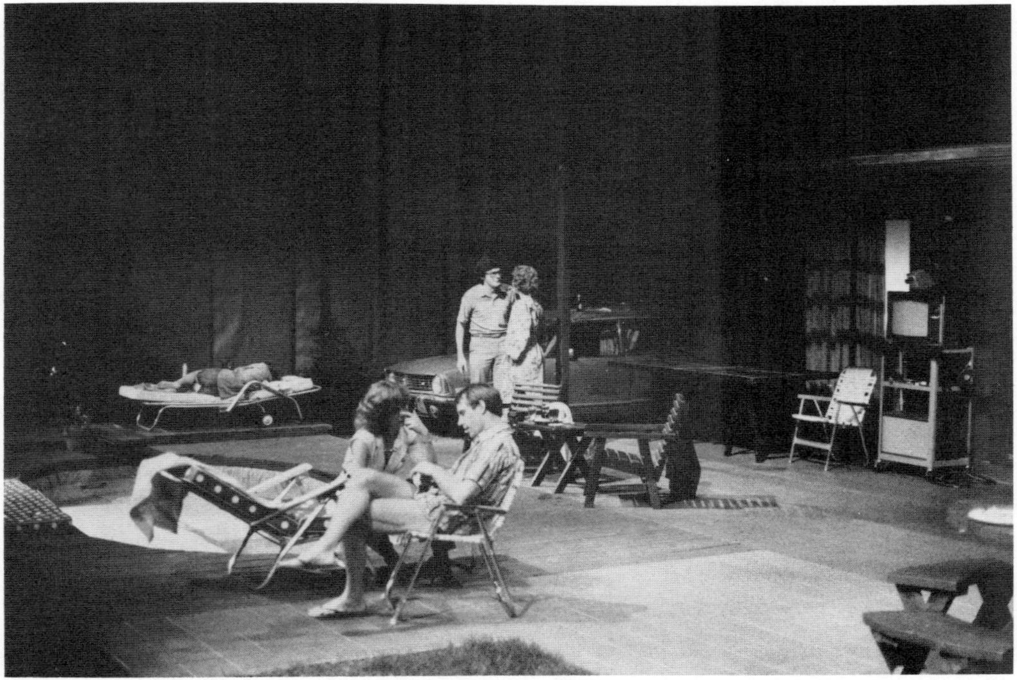

Late in the evening conversations become more private.

JOSH: Hey, that's no way to talk.

CHRISTINA: People make the same mistakes over and over and over again. It's dumb. (*Picks up her book and starts toward the gate.*)

JOSH: Hey, where are you going?

CHRISTINA: Home, where else?

JOSH: Maybe you shouldn't.

CHRISTINA: Why not?

JOSH: Well, you know, your folks . . .

CHRISTINA: What's the difference? They must have done it hundreds of times when he lived with us and it never bothered anybody then.

JOSH: It's different. You want to stay here tonight?

CHRISTINA: Where?

JOSH: In my car. With me.

CHRISTINA: Not tonight.

JOSH: Why not?

CHRISTINA: I'm not in the mood.

JOSH: OK, then the sofa in the family room.

CHRISTINA: I told you . . .

JOSH: Alone!

CHRISTINA: Why should I sleep on a sofa when I've got a comfortable bed next door? Just because my parents start acting like kids! Oh, all right. I'll read here for a while at least. That'll give them time to get settled anyway.

JOSH: Good night.

CHRISTINA: Good night.

JOSH: Good night.

> CHRISTINA *goes into the family room. She lies down on the sofa to read. Soon she falls asleep. A taxi is heard stopping in front of the house; doors open and close and it drives away.*
>
> JAMES *is sitting on the downstage left bench. It is now very late. He is drunk. He lies down, looks at the sky.*

JAMES: Beautiful evening. For love.

> COLLEEN *is sitting in a chair upstage smoking a cigarette.* JOSH *crosses to her and says something to her. She nods her head.* LOUISE *and* DANNY *move to the monitor and* LOUISE *speaks into the microphone and turns on the video camera.*

LOUISE: Anne? Honey?

ANNE: What?

LOUISE: Danny wants to talk to you, honey.

DANNY *sits down so that he can have a conversation with the monitor.* JOSH *crosses to his car, unlocks it, gets in and pulls the curtains closed over the windows.* GIDEON *comes out of the house and talks to* LOUISE *upstage and out-of-focus. He is saying goodbye.*

DANNY: Well, that was quite an entrance.

ANNE: I feel like an idiot.

DANNY: Why?

ANNE: Because I scared everyone and behaved like a little kid. I look silly in that thing.

COLLEEN: You can say that again. (DANNY *looks his disapproval at her; she makes a face at him.*)

ANNE: I can't see. Is someone there?

DANNY: (*Waves to* COLLEEN *to move further away.*) No, not really. (LOUISE *goes into the kitchen and we hear sounds of dishes being put in the dishwasher and general cleaning up.*)

ANNE: Where's Daddy?

DANNY: Over by the fence. Should I get him?

ANNE: No! Can't we go somewhere private?

DANNY: OK. Hold on. (*He moves the monitor downstage.*)

GIDEON: Colleen? It's time we were off.

COLLEEN: All right. I'll just see if I can help Louise clean up before we go, shall I?

COLLEEN *goes into the kitchen without waiting for his reply.* GIDEON *sighs and moves downstage, his back to the house.* JAMES *has fallen asleep.*

During the following conversation COLLEEN *goes from the kichen into the bedroom. She looks out the sliding glass doors. She thinks no one is watching and sneaks out the door, along the side of the house and around the car to the far side. She opens the door and gets into the car and disappears.* GIDEON *turns in time to see* COLLEEN *get into the car. He watches her, then turns away and sits on a chaise-longue downstage center, his back to the audience.*

DANNY: Anne, is something wrong?

ANNE: I need to talk to someone.

DANNY: Wouldn't it be easier if you came back outside? We could have a real talk.

ANNE: Isn't this real?

DANNY: It seems awkward to me.

ANNE: I can't come out. I feel like an idiot in that gear, but I haven't got anything else to wear.

DANNY: Where are your clothes?

ANNE: I haven't got any. I can't wear anything except that plastic suit.

DANNY: (*Embarrassed and uncomfortable when he realizes that, although he can only see her face, the rest of her body is naked.*) You mean you're . . . you're naked?

ANNE: Yes. I . . . it never mattered before.

DANNY: Borrow some clothes from your mother.

ANNE: I can't. I'm allergic to everything except plastic. (*She looks down at her body and smiles.*) Besides, they wouldn't fit.

DANNY: OK. Well. What was it you . . .

ANNE: I need some advice. It's kind of personal, I hope that's all right.

DANNY: Maybe I'm not the one you should. . . .

ANNE: There isn't anyone else I can talk to. Please, listen.

DANNY: OK. I'll do what I can.

ANNE: It's hard to know where to start. You see it's partly because things look different from in here. At least I think they do. Anyway, I watch things. I don't talk much because people don't, well, I guess it's hard for them. But I see a lot and I've noticed something lately that worries me.

DANNY: What is it, Anne?

ANNE: My mother. She isn't happy.

DANNY: She isn't?

ANNE: No. And I think I know why.

DANNY: Anne, I don't really think . . . (*Curiosity overcomes his sense of propriety.*) Why?

ANNE: She's having an affair with someone.

DANNY: Anne!

ANNE: Well, it would be natural enough. It's her turn. My father has been playing around for years.

DANNY: Anne, I think you must be wrong.

ANNE: Do you?

DANNY: Who do you think she's having an affair with?

ANNE: That's what I can't figure out. But I read that sixty-two percent of married women who have been unfaithful to their husbands feel guilty about it. So I figured that must be it.

DANNY: What?

ANNE: That must be why she's unhappy. She feels guilty.

DANNY: No, Anne, I'm sure you're wrong about this. Anyway your mother can take care of herself. She wouldn't want you worrying about her.

ANNE: I'm not exactly worried, but I think Mom and Dad would be better off if they'd just talk these things over and be honest with each other. It's very important to be honest about how you feel. That's why I want to say something.

DANNY: (*Uncomfortable about the direction of the conversation.*) Anne, I think it's a little late in the evening for . . .

ANNE: I just wanted to tell you. I like you, Danny.

DANNY: Well, that's very nice. I like you too. Anne, tell me, how long do you intend to live like this?

ANNE: I have to.

DANNY: That's not what your doctor says.

ANNE: Charles doesn't know what he's talking about. I know. I get bumps. When I used to come out I got bumps.

DANNY: There are worse things than bumps.

ANNE: Such as?

DANNY: Such as not having a real life.

There is a stifled giggle from inside the car.

ANNE: My life is just as real as yours.

DANNY: No. It's not. You're a little confused about reality. (*He suddenly makes a decision and stands up.*)

ANNE: Hey, come back, I can't see you!

DANNY: I'm sorry, Anne, but if you want to talk to me you are going to have to come out here and talk to me face to face. I want to be your friend, I will be your friend, but not like this.

ANNE: I see. (*A long pause.*) Good night, Danny.

The monitor goes dark. DANNY *starts to reach to call to her, but doesn't.* DANNY *sighs, then moves slowly toward the kitchen.* JAMES *snorts in his sleep.* DANNY *stops near* GIDEON *and calls softly.*

DANNY: Gideon? (*There is no response. He goes to the kitchen door and calls quietly.*) Louise? There's no one out here except Gideon and James and they're both asleep. Should I turn off the light?

LOUISE: (*Comes outside.*) Yes, I suppose. Where's James?

DANNY: Over by the fence. Should I help you get him into bed?

LOUISE: (*Crosses toward* JAMES *and looks down at him.*) No. Let him sleep. It doesn't matter. He'll be all right here.

DANNY: Is Gem asleep?

LOUISE: In the guest room. She thought you wouldn't mind staying overnight.

DANNY: Of course not, if it's not too much trouble.

LOUISE: Certainly not. Is Anne all right?

DANNY: Well, she's taking an interest in the rest of the world and that's a good sign, I should think. She's worried about you.

LOUISE: Me?

DANNY: She thinks you aren't happy.

LOUISE: Oh.

DANY: I'm not so sure I handled Anne right. If she ever wants to see me, you'll give me a call won't you?

LOUISE: Of course.

DANNY: (*They have been picking up the party debris.*) Anything else? Does all this stay out?

LOUISE: Yes. Just turn on the alarm system, would you? The switch is over by the bedroom door. (DANNY *turns to the switch as* LOUISE *changes her mind.*) No, wait. We'd better leave it off until Gideon and Colleen have gone.

DANNY: OK. (*He shuts off the shrubbery lights. It is completely dark except for the lights coming from the house. They both cross to the kitchen door and go in.*)

LOUISE: Would you like a nightcap?

DANNY: Not for me, thanks. You must be tired.

LOUISE: A little. There's clean towels in the bathroom next to the guest room. It's the second door on the left.

DANNY: Thanks, Louise. See you in the morning.

LOUISE: Good night. (*It is very dark and very quiet, the middle of the the night. Occasional night-time neighborhood sounds are heard.* LOUISE *turns off the kitchen light and comes outside.*) Gideon?

GIDEON: (*After a pause, he answers quietly.*) What?

LOUISE: Where's Colleen?

GIDEON: (*A long pause.*) I think she went for a walk. She does that sometimes. You go to bed. I'll wait here for her. Is the baby all right?

LOUISE: Sound asleep. Good night.

GIDEON: Good night.

LOUISE: (*Goes back into the family room.*) Christina? (CHRISTINA *mutters sleepily.* LOUISE *closes her book.*) Are you warm enough, dear? (CHRISTINA *mutters an affirmation.* LOUISE *turns out the lamp by the sofa.*) Sleep well. Good night, little baby. Poor, sweet, little baby.

LOUISE *shuts off the light in the family room. After a moment she can be seen moving in the bedroom. She shuts the sliding glass door and closes the drapes. It is very quiet.*

A train whistles and fades into the night. We hear the sound of a man's sob in the dark and come to realize that it must be GIDEON. *The sobbing is brief and again there are only neighborhood night sounds.*

JAMES *snores, then snorts himself awake. He sputters, coughs. It is too dark to see him.*

JAMES: Louise . . . ouise . . . I'm cold. (*Silence. There is a giggle from inside the car.*)

JOSH: Shhh! For Christ's sake!

JAMES: Need a blanket. Louise? (*Sits up.*) Huh? Hey, what the . . . oh. All gone home. Party over.

We hear JAMES *get up and try to make his way toward the house. En route he trips over something. There is a great crash and clatter as he knocks over an ashtray stand and a chair. He completes the pandemonium by falling head first into the swimming pool. As he flails around in the water unable to get his balance, lights come on in various parts of the house at various times.* GIDEON *calls out in alarm.*

GIDEON: Jesus! Help!

JAMES *is struggling in the water. The baby starts to cry in the family room.* GIDEON *dives into the water to "rescue"* JAMES. JOSH *has come out of the car.* CHRISTINA *comes running out of the family room.* LOUISE *comes out of the bedroom tying a bathrobe. She turns on the patio lights.* GIDEON *is pulling the choking, helpless, drunken* JAMES *out of the pool.* JOSH *and* GIDEON *arrange* JAMES *so that he can be given artificial respiration.* GIDEON *sits astride* JAMES*'s back and applies back pressure as* LOUISE *watches calmly.* COLLEEN *can be seen sitting up inside the car.* ANNE*'s face appears on the monitor and the light comes on on the video camera.* JOSH *runs to the left fence.*

LOUISE: It's finally happened.

ANNE: What is it! I can't see! What's happening?

DANNY *in his trousers and* GEM *wrapped in a blanket come out from the family room.*

JOSH: (*Shouts across the left fence.*) Charlie! Charlie are you there?!

GEM: What is it? What's happened?

CHARLIE: What is it?

JOSH: Come over here, Dad's in trouble!

CHARLES: I'm on my way.

GEM: Oh, my god! What happened to Jimmy?

LOUISE: He's had a heart attack.

DANNY: Have you called the fire department?

LOUISE: There's no need. It will all be over soon. (JAMES *sputters and coughs.*)

DANNY: (*Starts to go into the house.*) I'm going to call. If he's had a heart attack he needs the resuscitator.

JOSH: Sit down, Mom.

LOUISE: I'm all right.

CHRISTINA: I think he just fell in the swimming pool

DIANE *in bathrobe and* CHARLES *zipping his pants come running through the gate.* CHARLES *goes immediately to* JAMES *and bends over him.* DANNY *decides to wait for the doctor's advice before calling and returns to the group around* JAMES.

CHARLES: What happened?

LOUISE: He's had a heart attack.

CHRISTINA: I think he just fell in the pool.

GIDEON *relinquishes his position to the doctor and goes into the house to get his still crying baby. He sees* COLLEEN *sitting up in the car and motions her to get down out of sight.*

JOSH: He's going to be all right, Mom.

LOUISE: He is?

GIDEON *goes into the family room.* JOSH *also tried to signal* COLLEEN *to stay out of sight, but instead she gets out of the car and comes over to the group around* JAMES. *She is buttoning her blouse.* GEM *sees her get out of the car and looks at her with strong distaste, and then turns the same look on* JOSH *to his great discomfort.* CHARLES *is helping* JAMES *to sit up. He is still coughing and having difficulty getting his breath.*

CHARLES: Easy does it. Try to relax and breathe regularly. Jimmy, do you have any stomach pains?

GEM: Stomach pains!

ANNE: Josh! Someone tell me what's happening!

JOSH: Don't worry, Annie. It's going to be OK.

LOUISE: (*Numbly.*) He's going to be all right?

GEM: Of course he is. He's going to be fine.

DIANE: I don't understand, what happened?

CHARLES: Jimmy? Any stomach pains? Nausea? (JAMES *shakes his head.*)

CHRISTINA: I don't know for sure. I was asleep. There was a lot of racket and splashing. I think he tripped and fell in the pool.

LOUISE: Yes. He had a heart attack and fell in.

CHARLES: Jimmy, do you have any chest pains at all?

JAMES: (*Looks up at* LOUISE *who is staring down at him.*) No. No pain.

LOUISE: I thought it had come.

CHARLES: Any vomiting? Heaviness in the limbs?

GEM: He's going to be all right, aren't you, Jimmy? Tell her you're OK, for christ's sake.

LOUISE: You're not dead.

JAMES: Drunk. I fell down. (*He and* LOUISE *continue to stare at each other.* GIDEON *has come out of the family room with the baby. He feigns surprise to see* COLLEEN. JOSH *turns away in embarrassment.*)

GIDEON: Oh, there you are.

COLLEEN: Yes. Here I am.

GIDEON: I think we should be going.

COLLEEN: All right.

GIDEON: Unless there's something we can do, Louise?

LOUISE: No.

GEM: (*To* GIDEON.) Your clothes are wet. Aren't you cold?

GIDEON: No. I'll change when I get home.

GEM: (*Impulsively crosses to* GIDEON *and hugs him.*) Good night, Gideon. (*Pause.*)

GIDEON: (*In a soft voice.*) Good night, Mother. (COLLEEN *and* GIDEON *go into the house and exit.*)

GEM: (*Turns to* JOSH.) Oh, Josh, did you have to do that?

JOSH: I am sorry. It was stupid. Please don't say anything. It was a mistake.

GEM: (*Puts her arm around him forgivingly.*) It runs in the family.

DIANE: (*Begins shepherding people away.*) Come on, let's go home. Charles?

CHARLES: Coming. Louise? Are you all right?

LOUISE: (*Emerges a little from her shock.*) Yes. Yes. I'm all right.

CHARLES: A sedative?

LOUISE: No.

CHARLES: Well, he'll be all right, but some strong black coffee wouldn't hurt him any. I've never seen anyone so drunk. You know you can kill yourself drinking booze by the tumbler. (*Having been helped to a chaise-longue,* JAMES *tries to hide under a beach towel. To* LOUISE.) I'm just next door if you need me. (*We hear* GIDEON*'s car starting and then driving away. The sound fades in the distance.*

DIANE: Good night, Louise.

LOUISE *doesn't respond. The* TV *monitor goes dark but the video camera light stays on.* DANNY *puts his arm around* GEM *and they go into the family room and through to the guest room.* DIANE, CHRISTINA, *and* CHARLES *leave together through the gate.*

CHRISTINA: Daddy, I don't understand what stomach pains have got to do with heart attack symptoms.

CHARLES: Nothing. Forget it.

JOSH: You need anything, Dad?

JAMES: No. No, thanks, Josh.

JOSH: OK. Well . . . good night. (*Goes to his car, gets in and closes the door. The light inside the car goes out.*)

Again it is very quiet with soft neighborhood night sounds. It is just before dawn. LOUISE *tries to pull herself together. She is exhausted.*

JAMES: Well, well, well.

LOUISE: Do you want coffee?

JAMES: No. The shock has sobered me up.

LOUISE: You'd better come in the house. You'll catch cold sitting out here in wet clothes.

JAMES: And you wouldn't want that, would you?

LOUISE: Of course not.

JAMES: It's funny. You go along, oh, for years and years and things just pass by and seem ordinary and normal. And then something hits you, right between the old eyeballs.

LOUISE: I'll make coffee.

JAMES: No! I'm trying to tell you something! Everything's different than I thought it was. The thing is I can hardly believe it . . . I was choking and that ass Gideon was sitting on me and then I looked up and saw your face and the flashbulb went off.

LOUISE: You are talking absolute nonsense, you know that, Jimmy.

JAMES: I'm almost afraid to say it.

LOUISE: I hate these middle of the night melodramatics. Let's just go to bed, everything will seem all right in the morning.

JAMES: You don't love me, Louise. (*There is silence.*)

LOUISE: Charles said you should drink coffee.

JAMES: I don't give a good god damn what Charles said! You tell me the truth! Everything's been a fake, hasn't it? When you wait on me, when you bring me a drink, a pencil, fix my favorite food, put toothpaste on my toothbrush, you aren't doing it because you love me!

LOUISE: Oh, James . . .

JAMES: I don't understand it, but I know I'm right. Why do you hate me!

LOUISE: (*Speaks quietly after a pause.*) It . . . it's complicated. I don't exactly hate you.

JAMES: (*Mimicking her.*) You don't exactly hate me. What's that supposed to mean? I suppose you don't exactly love me either.

LOUISE: No. Not exactly.

JAMES: I see. Well, now we're getting somewhere. Just exactly what do you do?

LOUISE: Nothing.

JAMES: You nothing me.

LOUISE: That's right.

JAMES: Great!

LOUISE: I used to hate you. And before that I loved you. But even hate doesn't last. And then there's nothing.

JAMES: (*Awed.*) And I never knew the difference.

LOUISE: Never noticed.

JAMES: I don't believe you.

LOUISE: All right. It doesn't matter.

JAMES: If you say that once more I'm going to . . .

LOUISE: To what?

JAMES: I don't know. I don't know anything. All those things I thought were kindness turn out to be something else. (JAMES *is working things out as he talks, as if he had just been given the key to the puzzle.*) So maybe you give me things because you hate me. You give me booze to make me drunk and food to make me fat. You assumed, yes, assumed, I was having a heart attack. And you didn't care! Oh, my god! Do you really hate me that much!

LOUISE: Oh, James, don't be silly. You're drunk and you're jumping to stupid conclusions. Believe me, tomorrow morning everything will seem fine. Except of course that you are going to have one really horrific headache. (*She moves to go into the bedroom.*)

JAMES: Louise, it's no good. I won't ignore it. You have to tell me.

LOUISE: Tell you what.

JAMES: Why you stopped loving me and started hating me? When and why?

ANNE: (*Her face appears on the* TV *monitor. She has been listening to to the entire conversation without turning herself on—in fact she has been spying.*) It's because you've been screwing around. (JAMES *and* LOUISE *whirl around to face the monitor with angry surprise.*)

LOUISE: Anne!

ANNE: It's quite obvious, Daddy. It's because you have been putting your penis in other women's vaginas. Mother doesn't like that.

JAMES: Oh my god!

ANNE: That's what Josh said. He told me that a long time ago when I was real little and I didn't understand what he was talking about.

JAMES: Jesus Christ, my own kids!

LOUISE: That's enough, Anne! Turn yourself off and go to sleep right now!

LOUISE: Oh, Mom, don't be mad.

LOUISE: What are you doing up at this time of night!

ANNE: I couldn't sleep and I got lonely so . . . what difference does it make anyway? I don't see what you're so mad about.

JAMES: Oh, nothing at all. My daughter talks like a tart and my wife is trying to kill me that's all.

ANNE: Oh, don't be silly, Daddy. Why would she want to do that? (*Silence.*)

LOUISE: (*She and* JAMES *look at each other.*) Go to sleep, Anne.

ANNE: I can't sleep. Everything's such a . . . I've got too much thinking to do. (*She waits, hoping for a response, gets none, shrugs and turns herself off. The light goes off on the video camera as well.*)

JAMES: It isn't true, Louise. What Anne said isn't true. I haven't done anything.

LOUISE: Do you expect me to believe that!

JAMES: I don't really do anything, Lo'. I mean sure I've kissed a few women, but I don't . . . (*Laughing in spite of himself.*) I don't put my penis in their vaginas.

LOUISE: (*Laughs in spite of herself.*) You don't?

JAMES: No. I don't.

LOUISE: And what about Carol?

JAMES: Yes. OK, yes, I did have an affair with her, but Christ, Louise, that was . . . god that was twelve years ago.

LOUISE: Thirteen.

JAMES: But I never have since. I swear.

LOUISE: But you have! I've caught you. Don't lie about it now, please. There were, oh, I don't know hundreds of times, dozens of them. I've heard you talking to them on the telephone.

JAMES: No. I see women. I take them to dinner, I kiss them, and two times I tried to have sex with them—no, three times. But I . . . Jesus, Louise, nothing happened.

LOUISE: What do you mean nothing happened?

JAMES: I mean nothing happened.

LOUISE: You can't?

JAMES: No, I can't. Can't! You understand simple English! Can't! (*Silence.*)

LOUISE: But you . . .

JAMES: You've never actually seen me in bed with another woman have you?

LOUISE: No, but . . .

JAMES: Because I haven't been.

LOUISE: Except for Carol

JAMES: Except for Carol.

LOUISE: But why? Why do you do . . . do whatever you do.

JAMES: I don't know. Maybe I keep hoping. Maybe I think I'm supposed to. I didn't see what harm it did.

LOUISE: What about Colleen?

JAMES: What about her? We just had some fun, that's all, some drinks. I bought her dinner twice. I don't know what she gets from other men, but all she got from me was a little old-fashioned necking.

LOUISE: Oh. (*The sky has been getting lighter gradually and in a few minutes the sun will be coming up. Silence.*)

JAMES: It's getting light.

LOUISE: Yes.

JAMES: We should go to bed.

LOUISE: Yes.

JAMES: Lo'. It isn't true is it? I don't believe you hate me. It isn't . . . it isn't possible. I was drunk.

LOUISE: Yes. You were drunk.

JAMES: I ought to quit. No, cut down. I'll get the light. (*Turns off the patio light and turns on the alarm switch. They move toward their bedroom door in an ordinary way, as if they had just been discussing whether to redecorate the living room.*)

LOUISE: I think I'll take the phone off the hook.

JAMES: Good idea.

They go into the bedroom, close the door, and pull the drapes. The light goes out. All lights are off in the house. Silence except for neighborhood early morning sounds. Birds start to sing.

The family room door opens a crack; there is a pause and then the door opens wider. ANNE *steps out into the soft dim light. She is naked. She looks around, unsure and a little frightened. She goes to a lounge, picks up a beach robe and puts it on. She goes to the gate left, opens it, and as she walks through a screeching alarm sounds and very bright burglar lights flood the back yard.* ANNE *runs back to the house instinctively, then hesitates outside the family room door. She makes her decision and runs out through the gate as the sound continues.*

BLACKOUT

Hyperrealism in the Theatre: Shank Interviews Shank

At the request of West Coast Plays, *Ted Shank, the first director of* SUNSET/SUNRISE *and the author's husband, interviewed Adele Shank about the style of her play and some of its implications.*

TED: Did you begin *SUNSET/SUNRISE* with the idea of writing a hyperrealist play?

ADELE: That is what I started with. You and I were both interested in exploring the theatrical equivalent of the painting style of hyperrealism or photorealism. After studying the characteristics of the painting style we discussed how they could work in the theatre. For example, the paintings keep the viewer on the surface; there is no projection into the painting, no emotional involvement, no interpretation. What you see is what there is. I extended that into a theatrical style and made some basic decisions. The focus would always be on the present moment; there would be no projection into the future and virtually no past revealed. This meant little or no exposition.

TED: What do you think you gain by not having exposition and by not having the audience hanging on an evolving future?

ADELE: Well, setting aside for the moment the hanging on an evolving future . . .

TED: Suspense in other words.

ADELE: Yes. One of the things you gain by not giving the audience exposition is that you make people work much harder than they are used to working.

TED: And that keeps the audience in the present?

ADELE: Yes, and it keeps them interested. Martin Esslin said a number of years ago that audiences raised on television commercials are much faster at making assumptions and deducing information than most playwrights give them credit for. I took that comment very seriously. Most exposition is unnecessary. The audience can figure out from simple verbal or action clues very fast what a given situation is between two people, psychologically, economically, and culturally. By keeping the focus on the present moment you are creating a different kind of suspense. Not really suspense, but interest.

TED: Is is the interest of a voyeur? Is it like peeking through a hole in the fence into the backyard of people whom you do not know, trying to sort out what they are talking about, how they are related and so forth? When you first start looking you may have a curiosity, but you don't have an interest in the people as people.

ADELE: Yes, it's very much like that. There is a very distanced relationship between the spectator and the characters. We in the audience have almost no emotional involvement with the characters. Therefore we can see anew details which we have been accustomed to dismissing. In the theatre of psychological realism we become emotionally involved with the characters, we feel with them or through them rather than looking at them, at the setting, at the situation. This emotional involvement in fact prohibits the heightened perception that hyperrealism is after.

TED: But perhaps as we keep watching we get to know something about the people. Then we become interested in their relationships and how those relationships develop. We are not indifferent to the characters in *SUNSET/SUNRISE*, are we?

ADELE: What happens is that there is a recognition of the characters by the audience, not an emotional identification. As the play progresses the audience comes to see these characters as being in the same situation they are in. It starts with a recognition of certain generalized suburban circumstances—there would often be a recognition laugh on a sound effect because it was a sound normally disregarded, but typical of suburbia on a hot Saturday afternoon at five o'clock. A lot of the comedy comes from this recognition of psychological elements as well as physical circumstances. And gradually as the audience comes to understand more, there is a recognition of, an understanding that, for instance, there are some things about Louise's life which are very much like their own.

TED: Would you say that an exception to the lack of emotional involvement might be the sob of Gideon in the middle of the night?

ADELE: Not necessarily. Gideon's emotion is revealed and we understand why he sobs. But I have not tried to make the audience sob in empathy with him. I am interested in moving the perspective in and out of characters. At one moment the audience sees something, an event or a relationship, from the point of view of the character and they sympathize or at least understand. At another moment they see the same event from the perspective of another character or from their own objective point of view and it is quite ridiculous. I think Gideon is a good example of how that works. Sometimes he appears to be, as James says, a perfect ass; at other times he seems to be a somewhat sympathetic, pathetic character who has problems with which he cannot deal. But I don't think it's a matter of being involved with the character emotionally, I think it's a matter of the observer understanding something.

TED: Because it is a hyperreal play did you work on it differently than you have worked on other plays?

ADELE: Yes. One of the things that I did very early, soon after I had established the cast of characters, was to pick what we later called role models. As I developed the plot and wrote the dialogue I had a specific actual individual in mind for each character. The role models were usually quite different from the characters in the details of their lives, but I used them for their way of speaking, their energy level, and their personalities. Because it's a large-cast play and the characters don't make long speeches the role models helped me keep straight the differences between the characters so that even a four-word line would reflect a change in energy level and tempo.

TED: Did these people whom you had in mind as role models, did they actually live in suburban California?

ADELE: Yes. But some of them have since moved on.

TED: Your use of role models was very helpful to the actors. One of the early rehearsals was held at our house and was a kind of party for the cast and the role models who were available. The role models were told when they were invited to the party that they had, without their knowledge, been used as role models in the play and that if they were willing they would meet the actors who were playing the roles that had been modeled on them. They all found that quite interesting. What was particularly useful for the actors was to be able to observe at close hand the various mannerisms, ways of talking, and so forth that had been used as a guide by you in writing the play. It was also a lot of fun. the role models guessing what actors were playing them and vice versa.

ADELE: Almost everyone got it right within about a minute of coming into the room, because it turned out that not only did the role models and the actors have similar movement and ways of speaking, they actually looked a lot alike.

TED: The opportunity to make those observations was useful to the actors because imagination alone is not always valid. Observation is needed to check one's imagination. You had already done that in the writing process by using role models. You avoided the limitations of imagination without losing its benefits.

ADELE: How do you mean?

TED: I think imagination has become a lot less reliable than it used to be because now such a large portion of our experience comes from watching television or listening to records, or seeing films. The information has already been processed at least once, and if we rely entirely on our imaginations we are likely to come up with an idea influenced by TV or film rather than being based upon actual observation. I think it used to be different when almost all experience came from dealing directly with the world. The actors, being able to observe real people who had served as a basis for a character, were able to return to that first source of art.

ADELE: They also had the community in which the play was set to observe. When I was writing I thought of the play as taking place in a house on our block. In fact I started most writing sessions with a walk around the block, just listening to the neighborhood sounds. And I think it was helpful to the actors when you asked them to go into the community and record interviews with the "natives."

TED: Did you have a specific house and back yard in mind?

ADELE: Well, I couldn't use ours because we don't have a swimming pool. [*They laugh.*] The house in the play is really a composite of the houses in the neighborhood.

TED: Then Darrell Winn, the set designer, continuing along those lines, observed various houses in the area and came up with the design for a house that looked very much as if it should be in West Davis.

ADELE: It certainly did. I would hope that always when this is produced, the house would look as if it belonged in that neighborhood. If it's done in Solano Beach the house should look like it had been built by a Solano Beach contractor, and everyone should be able to recognize it as a house from their community.

TED: You have kept the plot very simple.

ADELE: A complex plot creates too much suspense. It involves the audience too deeply in the fictional world, so they hang on what might happen rather than being focused on the present moment.

TED: For twenty-five hundred years or so suspense has been one of the chief techniques for keeping an audience focused on the illusion. What is it do you think that keeps the audience focused in here?

ADELE: I think it's primarily trying to figure out what is going on. It engages the mind but not the emotions. I think this can't be too protracted, by the way. *SUNSET/SUNRISE* plays an hour and a half with intermission and I think it couldn't hold much longer than that.

TED: Because it's a strain on an audience conditioned to expect information to come easy in theatre?

ADELE: Yes. It becomes too tiring. And there has to be a kind of reward system built in where they do figure out who so-and-so is and what is going on, or rather what appears to be going on. The audience needs encouragement to keep at it. Then they can be thrown off again because the appearance has not been the fact.

TED: Someone has commented on what they called the bizarre elements in the play and wondered how they fit into the hyperreal style. For example the fact that Anne appears on a video monitor.

ADELE: I don't see that as particularly bizarre and I don't think it seems to be so in production. It is certainly unusual and interesting, but it seems quite natural that liberal California parents, with an attitude of never forcing anything, accept whatever their children do and attempt to deal with it as if it were normal. If your daughter refuses to leave her room you find a way of integrating her into family life in as normal a way as possible. I think their solution is pretty realistic.

TED: In production it seems a hyperreal element.

ADELE: Yes. But I think there's another area of confusion. Hyperrealism is not at all the same thing as documentation. *SUNSET/SUNRISE* is not a blow-by-minute account of family life in Davis, California. It is a contrived and structured play presenting an illusion of reality, based on observations. Like hyperrealist painting, I have attempted in *SUNSET/SUNRISE* to make the spectator perceive acutely, niot become involved in the psychology or emotions of the characters.

TED: And part of the pleasure comes from recognition. It seems to reflect objectively a part of the familiar world of the audience.

ADELE: Yes. But it has taken on a harder edge and a clarity that one never sees in the real world. Our perception of the real world is muddy and diffused—there's too much of it. This play focuses attention to things we don't normally notice.

Skaters
Ted Pezzulo

To Neil

Developed and originally presented in a workshop production at the Joseph Jefferson Theatre Company in New York City. Directed by Bill Herndon.

NURSE	Jennifer Dawson
CARRIE	Rosemary McNamara
NICK	Richard Zavaglia
KURTZ	Roger DeKoven
FREDA	Anita Bayless
ANDY	Demo Di Martile

First produced at the Los Angeles Actors Theatre March 3, 1978. Directed by Jeremiah Morris.

NURSE	Betty Bridges
CARRIE	DeAnn Mears
NICK	Frank Savino
KURTZ	Phil Leeds
FREDA	Ann Morgan Guilbert
ANDY	Joe Pantoliano

Photos courtesy of Los Angeles Actors' Theatre

Skaters

Ted Pezzulo

ACT ONE

SCENE ONE

The sundeck of a small country hospital. An early summer evening.

A few patio chairs and end tables, as well as a chaise longue, are about the area. Up right center we see the interior of a hospital room with two beds and the customary appurtenances. In one corner of the room there is a screen behind which someone is dressing. He is singing to himself.

After a moment we hear voices approaching. VIRGINIA DEDRICK, *a Registered Nurse, enters the sundeck escorting* CARRIE MONTE. *Both women are about forty.*

NURSE: Well, here's where the grand tour ends. Back where we started. Do you like our little home?

CARRIE: I'm impressed.

NURSE: Thought you would be. Everybody is.

CARRIE: Frankly, I'm amazed a little town like this can sustain such a hospital.

NURSE: We're small but we're modern. Right down to the very latest in drainpipes. Thing we love most though is our sundecks. Especially this one. Western exposure.

CARRIE: (*Calling out into the room.*) Nick, come on out and see this.

NICK: (*From behind the screen.*) Where's my pajamas?

CARRIE: In the suitcase.

NICK: Where's the suitcase?

CARRIE: On the bed. Now hurry up, will you!

NICK: Yeah.

NURSE: I think he's going to be fun to have around.

CARRIE: You'll earn your salary, I'll tell you that. My God, look at those birches.

NURSE: Yes. And the sugar maples, too. See there? You've never seen the sun go down till it sets behind those trees. We're proud of our sunsets, yes, we are. And Mr. Monte . . .

CARRIE: Nick.

NURSE: . . . being Italian and all, we figured he'd like it here. We call it the Sunset Side.

CARRIE: Let me tell you something about Nick . . . being Italian and all. The "all" is heaven. It's the "Italian" you have to prepare for.

NURSE: Can't wait till he meets his roommate.

CARRIE: Who's that?

NURSE: Old Mr. Kurtz. Used to be an actor. Pretty famous, too, to hear him tell it. Trouble is, he still thinks he's Romeo. I had to restrain him the other day with a syringe. Mrs. Monte, never underestimate the power of an enema. Now tonight when you go home, I want you to pour yourself a double scotch and drink a toast to me and Ralph.

CARRIE: Ralph, huh?

NURSE: Believe it or not, he's about to become my third husband. I buried the first, divorced the second, and hope to God that Ralph will see me through. The nights get long.

NICK: (*Comes in wearing robe, pajamas, and slippers.*) Hey, Bedpan, come here and button me up!

NURSE: (*Buttons him playfully.*) I thought you went home.

NICK: What for? Everything I need, you got. (*To* CARRIE.) Honey, get out of here, will you. I'm trying to be unfaithful.

CARRIE: Somehow I feel secure.

NICK: Oh, yeah! Well, don't take me for granted; that's all I got to say. Me and Nurse, here, we got plans.

NURSE: I'm going to get you something to eat.

NICK: Can I eat out here?

NURSE: Don't see why not. And Mrs. Monte . . .

CARRIE: Carrie.

NURSE: Carrie. I'll see you tomorrow.

CARRIE: Rain or shine.

NURSE: By the way, my name's Virginia.

NICK: (*Laughs.*) Did you hear the one about this hooker named Virginia. They called her Virgin for short. But not for long. (*He is beside himself.*)

NURSE: What do you want for dinner—beef stew or a fist in the chops?

NICK: I thought it was pretty good.

NURSE: I got that impression. Carrie, five minutes, OK?

CARRIE: Just leaving. A toast to you and Ralph. (NURSE *smiles and leaves.*)

NICK: Who's Ralph?

CARRIE: A little outside interest.

NICK: I'll change all that.

CARRIE: Honey, give her some rest.

NICK: You kidding? I just checked in. Anyway, I think she loves me.

CARRIE: So do I.

NICK: Yeah? How much?

CARRIE: Twenty years and five kids' worth.

NICK: Rub my shoulders.

CARRIE: Oh, no, you don't.

NICK: Why not?

CARRIE: You're the only person I've ever met in my life who's got an erogenous zone in his shoulder blades. That's not normal. So until you come home, I want you to just sit here and sublimate.

NICK: Do what?

CARRIE: Think holy thoughts.

NICK: I'm thinking one right now.

CARRIE: I bet.

NICK: Come and sit on my lap.

CARRIE: No!

NICK: Thanks a lot. That's all I got to say. Thanks a lot. My mother told me: "Nick, I want you to find yourself a nice Italian girl. She'll know how to take care of you. You marry that Irish girl, all you're going to get is heartache. Heartache . . . and lots of boiled potatoes."

CARRIE: You finished?

NICK: No. I want to pout for a while.

CARRIE: Good. You do that. When you finish, call me. I'll be at the Burger Pit.

NICK: (*No longer playing.*) Honey, come here.

CARRIE: Why?

NICK: I want to hold you, that's all.

CARRIE: (*Goes to* NICK. *They hold each other for a long time. After a while.*) Nick . . . Nick . . . you're shaking . . .

NICK: It's nothing.

CARRIE: (*Pulling away slightly.*) Honey, you're trembling . . .

NICK: Hey, give me a kiss and get out o' here will you. Tomorrow motning you take the kids shopping; get Timmy that new skateboard he wants, and Sunday afternoon we'll go on a picnic. Fair enough?

CARRIE: Fair enough.

NICK: Oh, yeah, call Mom and tell her I'm here. But tell her don't worry. Christ, she'll have a bowl of pasta down here before you hang up.

CARRIE: See you tomorrow.

She kisses him. During this, DR. MUELLER, *about sixty-five, appears.*

DOCTOR: I beg your pardon.

NICK: Sorry . . .

CARRIE: I was just leaving.

DOCTOR: I'm sorry to interrupt.

NICK: No problem, really. She's going home, and I'm waiting for Nurse to bring my supper.

DOCTOR: (*Consulting his clipboard.*) You are Mr. Monte?

NICK: Yes. Nick Monte.

DOCTOR: How do you do. I'm Doctor Mueller.

NICK: Pleased to meet you. My wife, Carrie.

CARRIE: (*Extending her hand.*) Hello, Doctor.

DOCTOR: I'm delighted. Again I apologize for interrupting . . .

CARRIE: No trouble at all.

DOCTOR: I was passing by, and they asked me to look in. Just routine, you understand.

NICK: Sure.

CARRIE: Nick, I'll go now.

NICK: Oh, sure, honey. See you tomorrow.

CARRIE: Doctor Miller . . .

DOCTOR: No, M*ue*ller. It's Austrian.

CARRIE: I'm sorry.

DOCTOR: Quite all right.

CARRIE: Did you want me to stay for anything?

DOCTOR: No, we'll talk tomorrow.

CARRIE: Good night.

NICK: Kiss the kids, eh?

CARRIE: Sure. Bye. (*Leaves.*)

DOCTOR: She's charming.

NICK: Best thing ever happened to me.

DOCTOR: And children too, yes?

NICK: Yeah. Five.

DOCTOR: Five!

NICK: Two girls and three boys.

DOCTOR: Remarkable.

NICK: Not so hot. We're going for eight.

DOCTOR: Mein Gott! You must be Italian.

NICK: Yeah. How'd you know?

DOCTOR: Intuition.

NICK: I got an award last year, you know. A beautiful scroll from Saint Alphonsus, that's my parish. "Outstanding Catholic Father of the Year." Not bad, eh?

DOCTOR: "Outstanding Father," eh? In Austria, where I come from, they would call you a sex fiend; and for that, they don't give a scroll. But let that go. Tell me, Mr. Monte, in your spare time, when you're not busy populating the earth, do you have time to hold down a job?

NICK: Yeah. Electric appliances. I'm a plant foreman.

DOCTOR: (*Marking this down.*) Fascinating. Now if you don't mind, a few questions, all right?

NICK: Go ahead.

DOCTOR: Just routine, you understand.

NICK: They all say that.

DOCTOR: What seems to be the problem?

NICK: That's what I'm paying you to tell me. I got to tell you?

DOCTOR: Mr. Monte, just answer the questions. When did you first notice something?

NICK: I don't know. Maybe five months ago. Yeah, five months.

DOCTOR: Will you describe it.

NICK: It's not so pretty.

DOCTOR: Just leave the esthetic judgments to me.

NICK: Well, it was blood. (DOCTOR *writes all this on his clipboard.*) Blood on my pillow. Look, Doc, I already answered these questions a hundred times before. Don't they keep a file or something?

DOCTOR: You saw blood on your pillow. Then what?

NICK: So I thought maybe I scratched myself during the night. That happens, you know. But I couldn't find anything. Then I remembered I was up coughing most of the night.

DOCTOR: Are you still coughing?

NICK: It comes and goes. Right now I'm not.

DOCTOR: Were you a heavy smoker?

NICK: (*Embarrassed.*) I hate to tell you.

DOCTOR: Force yourself.

NICK: Yeah, I was.

DOCTOR: How many?

NICK: Quite a few.

DOCTOR: Specifically . . . ?

NICK: Well . . . look, Doc, I know I was foolish . . .

DOCTOR: No moral judgments either, all right. How many?

NICK: (*By now squirming in his seat.*) Three packs a day.

DOCTOR: Mein Gott!

NICK: I know I was wrong . . . !

DOCTOR: Not wrong, Mr. Monte. It was stupid.

NICK: I'm sorry . . . Christ.

DOCTOR: Monumentally stupid!

NICK: I said I was sorry. What do you want?

DOCTOR: I hope by now you've had the sense to stop.

NICK: I have.

DOCTOR: Thank Gott. So then what happened?

NICK: So I went to my company doctor, they took a few x-rays, and they put me in a T.B. clinic for a month and a half.

DOCTOR: T.B.?

NICK: Yeah. But I wasn't responding to treatment so they figured they must have made a mistake. So back to the doctor, more tests, and tonight they put me here for observation.

DOCTOR: Very well.

NICK: My lab tests are coming back tomorrow, and then I go home on Sunday. See, if I don't get back to work by Monday, they start docking my pay. Five kids, you know. Got to get back to work.

DOCTOR: Take off your tops and sit up here. (NICK *goes to a table in the corner and sits on it.*) We'll get a blood sample later.

NICK: Another one? How much blood you think I got?

DOCTOR: Just routine.

NICK: I bet Dracula said that, too.

DOCTOR: Quiet. (*Takes* NICK*'s pulse.*)

NICK: How is it?

DOCTOR: Hmmmm.

NICK: I said how is it?

DOCTOR: Not bad for three packs a day.

NICK: Look, I told you I was sorry . . .

DOCTOR: Still it was colossal stupidity to smoke so much. Your lungs must be a sewer.

NICK: Christ! Hey, Doc, you know how I feel now? Same way I feel when I go to confession. I tell the priest I'm sorry, he says no, that's not good enough. First he's got to call me names. What do I have to do to prove I'm sorry.

DOCTOR: Take off your tops and breathe deeply.

NICK: (*Doing as he is told.*) Madonn'!

DOCTOR: Breath in . . . hold . . . out. In . . . hold . . . out. Hmmmm.

NICK: What?

DOCTOR: I said, "Hmmmm."

NICK: Yeah, you keep saying that. What's it mean?

DOCTOR: Nothing in particular.

NICK: You know, Doc, you got a way about you scares the crap out of me.

DOCTOR: Put your mind at rest.

NICK: No, *you* put my mind at rest. I want my own doctor.

DOCTOR: One more question.

NICK: I talked enough. I want Doctor Grasso. He's Italian. He understands me.

DOCTOR: Lie down.

NICK: What for?

DOCTOR: (*Taking a thermometer from his lapel pocket.*) Routine temperature. (NICK *opens his mouth.*) Not in your mouth.

NICK: No!

DOCTOR: Jawohl!

NICK: (*Lying down.*) Christ!

DOCTOR: This hurts me more than you.

NICK: Ow! Want to bet!

DOCTOR: Now. Tell me, Mr. Monte. Are you a religious man?

NICK: You know, you got lousy timing.

DOCTOR: Are you?

NICK: What, have you got a priest waiting in the wings already?

DOCTOR: Just a point of curiosity, Mr. Monte.

NICK: All right. I go to church. You satisfied?

DOCTOR: I didn't ask you that. I said, are you a religious man?

NICK: Yeah! When business is bad. O.K.? Geez . . . Doc, what's all this got to do . . .

DOCTOR: Mr. Monte, you are an amazing specimen. Truly something to behold. Where shock and fear may have catastrophic effects on one person, on another there seems to be no effect whatsoever.

NICK: I'm fine.

DOCTOR: That is precisely my point. Against all odds, you are fine.

NICK: Except for this goddamn thermometer. Now when are you going to take it out?

NURSE: (*Enters with dinner tray.*) Here's din-din. Just the way you like it. (*Noticing* DOCTOR MUELLER.) Mr. Kurtz . . . ! What are you doing?

DOCTOR: Nothing.

NURSE: Mr. Kurtz, you get away from him right now.

DOCTOR: I didn't do a thing.

NURSE: Are you all right, Mr. Monte.

NICK: Get this thermometer out o' me . . .

NURSE: (*Running to him; removing the thermometer.*) My God . . . (KURTZ *is trying to sneak out.*) Mr. Kurtz, I'm not through with you. You stay right where you are.

KURTZ: I have another appointment.

NURSE: I said sit down. (KURTZ *mutters as he sits . . . reluctantly.*) Mr. Monte, since Mr. Kurtz won't do it himself, I'll apologize for him.

NICK: What's this Mr. Kurtz . . . He's not Doctor Mueller?

NURSE: No, he's not.

NICK: He said he was.

NURSE: He's not.

KURTZ: But he believed me. I made him believe me. Right over his eyes, I pulled the wool. I was spectacular.

NICK: Who the hell is he anyway?

KURTZ: For your information, Mr. Monte, I am Wilhelm Kurtz, expatriate of Vienna and actor sublime.

NICK: He's nuts.

KURTZ: I apologize for my shaky performance today, but I only learned my lines this morning.

NICK: I really think he's nuts. Get him out of here.

NURSE: I'll report him to the authorities.

NICK: No. Just leave him to me.

KURTZ: Don't you touch me, you barbarian. Never put your hands on an artist.

NICK: You come near me again, I'm going to throw you right over that wall.

KURTZ: Overreaction, Mr. Monte. You're giving a bad performance.

NURSE: Mr. Kurtz, do you want another enema?

KURTZ: You wouldn't dare.

NURSE: Try me. Just you try me. The syringe is in readiness.

NICK: Just get him away from me.

NURSE: I'm . . . afraid that won't be possible.

NICK: Why not?

NURSE: Mr. Monte, I'd like you to meet your roommate.

NICK: You're kidding!

NURSE: Afraid not.

NICK: What did I do wrong! I paid my Blue Cross, I paid my Blue Shield . . . I got to take him for a roommate?

KURTZ: Let me assure you, Mr. Monte, that in good time, you'll be thankful to have a roommate.

NICK: Don't get up your hopes.

KURTZ: In fact, I think you'll find me very affable indeed. I don't snore, I never toss in the night . . .

NICK: Sure, I'm stuck with a raving lunatic, I got to be thankful you don't snore?

NURSE: Let's have peace. All right, boys. You've got a half hour till lights go out. (*To* KURTZ.) You go inside.

KURTZ: I won't go without my roommate.

NICK: Look, we got two days together, OK? I don't want to hear your voice till I leave on Sunday morning. Then you say "bye-bye," and that's it. Fair enough?

KURTZ: So. You think you're leaving Sunday, eh?

NICK: Goddamn it . . . !

NURSE: No! (*After a silence.*) Mr. Kurtz, you go inside. You go inside at once.

KURTZ: I'm sorry, Mr. Monte. (*Leaves.*)

NICK: What did he mean?

NURSE: Just talking. Don't pay any attention to him.

NICK: What, does he get his jollies scaring the hell out of people?

NURSE: Some take kindly to him, others don't.

NICK: Three guesses where I stand.

NURSE: Just try to understand, he doesn't mean any harm. He used to be an actor. But now . . . he doesn't have a stage.

NICK: So I have to be his audience?

NURSE: If you don't mind.

NICK: Yeah, well I do mind. I want to know what he meant: "So, you think you're leaving Sunday . . ."

NURSE: Mr. Monte, he's an old man. He likes to babble. Get to be that age, no family, you can't help being lonely, I guess. Little bit afraid . . .

NICK: Afraid of what?

NURSE: Hey, I'll make a deal with you.

NICK: I don't know. What?

NURSE: You put up with him, just these couple of days, humor him, keep him happy . . .

NICK: What's in it for me?

NURSE: I'll see if I can't arrange some extra privileges.

NICK: Like what?

NURSE: Oh, I don't know. How about double desserts every meal?

NICK: A bowl of linguini, a big glass of wine, and you're on!

NURSE: What about lights out a half hour later than usual?

NICK: Oh, no, you don't. Longer I'm up, longer he's got to drive me nuts. Sorry.

NURSE: You know, you're a hard man to deal with.

NICK: I never promised I'd be easy.

NURSE: I know! How about a nice private room?
NICK: You're kidding.
NURSE: No.
NICK: You mean a real private room? All by myself?
NURSE: Absolutely.
NICK: Baby, you're on. Let me get my stuff.
NURSE: Wait a minute. Not so fast. A bargain's a bargain. First you have to do your part.
NICK: Keep the old fart company, eh?
NURSE: Just a day or two.
NICK: How long?
NURSE: Just through the weekend, that's all. Then Sunday we'll have a nice private room for you. Right down the hall.
NICK: Sunday, eh?
NURSE: Yessir. (*A silence. They stare at each other.*)
NICK: Except . . . I'm going home on Sunday. Remember? And I'm not going to be needing a private room. You got that? (*A moment. Three bells.*)
NURSE: (*Checking her watch.*) Well, off duty . . .
NICK: I said have you got that!
NURSE: You're right, Mr. Monte, of course. I'm just so used to making special arrangements for all our guests . . .
NICK: I don't want any special arrangements except for you and that bastard in there to leave me the hell alone.
NURSE: Mr. Monte . . .
NICK: Look, you heard the bells, didn't you? You said you were off duty. So just leave me alone and go home.
NURSE: I didn't mean it the way it sounded, believe me. I told you I'm so used to doing favors for the guests . . . I just accepted you as one of the family . . .
NICK: But I'm not one of the family, and I'm not a guest. I'm me, Nick Monte, and I'm a goddamn patient here, and I'm here for tests and observation, and I'm getting out of here on Sunday . . . you taking this down? . . . I don't want you to forget it.
NURSE: I'm sorry.
NICK: Prove it by leaving me alone.
NURSE: What about your dinner.
NICK: I don't want it.
NURSE: (*Picks up the tray.*) I'll leave the tea.
NICK: I hate tea.
NURSE: Please drink it, Mr. Monte. I'll send the night nurse later to look in on you.

NICK: She go to the same school you did?

NURSE: Drink the tea. There's a chill coming up; you'll want it.

NICK: Yeah.

NURSE: Don't stay here too long. And, Mr. Monte . . . welcome to the Sunset Side.

NICK: Yeah. (NURSE *leaves.* NICK *feels a slight chill and closes his robe around him snugly. He moves to the edge of the sundeck to look at the sunset.*)

KURTZ: (*Poking his head in.*) Pssst! Pssst!

NICK: What! What the hell do you want?

KURTZ: Is she gone for the night?

NICK: Yeah. Now go to bed.

KURTZ: I have to talk with you.

NICK: Nothing more to say. Just keep your distance.

KURTZ: I only want to say . . . I'm sorry.

NICK: You ought to be.

KURTZ: I am. I had no right.

NICK: Look, Pop, you get me straight, OK? From now on you keep five feet away from me at all times. You and your goddamn thermometer. You know you hurt me.

KURTZ: Really?

NICK: I can still feel it.

KURTZ: I'll be more careful next time.

NICK: I'm warning you . . .

KURTZ: I don't mean you. I mean the next person.

NICK: What, do you do that to everybody?

KURTZ: Only the newcomers. Before they get to know me.

NICK: And to know you is not necessarily to love you. You understand that, don't you.

KURTZ: Except for Freda.

NICK: Who the hell's Freda?

KURTZ: You don't know Freda? Freda Belden from the East Wing. Former librarian, pushing seventy. And jugs . . . right out to here!

NICK: Yeah?

KURTZ: Yeah.

NICK: Sounds like a monument. She loves you, huh?

KURTZ: You bet your boots she does. When she found out I'm not Doctor Mueller, she laughed and forgave me right away.

NICK: You played Doctor Mueller with Freda . . . !

KURTZ: Sure.

NICK: Thermometer and all?

KURTZ: You ain't just whistlin' Dixie. Her temperature was normal. For a while. You never saw such jugs.

NICK: Out to here, eh?

KURTZ: Jawohl! (*They laugh together.*)

NICK: You know, you're OK, Pop.

KURTZ: You forgive me?

NICK: What the hell. Why not?

KURTZ: That's good. Now I have a little something for you.

NICK: What?

KURTZ: Go stand by the door and keep watch.

NICK: What's going on?

KURTZ: You'll see. Just keep watch over there. If anybody comes, you give me a signal. Go on. (NICK *stands by the door.* KURTZ *crosses down to the edge of the porch. Very cautiously he removes one of the stones from the wall. He reaches in and pulls out a bottle of booze and a small glass.*)

NICK: My God!

KURTZ: Shhh! If Nurse finds out, we're cooked.

NICK: You're cooked. Not me. Where'd you get that stuff.

KURTZ: I have my sources. Now come and have a nip.

NICK: Oh, no. I got blood tests tomorrow.

KURTZ: This stuff will never touch your blood, believe me. It goes directly to the brain. Come on. (*He pours a shot and offers it to* NICK. NICK *refuses it.*) Ach! I'll show you. (KURTZ *downs it in a gulp.*) Good for the doldrums, but wicked for the stomach.

NICK: You're something else, Pop.

KURTZ: (*Puts the bottle and glass back.*) Remember. Not a word.

NICK: Don't worry. I might want it later.

KURTZ: So now we're friends, eh?

NICK: Sure. Hey, you really used to be an actor?

KURTZ: Not used to be. I *am* an actor. You saw my Doctor Mueller.

NICK: Yeah, I was moved.

KURTZ: A crackerjack creation. One of my best.

NICK: Ever do TV?

KURTZ: You must be mad.

NICK: No. I hear there's lots of money on TV. Commercials and all.

KURTZ: Commercials! Mr. Monte, I am an actor. I'm not in the toothpaste and armpit business.

NICK: Just wondering, that's all.

KURTZ: May I say something to you.

NICK: Sure.

KURTZ: In all modesty, of course.

NICK: This ought to be good.

KURTZ: In Austria, before the war, I was on the verge of greatness.

NICK: I like your modesty.

KURTZ: It's true.

NICK: I believe you.

KURTZ: No, you don't. But never mind. Let's not talk about me.

NICK: Ever hear of Andrew Monte?

KURTZ: Who?

NICK: My brother. Andrew Monte. Andy.

KURTZ: Where could I have heard of him?

NICK: He's a writer.

KURTZ: Give him my condolences.

NICK: Damn good one, too. Published his first book last year. *End of Grace.*

KURTZ: *End of Grace,* eh?

NICK: Yeah. You heard of it?

KURTZ: No.

NICK: See, it's about this group of people . . .

KURTZ: So far, so good.

NICK: . . . and every one of them is running from his past, you know. They all got their secrets, and one by one they're forced to open up . . . lay their cards on the table . . .

KURTZ: Lay their card, eh? That's good . . . go on.

NICK: So by the end of it, they all got a choice. Either keep on living a lie or face up to the truth and go on from there.

KURTZ: (*Sardonically.*) Sounds absorbing.

NICK: It's a powerhouse. Hey, Freda's a librarian. Maybe she read it.

KURTZ: I doubt it. She would have recommended it.

NICK: Critics killed it, the sons of bitches. Poor kid busts his ass two years on that book, and overnight the critics try to knock it out of print.

KURTZ: Mr. Monte, it's possible the book is no good. Have you thought of that?

NICK: What, do you want to join the enemy? Two years he spent . . .

KURTZ: Two years . . . ten years . . . crap is still crap!

NICK: Well damn it, I say it's not fair.

KURTZ: Fair? You ask for fair? Mr. Monte, there is no democracy in art. You teach that to your brother when you see him next. He must work until he drops, and he must expect nothing in return. Art is a lottery and talent only buys the ticket. The drawing comes later and it's out of our control.

NICK: OK, you never heard of Andy, eh? You will someday, you watch. Boy, he's some kid, Andy is. Fifteen years apart, but anybody's think we're the best of friends to look at us. Fishing, drinking beer . . . boy, we used to have good times. Our father died, so I had to teach him everything he knows. I remember once, he was five and I was twenty. I was shaving and Andy's taking a bath in the tub. All of a sudden he says to me, "Hey, Big Brother, what's this?" "That's your pecker, kid; now you leave it alone and save it for a rainy day." Just discovering himself, only five years old. Anyhow, couple of weeks later, I was getting ready for dinner and this big storm blew up. Thunder and lightning and pouring down rain. All of a sudden Andy comes running in the kitchen, his pecker hanging out: "It's raining, Big Brother, it's raining! Now, what do I do with this?" What a kid he is! (*A moment.*) A writer now. In the big city. Christ.

KURTZ: Do you always babble so about the past?

NICK: What are you talking about?

KURTZ: The past, Mr. Monte. It's dead. Forget it.

NICK: The hell I will.

KURTZ: There's only the present. And maybe the future, but don't count on that.

NICK: You know, you ought to go down to the lobby and set up a Welcome Wagon. You really got a way with people.

KURTZ: Just think about the present.

NICK: I'm not saying another word. You want to talk about the present? Go ahead. Talk.

KURTZ: I'll go to bed.

NICK: No, let's talk. How long you been here?

KURTZ: A few months.

NICK: What are you here for?

KURTZ: (*After a moment.*) Tests.

NICK: Come on. A few months, you're still taking tests?

KURTZ: Oh, yes. But don't despair; I've finished all but one. It will be the test of my life, and I hope I shall pass it magnificently. So now, to bed. Will you come in?

NICK: I'm . . . just going to stay here a minute.

KURTZ: Fine. But you're not to worry.

NICK: About what?

KURTZ: Anything.

NICK: Who's worried?
KURTZ: You will go home on Sunday.
NICK: You bet I will.
KURTZ: Tomorrow your test results will come, and everything will be as you wish.
NICK: You're damn right.
KURTZ: It's just no good to worry.
NICK: Look, can we drop it!
KURTZ: The present tense. That's all there is. I am . . . you are . . .

KURTZ *leaves.* NICK *stands staring after him. He sips a bit of tea, but it is cold. He walks to the edge of the sundeck and he is captured by the light of sunset. Slowly he undoes his robe and lets it fall to the floor in a pile. He removes his pajama tops, steps out of his slippers and gradually begins to jog in place.*

NICK: Easy, boy. That's it, kid. Yeah. Little more speed there. Lift those legs. In rhythm, baby; in rhythm. Touch soft, boy. Like a kiss. Kiss the earth with your feet, boy. Run, boy. Run, boy. Run . . . you son of a bitch, boy . . . RUN!

Lights out.

SCENE TWO

The next morning, about eleven o'clock. A brilliant sun is shining. KURTZ *is lying in his bed, fast asleep.* NICK *is up and about, getting things in order. He is singing a little Italian song to himself. He checks himself in the mirror, likes what he sees and begins to brush his hair.*

NICK: Hey, Pop, you going to get up or what? Come on; my wife's due any minute. I don't want her seeing you like that. (*Opening his bag.*) Case you change your mind, here's Andy's book. I'm putting it on the table. (*He looks around for something else to do. He checks his watch, paces about a little, then sits on his bed staring at the sleeping figure of* KURTZ.) Pop, you're really something else, you know? You just slept through the most important part of my life. What do you make of it, Pop? You struggle all your life trying to make something of yourself, find a little star out there, pin your hopes on it and what do they want . . . ? A little blood, a bottle of piss, and go on back to bed. Madonn'! . . . You just

NICK: She hasn't.

NURSE: Well, now, she must have had a little business to take care of; and I'm sure she'll be up as soon as she's finished.

NICK: What kind of business?

NURSE: Probably going to bawl out the cook 'cause you didn't eat your dinner last night.

NICK: Come on . . .

NURSE: And speaking of the cook, she wants your lunch order.

NICK: It's on the table.

NURSE: You want two desserts?

NICK: I want Carrie, OK? If you see her, tell her to come up.

NURSE: I will. Now why don't you go out there and enjoy that sunshine?

NICK: Yeah . . . sure.

NURSE: (*Indicating* KURTZ.) See if you can't get him out there, too. It'll do you both good.

NICK: He's not talking to me.

NURSE: So drag him by the ankle.

NICK: Tell Carrie I'm waiting, OK?

NURSE: Sure, honey. Sure.

NURSE *leaves.* NICK *moves about aimlessly, not knowing what to do with himself. He steps out to the sundeck and after exploring a bit, sits in one of the chairs to think.*

After a time, FREDA BELDEN, *a woman of sixty-five or seventy, enters onto the sundeck from the opposite side. She is thin and hunched, and walks with the demeanor of one who has given her best years to the reference room of a little village library.*

FREDA: (*Calling.*) Willy! Willy! (*She approaches the window of* NICK'*s room.*) Willy!

NICK: I ain't Willy, but I'll do in a pinch.

FREDA: Who are you?

NICK: Just going to ask you the same thing. Who are you?

FREDA: The Ghost of Christmas Past. Now where the hell's Willy?

NICK: Look, Mom, I'll make a deal with you. This Willy . . . you tell me *who* he is, I'll tell you *where* he is.

FREDA: (*Seeing* KURTZ *asleep.*) There he is. Willy!

NICK: You mean . . . Pop? That's Willy? (*Laughing he runs in to shake* KURTZ.) Hey, Willy . . . shake your ass. You got company.

KURTZ: (*Startled awake.*) What . . . no! Take your hands away . . . you brute!

NICK: Look, Pop . . . it's the Tooth Fairy.

going to lay there? Sure, sugar plums for the old man. Me, I got to babble to the walls. . . . If my father was alive today, he'd be just about your age. You even look like him, too. Except for the forehead. My father's forehead was very aristocratic. (*Checking his watch.*) Wonder what's keeping Carrie. She said eleven o'clock. (*He notices the bedside phone. He dials home, props himself up on the bed for a good conversation, then waits. No answer. He hangs up. He tries to read. Finally:*) Damn it all! Talk to me, will you!

NURSE *enters carrying a juice tray.*

NURSE: Good morning, boys.

NICK: Hey, where you been? I missed you.

NURSE: Just came on duty. You're not still mad at me?

NICK: Forget it.

NURSE: You sleep all right?

NICK: You ever sleep with a dragon?

NURSE: I heard you were a good boy down in the lab.

NICK: Except they drained me dry. What the hell they going to do with all that blood?

NURSE: Here's a little juice for you and a nice little pill.

NICK: What for?

NURSE: Calm your nerves. Take it. (*Going to* KURTZ. *She takes his pulse.*) You awake, honey? (*No response.*) Have you had your movement yet, or should I get the syringe?

KURTZ: (*Sitting up.*) Don't you dare! I already moved. Why do you insist upon abusing my body?

NURSE: Honey, you are so gorgeous, I just can't keep my hands off you.

KURTZ: Well, today I must insist that you restrain yourself. I'm going back to sleep and I do not wish to be disturbed. (*To* NICK.) And you! Don't you talk to me again.

NICK: What'd I do now?

KURTZ: Between us, it is finished. Kaput! Goodbye. (*He goes back to sleep.*)

NURSE: All right, what happened?

NICK: Do I know? He keeps me awake all night snoring, and now *he*'s pissed at *me*. Nurse, have you seen Carrie?

NURSE: Carrie? Well, yes; downstairs when I came on duty. She hasn't been up?

NICK: No.

NURSE: I just assumed she had.

KURTZ: Freda!

FREDA: Good morning, Willy.

NICK: You're Freda? The librarian? What do you say, Freda? Hey, no kidding, you really got a thing going with Pop, huh?

FREDA: I do.

NICK: Funny, I had a different picture . . . the way Pop described you . . .

KURTZ: Mr. Monte! Give me my robe.

NICK: (*Tossing it to him.*) Here, catch!

FREDA: Willy, shall we have our walk?

KURTZ: (*Putting on his robe.*) Right away, Freda.

NICK: Going for a walk, huh?

KURTZ: Yes. And you are not invited to join us.

NICK: Who said I wanted to join you?

KURTZ: Just in case you took the notion.

NICK: Hey, what's eating you anyway?

KURTZ: So . . . you don't like my forehead, eh? Well . . . pish-posh!

FREDA: Well said, Willy!

KURTZ: Now, why don't you sit in the corner and read your book. Freda, come.

NICK: OK. Go ahead, take a walk. But when you come back, don't say hello. Far as I'm concerned you're dead.

FREDA: No!

NICK: You hear me. You're dead!

KURTZ: Stop! (KURTZ *stares at* NICK *deeply hurt. Slowly he wilts and starts walking outside.*) All I want . . . is to have my walk with Freda.

NICK: (*After a moment.*) What happened to him?

FREDA: Are you so blind?

NICK: Tell me.

FREDA: Just open your eyes and look. Can't you see that he's a dying man?

NICK: Pop? Come on, he's a laugh a minute.

FREDA: What would you expect, self-pity! That happens early on. Now he wants to laugh.

NICK: You mean he knows?

FREDA: How does one not know when one is dying?

NICK: Jesus . . . I'm sorry . . . I didn't understand.

FREDA: You've much to learn, Mr. Monte. (*She exits to the sundeck.*) Willy! Walk time.

KURTZ: (*Extending his arm.*) I'm ready, Freda. (*Very slowly and gracefully, as though in a dream, they promenade about the entire circumference of the sundeck, now and then pausing to acknowledge passersby.*) Ah, Herr Schmidt! Frau Schmidt, you're ravishing today. May I present to you, Fräulein Belden.

FREDA: Howdy. Pleased to meet you, I'm sure.

KURTZ: She comes from America. (*They turn and walk back, exactly the way they came.*) They say he's cheating on his wife.

FREDA: No!

KURTZ: Jawohl! Ah, Fräulein Hoffer . . . (*To* FREDA.) With her. (*They continue their promenade.*)

FREDA: (*Finally.*) Willy, I need to rest.

KURTZ: Waiter, two coffees. (*They sit.*)

FREDA: A lovely café.

KURTZ: But the service is impossible. Well, what can you expect?

FREDA: . . . in this day and age.

KURTZ: What's that?

FREDA: I said, in this day and age.

KURTZ: Ah, yes. You're right of course. Well, anyway . . .

FREDA: Oh, I agree.

KURTZ: All is not lost.

FREDA: Thank God for that, at least.

KURTZ: In this day and age . . .

FREDA: . . . these times of change . . .

KURTZ: I'm proud to say . . .

FREDA: . . . you ought to be . . .

KURTZ: That all . . . is not lost. (*A moment.*) They've asked me to play King Lear!

FREDA: Oh, no!

KURTZ: Yes! Yes! The greatest of them all!!

FREDA: You must be proud.

KURTZ: Oh, yes. And scared. So long I've waited . . .

FREDA: And the contract . . . ?

KURTZ: . . . comes tomorrow. I'll sign of course.

FREDA: That's right. No fear.

KURTZ: Forget my fear. My art comes first.

FREDA: And art . . .

KURTZ: . . . after all . . .

FREDA: . . . is art!

KURTZ: Freda . . . look!

FREDA: Look where?

KURTZ: You see. Right there.

FREDA: A boy! Like you.

KURTZ: A boy! Like me. (*They watch a moment.*) He's standing by the water . . .

FREDA: . . . the rippling water . . .

KURTZ: Yes. Rippling, rippling . . . and he's waving at the ships.

FREDA: . . . huge merchant ships, so proud . . .

KURTZ: Don't go too close; they'll eat you up . . .

FREDA: . . . the ships . . . the sea . . .

KURTZ: . . . they'll eat you up. He's turning back; but look, he sees a cloud.

FREDA: A cloud?

KURTZ: A black storm cloud.

FREDA: No . . .

KURTZ: He does!

FREDA: No, Willy!

KURTZ: The sky is black.

FREDA: He never saw the clouds before.

KURTZ: Over his father's house.

FREDA: Willy, please . . .

KURTZ: Over his Fatherland. Afraid to go back. He runs to the ships instead.

FREDA: No, not the ships. Don't leave your home, little boy.

KURTZ: Hurry, boy, hurry! (*Silence.*) He's on the ship. Sailing . . . to the horizon. And the boy. Afraid to go back, afraid to swim . . . What is he to do? Don't look back. Just go . . . go . . . but where? . . . to what? (*We see* CARRIE *who has entered the room.* NICK *does not see her; he's watching* KURTZ *and* FREDA. KURTZ *collects himself.*) Freda, did the coffee come?

FREDA: I sent it back. Too cold.

KURTZ: You did right. (*They sit quietly,* KURTZ *collecting himself.*)

CARRIE: (*She has been standing behind* NICK, *watching him closely; she goes to him, puts her head on his shoulder.*) Hi, lover.

NICK: Hey, where you been?

CARRIE: Missing you.

NICK: Nurse said she saw you.

CARRIE: Yeah. She did.

NICK: Come here. Take a look. (CARRIE *looks out and sees* KURTZ *and* FREDA, *who are still in the "café," now sipping fresh coffee. She cannot see their faces.*)

KURTZ: (*Relishing the coffee.*) Ah. Exquisite.

FREDA: At least it's hot. I told that waiter, my Willy likes his coffee hot.

KURTZ: That raises an interesting philosophical dilemma. Should I insist my coffee be hot and risk the unbridled anger of a surly waiter . . . or, on the other hand . . . should I recognize the basic humanity even of a goddamn waiter, and take my coffee cold? Hmmm.

FREDA: I wouldn't leave him a tip.

KURTZ: That's true. We mustn't encourage the help.

FREDA: After all . . .

KURTZ: . . . in this day and age . . .

FREDA: . . . this day . . .

KURTZ: . . . and age, we have to . . .

FREDA: . . . have to . . . (*They grow silent and stare off into space.*)

NICK: They're in love.

CARRIE: Me, too. Think they'll move if we ask them nicely?

NICK: Why?

CARRIE: So we can talk.

NICK: You can't just ask them to move.

CARRIE: Why not? He owes you one.

NICK: What do you mean?

CARRIE: (*Laughing.*) He really got you with a thermometer, huh?

NICK: How'd you hear?

CARRIE: From Nurse. You have to admit it's kind of funny.

NICK: I don't have to admit anything. That thing hurt, you know.

CARRIE: Poor baby. Now watch and learn.

NICK: Where you going?

CARRIE: I'm going to clear the sunporch. (*She goes out.* NICK *stays behind and watches.*) Hello.

FREDA: Hello, dear.

KURTZ: Mrs. Monte!

CARRIE: Dr. Miller.

KURTZ: No, M*ue*ller.

FREDA: Willy!

KURTZ: (*Trapped.*) Oi . . . ach!

FREDA: Have you been playing Dr. Mueller again?

KURTZ: (*To* CARRIE.) I must apologize for my patient, Mrs. Monte. She insists that I am some lost love named Willy, so I humor her, you understand.

CARRIE: No matter. Please sit. You're just the people I wanted to see.

FREDA: Did you hear that, Willy? She wants to see us.

CARRIE: Yes. As you know, I'm a very busy woman. My husband there, five kids to drive to school; there's just no end to my day. But somehow I manage to keep active in my church group and different civic functions . . .

KURTZ: Church group?

CARRIE: Yes.

FREDA: And different civic functions.

CARRIE: Right. And at the moment I'm very involved trying to organize a little social club for children. We call it the Society of St. Aloysius . . . he loved children, you know.

KURTZ: Aloysius, eh?

CARRIE: Yes. And to do our work, we depend absolutely on the generosity of other caring people . . . private contributions.

KURTZ: Contributions, eh? Freda, you seem to be trembling.

FREDA: I think it's time for my medicine.

KURTZ: (*Checking his watch.*) Ach! You're right. Mrs. Monte, if you don't mind, my patient must return to her room. We don't want to exhaust her.

CARRIE: I see.

KURTZ: Perhaps we can discuss this matter at a later time.

CARRIE: I'll be here awhile.

KURTZ: At some later date, perhaps. Come, Freda. (*Arm in arm* KURTZ *and* FREDA *start off.*)

FREDA: You never know, do you?

KURTZ: I should say you don't.

FREDA: Wouldn't you think . . .

KURTZ: . . . in this day and age . . .

FREDA: They'd let you live in peace?

KURTZ: Aloysius . . . contributions . . . Gott! (*They exit.*)

CARRIE: (*To* NICK.) You want to talk now?

NICK: Amazing.

CARRIE: Never fails.

NICK: Poor old guy. I just found out he's dying.

CARRIE: Oh, no.

NICK: Yeah. Christ, what a lousy break.

CARRIE: Does he know?

NICK: That's just it. He knows. But to watch him, you'd think he was going to check out of here with me tomorrow. Don't know where the hell he gets the strength. I always figured if a guy knew he was going to die, he'd just . . . sort of sit around and cry all day. Not Pop. Christ, what a break. (CARRIE *is silent, watching* NICK.) You better tell me what to do, honey. 'Cause when he comes back, I got to try to act natural, you know. Like nothing's wrong.

Ann Guilbert (FREDA) *and Phil Leeds* (KURTZ), *foreground, and DeAnn Mears* (CARRIE) *and Frank Savino* (NICK), *background, in the Los Angeles Actors' Theatre production.*

CARRIE: I don't know what to tell you. Just be yourself. Just always be my Nick. That's all.

NICK: Hey, let's not worry about it, huh? He's a great old man, but he's had a long life and there's nothing we can do to help him. So what's the point of worrying? How's the kids?

CARRIE: Collectively, they're fine. Not allowing for Timmy's nosebleed last night.

NICK: What happened?

CARRIE: Well, in his hurry to get to the softball game, he gulped down his dinner and ran out through the back screen door.

NICK: So?

CARRIE: *Through* . . . the back screen door. He forgot to open it.

NICK: (*Laughing.*) Crazy kid! (*Chokes on his laughter as cough spasms take hold of him.*)

CARRIE: Nick . . .! (NICK *turns away from* CARRIE.) Nick . . . sit down. (*He covers his mouth with a handkerchief to muffle the sounds. He moves to a chair and sits. After a time,* CARRIE *goes to him and stands behind, rubbing his shoulders.* NICK *has collected himself.*)

NICK: So?

CARRIE: Carrie?

NICK: What's wrong?

CARRIE: You mean besides having to sleep alone last night?

NICK: I mean you're late. You never been late a day in your life.

CARRIE: I was here on time.

NICK: You were downstairs on time. Coming to see me, you're an hour late.

CARRIE: Nurse and I were having a chat. OK?

NICK: You're a lousy liar.

CARRIE: I'm not!

NICK: Come on, where you been?

CARRIE: All right. I just saw the doctor. He says you're a model patient; about the best he can remember.

NICK: Look, honey, it's me . . . Nick. Remember?

CARRIE: What's wrong?

NICK: You saw the doctor, right?

CARRIE: Yes.

NICK: So what did he say?

CARRIE: I'm trying to tell you.

NICK: Stop trying. Just tell me.

CARRIE: He . . . wants you to stay here a couple more days.

NICK: (*A moment to receive the news.*) Tell him I don't like the food. Hey, what time's checkout tomorrow? Twelve o'clock, isn't it?

CARRIE: Just a day or two . . .

NICK: Soon as we get home, we'll pack a lunch and have that picnic we promised the kids . . .

CARRIE: Nick . . . ?

NICK: . . . then a good night's sleep, I'll be back on the job with the other guys.

CARRIE: Will you let me finish?

NICK: Yeah. Sure. Go ahead.

CARRIE: It's not much to ask.

NICK: It's not, huh?

CARRIE: Not considering everything.

NICK: What? Considering what?

CARRIE: That we shouldn't take any risks if there's a chance of complications.

NICK: What complications? What the hell are you talking about?

CARRIE: I didn't say there were any.

NICK: And you didn't say there weren't.

CARRIE: (*Collecting her thoughts.*) Remember the other hospital?

NICK: Six weeks nursing the wrong sickness, you want to know if I remember. Vaguely, yeah!

CARRIE: There was a little shadow in your x-rays . . . just a pinpoint . . . nothing to worry about.

NICK: What a relief!

CARRIE: And your tests this morning just confirmed it. There's a tiny spot . . . no cause for alarm.

NICK: You keep saying that.

CARRIE: So as long as you're here, they figured you might as well stay another day or two . . . they can do a little exploratory surgery.

NICK: Surgery!

CARRIE: *Exploratory* surgery!

NICK: Oh, Lewis and Clark, huh! I hope you told 'em no.

CARRIE: I wanted to talk with you first.

NICK: Fine. You talked. We finished. Go tell 'em no.

CARRIE: I can't do that.

NICK: Then I will.

CARRIE: Nick, for God's sake . . .

NICK: Day after tomorrow, nine o'clock in the morning, I'm due back on the job. You want bread and butter on the table, I go back to work.

CARRIE: I'm not concerned about bread and butter.

NICK: How the hell can you say that! You spent your whole goddamn childhood without a dime.

CARRIE: Nick!

NICK: I just want to do what's best for you!

CARRIE: Then prove it!

NICK: How! By letting some butcher come at me with a knife! I'm telling you *no!*

CARRIE: And I'm telling you you'd better.

NICK: Look, get off my back about it. I'm not having any operation. Nobody ever cut me up before, they're not going to start now. How do we know these guys are right anyway?

CARRIE: We'll have to trust them.

NICK: We trusted the last place, too; and look what the hell they did. Six weeks and nothing!

CARRIE: It's different here.

NICK: How do I know that?

CARRIE: You'll have to take that chance.

NICK: Go on home, will you?

CARRIE: Do it, Nick.

NICK: I said get out.

CARRIE: Nick.

NICK: Shut up and get out!

CARRIE: It's the only chance you've got! (*A long silence.*)

NICK: (*Finally.*) Funny, I'm trying to think of a proverb I heard once, but nothing comes to mind. Hey, how about: "Shape up or ship out!" Naw, it's not good. Or maybe: "A stitch in time . . . saves nine." Yeah, that's a good one. Wait a minute. Nine what? "A stitch in time saves nine . . . what?" Wouldn't you think some dumbass guy wants to make a proverb, least he could do is finish the goddamn thing! Boy! I never went to college, but I know how to put the finish to a . . . (CARRIE *watches him silently.*) What are you looking at? Look like you see a ghost. Come on, it's me . . . Laugh-a-Minute Monte, remember? You married me for the laughs, so let's do it. Look at me. I'm fine. Don't I look fine? I mean that's a stupid thing those doctors want to do. Well, let me tell you something; they got the wrong party. Hell, I was out here jogging for a full hour last night. . . . And come to love, I'm just as good as I always was, right! Haven't heard you complain. I mean, if I wasn't as good as I always was, stands to reason the old lady would complain. Like your friend . . . what's her name . . . Lucille . . . always grousing her husband can't get it up anymore. Hell, married twenty-five years to her, no wonder he can't get it up. But you can't say that about me, now can you? Can't go squealing to your bridge club that Nick's no good. Oh, no. I'm good! And I'm going to stay good for a lot of years to come. (*Pause.*) Carrie, baby? Remember that coat you wanted? Why don't you go buy it, huh? Go get your hair done, get yourself a new coat, and tomorrow we'll take the kids for that picnic.... What, are you some kind of statue! Just going to sit there and let the pigeons dump on you? Come on, wake up. Only a princess gets to sit around like that. Let's face it, honey, you're no princess. I mean you're pretty and all, but the bloom just naturally tends to wear off after... what is it... forty years, forty-one? The petals begin to fall.... Look at it this way. Things are going to be fine. New coat, new house. Hell, there's no limit to what you can buy once you get your hands on that insurance money.

CARRIE: Oh, Jesus!

NICK: You say something?

CARRIE: Stop it, Nick.

NICK: No!

CARRIE: Please stop.

NICK: Why? You said I'm dead already.

CARRIE: I said there's a chance.

NICK: (*Grabbing hold of her.*) If I let 'em slice me up, right!

CARRIE: Nick, I'm only the messenger!

NICK: Am I right?

CARRIE: Let go!

NICK: Am I?

CARRIE: I said let me go! (*A long silence.*) Do you want to beat me, Nick? Come on. I wish you would. Do you want me to go? Tell me. I will. I'll do anything you want, Nick. Anything at all. But you're not going to make me lie to you. I can't give you that.... If I could lie with an easy heart and let you rest tonight, you know I would. If I could take away what you feel right now and lay it on myself, you know I would. And if I could take that doctor's knife and cut away this day, by the bitter tears of Jesus, you know I would.... I'm telling you as simply as I can that I love you. I don't know how else to say it except... I love you. But you know what? So do you! (NICK *grabs at her again, but she avoids him.*) Oh, that hurt, didn't it? Well, you just hang on, because I'm not finished yet. While you stand there deciding whether to leave me or murder me, how about a passing thought for your kids! They want their father, you know. They like him quite a bit. And I can tell you now, they're not going to cotton to being orphans, and I sure as hell won't cotton to being a widow.

But if that's what you have in mind, if you have any intention of refusing the doctor's orders, then you go ahead and do it. But remember, you do it without me and you do it without the kids. We're going to have that picnic, the kids and I, and you can goddamn die alone!

NICK: Baby.

CARRIE: Alone, you hear me!

NICK: Oh, Baby. (*He holds out his arms but she stands firm. Finally,* NICK *sits.*) O my God. I am heartily sorry . . . (CARRIE *comes behind and rubs his shoulders.*) Holy Mary . . .

CARRIE: . . . Mother of God . . .

NICK: . . . pray for us sinners . . .

CARRIE: . . . now and at the hour . . .

NICK: . . . now and at the hour . . .

CARRIE: . . . of our death. Amen.

Lights out.

ACT TWO

SCENE ONE

About three months later. Near the end of summer. NICK *and* KURTZ *are both in their beds.* NICK *is watching* TV. KURTZ *is wearing bright red pajamas with a matching red stocking cap. If Santa Claus were terminal, here he would be.*

KURTZ: (*After a long time.*) Things are looking up, Mr. Monte. You have a TV, you have a new plant; what more can you ask? (NICK *pays no attention.*) And for myself, today we go to the opera, Freda and I. Ponselle is singing *Norma,* and I have to look my best. (*He sings a few bars.*) "Mira, O Norma, a' tuoi ginocchi . . ." (NICK *turns up the volume of his* TV.) Ah, yes. I have to give it to the Italians. They know how to slap together an opera. And I ain't just whistlin' Dixie. Mein Gott! (*Silence.*) I have always felt, if ever I had a daughter, that I should call her Norma. Brunhilde does not make it. But Norma . . . yes! (*A moment.*) What did you say? (*Finally.*) Ach! (*Pulls the covers up and snuggles down in bed. After a moment* NICK*'s telephone rings.*)

NICK: (*Eagerly, after turning down the* TV.) Hi, honey, how are you?

KURTZ: (*Sits up holding his telephone, which he had concealed.*) Fine, my darling; I thought you would never speak.

NICK *slams down the receiver, turns off the* TV, *and* KURTZ, *of course, is beside himself.* NICK *hurriedly gets out of bed, tries to walk, and goes to the floor as his legs give way beneath him.* KURTZ *makes an attempt to help him.*

NICK: (*Grabbing his cane.*) No! Don't!

NICK *struggles up, takes a few steps, picks up his new plant and walks out to the sundeck. He looks around and finds a place in the sunshine. He sets down the plant and waters it from a nearby pitcher. Then he sits for a long, long time staring at the plant.*

KURTZ, *meantime, has gotten up and slowly walked out. He is noticeably weaker, too, but still able to support himself. He stands behind* NICK *and stares at the plant, too.*

KURTZ: (*Finally.*) Look. It's growing.
NICK: Pop, do you mind?
KURTZ: What?
NICK: I'd like to be alone.
KURTZ: Why?
NICK: I'd like to be alone.
KURTZ: In good time you'll be alone. Meanwhile, enjoy my company. We have a few minutes till Freda comes. How shall we pass the time?
NICK: Pop, don't you understand?
KURTZ: Only too well. So, let us have a drink. (*Goes to the wall and removes a bottle of wine.*) Good wine your mother brought. Vintage stuff, you should know. Will you drink? (NICK *shakes his head no.* KURTZ *pours for himself.*) An attractive woman, your mother. A bit sentimental, I suppose, as mothers tend to be, but we all have our faults. Most people do, that is. To your health! (KURTZ *savors the wine.*) Ahhh! Straight to the brain. (*He sits.*) Now, shall we philosophize? (NICK *finally laughs in spite of himself.*) You still know how to laugh, you see. Let's philosophize. So, what do you make of it?
NICK: What?
KURTZ: This boat we are in together.
NICK: (*Thinking a moment.*) It sucks.
KURTZ: Well put.
NICK: Pop?
KURTZ: Yes?

NICK: I'm sorry.
KURTZ: Pish-posh!
NICK: I guess I'm afraid.
KURTZ: Who is not?
NICK: You too?
KURTZ: Who is not? (*A silence.*) But they say it passes.
NICK: Who says?
KURTZ: They do.
NICK: Ah. (*A silence.*) I wonder when.
KURTZ: In time. In time.
NICK: I'm only forty-five.
KURTZ: I know.
NICK: I used to jog. The peak of health.
KURTZ: Yes, yes.
NICK: Outran 'em all. I was strong.
KURTZ: Of course.
NICK: Why me!
KURTZ: Ah, yes. Why me? The primal question. Congratulations, Mr. Monte. You have now reached the third plateau. Step three . . . why me?
NICK: What are you talking about.
KURTZ: The natural progression from life to . . . the other place.
NICK: Death.
KURTZ: Bravo! From life to death. It goes in steps. It's all charted out. I have it inside.
NICK: To hell with the charts. I'm telling you how I feel. I'm young and I'm strong and I want to know why me?
KURTZ: Or me, Mr. Monte. What of me! I've asked the question, too.
NICK: Yeah, but you're old. I'm not.
KURTZ: With a little dash of cruelty, eh? You've still a way to go.
NICK: I'm sorry.
KURTZ: Look there. I've never seen the maples look so sweet. Or the birches any prouder. Can you imagine that?
NICK: (*Truly apologetic.*) Please, Pop . . . I'm sorry.
KURTZ: Mr. Monte, let me caution you. You must not ask *why me.*
NICK: I got a right to know.
KURTZ: Don't flatter yourself. You have no such right. Hope as much as you wish, but do not make demands. The best you can do is to learn the way the wind is blowing, but don't be so foolish as to think that you can change it, or even explain it. All your demands do not alter for a single moment the fact of your mortality.

NICK: Jesus, have a heart.

KURTZ: I have a heart, Mr. Monte. Yes, I do. Now have a sip of wine with me. (NICK *takes the glass, stares at* KURTZ, *then drinks. For a long while after,* NICK *and* KURTZ *stare at the trees. Softly,* NICK *begins to whistle "Dixie."*) You ain't just whistlin' Dixie. (*And they laugh together.*)

NURSE *enters with a* TV Guide. *She is excited.*

NURSE: My God, will you look at this!

NICK: What is it?

NURSE: Biggest thing to ever hit this place.

KURTZ: What?

NURSE: I tell you the Sunset Side is going to be a monument some day.

NICK: Come on, what are you talking about?

NURSE: (*Handing* NICK *the* TV Guide.) Look right there.

NICK: Where?

NURSE: There, you see. Tomorrow. Channel 3.

NICK: (*Finding it.*) The Midday Movie. *The Fiend of Berlin.* So?

KURTZ: The what!

NICK: *The Fiend of Berlin.*

KURTZ: No!

NICK: Hey, wait a minute. 1943. Starring Wilhelm Kurtz. Hey, Pop, that's you!

KURTZ: Let me see! (*Grabs the magazine.*)

NICK: See. Right there.

KURTZ: Gott! "Madman tortures young women for the Fuehrer's pleasure."

NURSE: Sounds wonderful.

KURTZ: It was not my best work.

NURSE: Never you mind. I've told everybody. They want you to make a speech after.

KURTZ: We will not watch it.

NICK: The hell we won't.

NURSE: Who plays the madman?

KURTZ: I do, of course.

NICK: Yeah, that figures.

KURTZ: I always took the leading roles. (*Checking the* Guide *again.*) What's this! "If you believe this, you'll believe anything." Who said that!

NICK: One man's opinion. Forget it.

KURTZ: He had no right. They might be showing any one of my films. Why this one! It is not representative.

NURSE: Relax, Mr. Kurtz. What do we care? For us it's going to be the best movie ever made.

NICK: Yeah! I want to see you torture them broads.

KURTZ: One broad in particular. The leading actress . . . ach! I could have strangled her with my own bare hands, but the director made me stop.

NURSE: Then it's true!

KURTZ: What?

NURSE: Temperamental actresses and all that.

KURTZ: No, my dear, she was not temperamental. She was inept. An Olympic figure skater from Czechoslovakia who came to Hollywood with three gold medals and tried to be a star. I think she learned to act from a block of wood. But, mein Gott! Could she skate. So, no matter what the story, the studio insisted she have a skating scene. Tomorrow, you'll see. Imagine this: I abduct her from the Olympic Arena and drag her screaming to the Fuehrer's bunker and I fasten her with chains. "Tomorrow," I say, "the Fuehrer vill come to haf his vay vit you" . . . we had to speak mock German, you understand . . . "But before he comes, I intend to haf my own vay vit you! Vat do you tink uf dat!" "I vant my shkates," she cries: "I vant my shkates!" So then she passes out and in her delirium she has a dream. Fade out, fade in. A chorus of Rhine Maidens dancing to the tunes of Strauss . . . on skates.

NICK: Did you have your way with her?

KURTZ: No! By a colossal act of Providence and a twist in the mind of the author, her lover Bruno appears, disguised as Der Fuehrer, and they go skating away to freedom. End of movie. End of career. (*A moment.*) I wonder what happened to Bruno?

FREDA *enters in street clothes.*

FREDA: Willy! Willy, have you heard?

KURTZ: Yes. But we won't be watching.

FREDA: Oh, not that. I mean about me. Excuse me, would you mind if I talk with Willy?

NICK: No, I don't mind.

FREDA: Alone.

NURSE: Come on. You have a surprise coming tomorrow.

NICK: Me? What kind of surprise?

NURSE: Nope. Can't tell.

NICK: Come on.

NURSE: Uh-uh. I promised. But if you're good, I'll give you a hint. It's from New York.

NICK: New York? You mean . . . Andy! Hey Pop, d'you hear that? Andy's coming!

KURTZ: When I see it, I'll believe it.

NICK: He's coming. (*To* NURSE, *as they exit.*) I'm going to haf my vay vit you. Vat do you tink uf dat?

KURTZ: For three months he's talked of nothing but that boy. Shall we walk to the opera, or shall I call for my carriage?

FREDA: It doesn't matter, Willy.

KURTZ: Good. Then we shall walk. Herr Schmidt will join us later.

FREDA: You tell him that won't be necessary.

KURTZ: Not necessary? We mustn't offend Herr Schmidt.

FREDA: I'm afraid I won't be joining you for the opera, Willy.

KURTZ: Not join me . . . pish-posh! Who else should take my arm?

FREDA: I'm leaving, Willy.

KURTZ: (*A moment.*) After all, Ponselle is singing today . . .

FREDA: I'm going home.

KURTZ: A benefit performance . . . a gala, don't you know?

FREDA: I'm well. They're sending me home today.

KURTZ: They'll all be there to hear . . . the famous, the near-famous . . . (FREDA *is silent.*) Home?

FREDA: Home, Willy.

KURTZ: But . . . you can't . . . just go.

FREDA: I'm better.

KURTZ: But the walks . . .

FREDA: They were fun.

KURTZ: The museums, the café . . .

FREDA: Yes, Willy. You always showed me the best. But now it's time. My sister's coming soon to drive me home. And you'll never guess what's happened. We're taking a place in Florida. A condominium by the sea.

KURTZ: But that's so far away.

FREDA: Nonsense, Willy. The world is shrinking. Why, in no time flat these modern jets can whisk us away and back again before you know I've gone. Imagine me in Florida. A whole new life. Be happy for me.

KURTZ: Of course.

FREDA: And come next spring, I'll be back to say hello. You'll see. Make a clean break, you always said. The past is gone. Face tomorrow.

KURTZ: You have learned your lesson well.

FREDA: I had a splendid teacher. (*A moment.*) It was fun, Willy. Remember that.

KURTZ: What was fun?

FREDA: The walks . . . you know.

KURTZ: What walks? (*They stare at each other, their lessons learned.*)

FREDA: (*Extending her hand.*) Goodbye.

KURTZ: (*Not accepting it.*) You'll be late.

FREDA *leaves.* KURTZ *stares after her for a while, then begins to move about aimlessly. He sits and waits, staring off into time. We see a smile appear. He takes the remaining wine and offers a toast.*

KURTZ: (*Continued.*) Herr Schmidt! Frau Schmidt! How good of you to come. You'll join me, of course. I've ordered wine. Herr Schmidt . . . ! Frau . . . ! (*They vanish and* KURTZ *is alone.*) Waiter, coffee for two. And bring dessert; we're famished. The opera was long. (*A moment.*) Closed? Impossible. The café is never closed. We demand to see the manager. You'll get no tip for this. We'll take our business elsewhere . . . we'll . . . (*He gradually assumes the posture of an actor acknowledging the cheers of an audience on an evening of triumph.*) Thank you. Thank you so very much. Without your encouragement my art is nothing.

"Blow, winds, and crack your cheeks! Rage! Blow!
You cataracts and hurricanoes, spout
Till you have drenched our steeples, drowned the cocks!
You sulphurous and thought-executing fires,
Vaunt-couriers to oak-cleaving thunderbolts,
Singe my white head."

(*He begins to stammer and forget the words.*) I'm sorry. It's such a long time, you understand . . . (*He goes back to recover and stammers again.*)

"I will have such revenges . . .
. . . I will do such things . . ."

Please bear with me. The words will come . . . I know the words . . .

"You think I'll weep.—
No, I'll not weep.
O fool, I shall go mad!"

Ladies and gentlemen, please take your seats. Understand, I didn't mean to run away. I tried to go back, but I was on the ship, and the ship had left the shore. Was I to swim! . . . I saw the storm clouds rising. I heard my father, I heard my mother. "Come back; don't leave us here . . ." I sent for them; I did. But they had gone. Six million had gone. The clouds had covered my land . . . had covered the world . . . Who would have thought? (*A silent scream.*)

NICK: Hey, Pop? Pop . . . you all right?

KURTZ: What? Oh . . . yes . . .

NICK: Pop, what's wrong?

KURTZ: I'm fine.

NICK: Where's Freda? I thought she was here.

KURTZ: Freda? No.

NICK: Pull yourself together. You're going to the opera.

KURTZ: Don't be foolish. Ponselle retired years ago. You should know that.

NICK: It's getting late. Let me help you to bed.

KURTZ: Not yet. I want to tell you what I saw. Just now. I looked into the Eyes of God, Mr. Monte . . . and there was a void.

NICK: Come on, don't talk like that.

KURTZ: A void, do you hear me? So much for justice. They told me to act, so I acted. Oh, boy, the guns went off when I set foot upon the stage. "Wilhelm Kurtz give an astonishing performance as Mercutio!" That's what they said. About me. And I might have been a Hamlet, too, with just a little time. All I needed was just a little time . . .

NICK: Never mind. It's past. You don't have to talk about it.

KURTZ: I do! Finally . . . I do. The war came to Vienna. And they took away my stage. I was forced to run, and they took away my language. What in the hell is an actor without his language! Cheap impersonations in second-rate stock companies, specializing in lunatic scientists and demented counts. In America, I built a career out of broken English! Imagine . . . me, a Jew . . . playing Hollywood Nazis in the old war films. "Sieg Heil! Sieg Heil!" I had to say. O my God, Sieg Heil! . . . till I thought that I would die. (*Turning to* NICK.) And now I am. Please . . . help me to my bed. (*Slowly they go in,* NICK *struggling with his cane to support the additional weight of* KURTZ. *Once inside,* KURTZ *opens the drawer of his night table and takes out a pamphlet. He gives it to* NICK.) You'll want to read this.

NICK: What is it?

KURTZ: Not now. You read it later.

NICK: You want the nurse.

KURTZ: Pish-posh. I want to sleep, that's all. The bed feels good.

NICK: You sleep, Pop. You sleep good, and tomorrow you meet Andy. He's a great kid. You're going to like him.

KURTZ: I'm sure of it. But I must give him some advice. I must tell him . . . (*He has fallen asleep; snoring softly.*)

NICK: (*Sitting on his own bed, as if keeping watch.*) You sleep, Pop. I'm here. It's OK. I'm going to be right here.

Lights fade.

SCENE TWO

The next morning. NICK *is still in the sitting position he assumed to keep watch over* KURTZ. *But he is fast asleep.*

KURTZ*'s bed is empty. It has been stripped during the night, and all trace of* KURTZ *is gone.*

After a time, NURSE *enters with some pills. She stands looking at* NICK *awhile, as though steeling herself for the inevitable.*

NURSE: (*Gently tapping* NICK.) Good morning. Come on, lover. Pill time.

NICK: (*Rousing.*) What time is it?

NURSE: (*Looking at the pills.*) Time for the pink, the blue, and the yellow.

NICK: Christ! (*Taking the pills.*) Well, at least I'm going out in technicolor. How come I feel so groggy?

NURSE: Don't you remember?

NICK: What?

NURSE: You woke up in the night. We gave you an injection.

NICK: With my permission?

NURSE: Sure.

NICK: I don't remember.

NURSE: Miracle drugs. They work wonders. You slept right through breakfast.

NICK: Hey, where's Pop?

NURSE: Carrie called. She'll be here soon.

NICK: Where's Pop?

NURSE: With a surprise, remember? From New York.

NICK: (*Struggling out of bed.*) What happened here? Where'd Pop go?

NURSE: Go? I just got on duty . . .

NICK: (*Going out to the sunporch.*) Pop? Hey, Pop . . . ? Where'd he go?

NURSE: Come on. Take it easy . . .

NICK: We were having a talk last night and he fell asleep. And I told him I'd be here when he woke up. And I'm here. I kept my promise. Where's Pop?

NURSE: He was discharged.

NICK: Hey, it's me you're talking to, OK? Pop . . . !

NURSE: It was time for a private room.

NICK: No, it wasn't. Not yet.

NURSE: Mr. Monte, if you'll relax, we can have a little talk.

NICK: I don't want a little talk. I want a big talk; you hear what I'm saying! When the hell is it going to start!

NURSE: I don't know what you're talking about.

NICK: I'm talking about the truth! The truth, for Christ's sake. When do you start leveling around here?

NURSE: I am trying to tell you.

NICK: Jesus, you getting paid to go around like this.

NURSE: Like what?

NICK: Like that. Like what you're doing right now. That goddamn "God's in His Heaven" kind of smile you put on just before the roof comes crashing down.

NURSE: What do you want . . . funeral music!

NICK: I want you to look at me . . . here . . . right here in my eyes . . . and I want you to serve me up the truth.

NURSE: You big enough to take it?

NICK: Try me.

NURSE: Very well. Mr. Kurtz died last night. No fanfare, no flourishes, he just died. We thought he'd be another month at least, but he up and surprised us. He was funny that way. He liked to have the last word. So, when someone dies around here, we do what we have to do. We take away the body, we strip the bed, and we make room for the next one. Anything else you'd like to know?

NICK: Jesus . . . it's not a piece of meat . . . it's Pop!

NURSE: In the end it's a cold, cold carcass and we have to wheel them out. Esthetics, you know. You asked for the truth. There it is.

NICK: (*Contemptuously.*) Not even a little feeling?

NURSE: You didn't ask for feeling. You said, "The Truth!" Now, what do you want for breakfast?

NICK: Breakfast?

NURSE: Yeah, breakfast! They got a wagon full of trays downstairs and it's up to me to serve them. And with your cooperation, I would very much like to do that.

NICK: Don't you understand . . . ? Pop is gone!

NURSE: But you're not and you've got to have your food.

NICK: OK . . . sure . . . go ahead. Bring the food. Christ, what the hell happens when I go?

NURSE: Maybe I go home . . . and maybe I drop a tear or two . . . but for sure, I come back and serve lunch. Banana with your cereal? (NICK *starts to laugh in spite of himself.*) Well?

NICK: No, thanks. No bananas. Just let me digest all this.

NURSE: Let me tell you how. Ever hear of a kid named Pollyanna? Frankly, I always thought she was a little puke; but she invented this nice little game, see, and I think it's time to play it. You see that rainbow up there?

NICK: No.

NURSE: Well, you just keep looking and one of these days you will. See you around. (*Exits.*)

NICK: You hear that, Pop? Bananas and rainbows. Some Fun House they got here, huh? . . . Hey, you know you could have said goodbye or something. I mean, considering everything. It's not like I ran off and left you. I kept my promise. I was sitting right there, just like I said I would. It's not fair just leaving me with nothing. I got to know what I'm supposed to do, that's all. What to expect . . . how to prepare. Some buddy you turned out to be. Some buddy . . . and some bastard. And I hate bastards; you ought to know that about me. . . . What in the Name of God am I going to do . . . ?

NICK *tries to control his hurt and rage. After a moment he hurries out to the sundeck and begins to water his plant.*

ANDY *enters the room, and not seeing* NICK *steps out to the sundeck. He watches* NICK *for a long time before speaking.*

ANDY: Hello, Big Brother.

NICK: Andy? Jesus, Andy, is that you?

ANDY: Sure it's me. How many baby brothers you got, anyway?

NICK: Only one crazy enough to visit this dump. Come on around here. I can't see you.

ANDY: I came right over.

NICK: What's the suitcase?

ANDY: I just got off the plane and hopped a cab right over.

NICK: You took a plane?

ANDY: I figured I'd save some time.

NICK: You look great, Andy.

ANDY: Yeah. Thanks.

NICK: Pull up a chair.

ANDY: This one's fine right here.

NICK: C'mon, pull it over a bit closer. I'd get it myself, but my goddamned legs have gone to toothpicks. (ANDY *moves slightly closer.*) How's it going in New York?

ANDY: Pretty good, again. Things are looking up for a change.

NICK: Still writing?

ANDY: What else? Hey, I got some great news. They're going to publish my new book.

NICK: No kidding! When?

ANDY: Should be on the bookstands of the world by next summer.

NICK: (*Trying to conceal his sadness.*) Oh. Next summer.

ANDY: Yessir. Simultaneous publications in Great Britain, Canada, and the good old U.S.A.

NICK: How about an Italian translation for Mom.

ANDY: Christ, she'll kill me when she reads it!

NICK: I'm really happy for you, Andy. That's all I can say. I'm just so goddamned happy for you.

ANDY: Thanks. It's a good break.

NICK: You've got it all ahead of you, kid. Make it grow, whatever you've got.

ANDY: Come on. You've got a lot ahead of you, too. You'll be back on the job in no time.

NICK: Nope. Not me. They pensioned me off last month.

ANDY: It's only temporary.

NICK: You should see my rewards for twenty years' service. A case of Scotch I can't have and a color TV I can't stand. (*Off the cuff.*) Well, maybe drunk and blind is the best way to go after all.

ANDY: Hey, uh . . . how's Carrie?

NICK: Fine.

ANDY: I'll go over when I leave here.

NICK: Carrie'll have lunch for you.

ANDY: Great. I'm starved.

NICK: Me, too.

ANDY: You want something?

NICK: I can't have it.

ANDY: Sure. I'll call a nurse.

NICK: Never mind.

ANDY: No. If you're hungry, I'll call a nurse.

NICK: Don't call a nurse.

ANDY: Sure, just a second . . .

NICK: I don't want a goddamned nurse! (*A moment.*) Jesus . . . I'm sorry.

ANDY: What's the matter, Nick?

NICK: Nothing. Just a bit edgy, I guess. It'll pass.

ANDY: I'll pour you some water.

NICK: Forget it. The glass is full.

ANDY: Here. Just cool it off a bit.

NICK: Andy, relax.

ANDY: I am. Just drink some water.

NICK: Don't try so hard to please me, huh?

ANDY: I wasn't.

NICK: Everybody else is doing that. Come on back and sit down. I don't need a thing. (ANDY *sits. There is an awkward silence.*)

ANDY: Pretty nice set-up you've got here.

NICK: You like it, huh?

ANDY: Beautiful.

NICK: Yeah, we're proud of it. The Terminal Hilton.

ANDY: I mean, you even get a private room.

NICK: Yeah . . . that's right.

ANDY: Most hospitals, you wind up with some old fart who won't give you a minute's peace.

NICK: Not here.

ANDY: You're lucky.

NICK: You bet.

ANDY: Hey, uh . . . you're really looking good, Nick.

NICK: In contrast to what?

ANDY: No, I mean it.

NICK: Sure. Thanks. (NICK *thinks a moment and then laughs to himself.*) Mom says I look like death warmed over.

ANDY: God, what a rotten thing to say.

NICK: Hell, it's the first honest judgment I've heard around here. Her old heart's on her sleeve every minute. Guess that's why we love her, huh?

ANDY: Yeah. I guess.

NICK: You know she sneaked in here after hours one night last week. Walked right by the front desk, the administration office, and the head nurse with a lunch basket full of homemade bread and a bottle of red cellar wine. Said she wouldn't leave till I ate. So we came out here, both of us, and we ate the bread, and we drank the wine . . . like the goddamned Last Supper! Then, when we'd finished eating, she pulled out this plaster of paris Sacred Heart of Jesus statue and made me promise on her life I'd pray to it every night.

ANDY: Have you done it?

NICK: Hell, I'm afraid not to. You know, that thing comes equipped with an extension cord and a red bulb, so at night if you feel the need for a little inspiration you can just flick it on and watch that heart pump away... ba-ba-boom, ba-ba-boom... scares the piss out of me. (*They both laugh uneasily; then a silence.*) It's... been a while, Andy.

ANDY: Yeah. I'm really sorry about that.

NICK: Almost a year.

ANDY: I came as soon as I could. I got so damned tied up with the editor and rewrites... I didn't even know how sick you... I mean...

NICK: Even I was spared that little bit of news. I felt on top of the whole damn world in March, and in April all of a sudden my ass starts dragging on the pavement. Figured I was smoking too much, so I cut down to a pack a day from three and took up jogging. I tossed down a few Vitamin C's, a couple of aspirins, and just kept running like I was going cross-country and no son of a bitch this side of the Mississippi or the other was going to touch me. One week later I found to my surprise that my ass was still dragging and I'm coughing up blood all over my bed... all over Carrie... in the night.

ANDY: Come on, Nick. Don't.

NICK: (*Bitterly.*) Carrie's my wife, goddamn it! I love her. I got no goddamned business spitting up blood all over the woman I love! (*A pause to collect himself.*) So off I go to pay my respects to the company M.D. "Ouch," he says, "it's serious." "Zap! Let's operate. Whoops! Inoperable!" How was your week?

ANDY: Nick, you're going to wear yourself out talking.

NICK: Then you talk, for God's sake.

ANDY: (*Going to his suitcase.*) Hey, I almost forgot. Here's that book you asked for.

NICK: Thanks a lot.

ANDY: I never knew you were interested in plants.

NICK: I never was much. Not until I read about this experiment in California. Some guy out there had a theory that plants communicate, so he planted two lots side by side with a brick wall between. Every day he gave all his attention to one lot and let the other go to hell. So naturally one side was strong and healthy, and the other was dying fast. But then the funniest damned thing... One night the healthy plants started sending out vines ... almost as if they understood the need of the sick... they send out vines over the wall, under the wall, giving help and juice and life...

ANDY: Do you believe it?

NICK: Yes. I think so.

ANDY: It's a nice story. (*A nervous pause.*) What time are visiting hours over?

NICK: You've got time. Getting impatient?

ANDY: No, I just wondered.

NICK: Do you have to go?

ANDY: Not really.

NICK: Look, Andy, if you want to go . . .

ANDY: (*Almost too defensively.*) I didn't say I want to go!

NICK: Come on, now. Let's not get testy with the dying.

ANDY: Nick, do me a favor, will you?

NICK: Sure.

ANDY: Will you stop talking about it all the time.

NICK: About what?

ANDY: Dying.

NICK: Makes you uncomfortable, huh?

ANDY: Well . . . yes.

NICK: That's a dirty shame, now, isn't it?

ANDY: Let's drop it.

NICK: No. I don't want to drop it. I don't have a hell of a lot else to dwell on except that fact, do I? Besides, if I keep saying it . . . I'm dying, I'm dying . . . maybe I'll even get to understand what the hell it means. (*A pause.*) You can go if you want.

ANDY: I didn't say I want to go!

NICK: You've been saying it since you got here.

ANDY: What are you talking about?

NICK: Come on. You've stayed five paces away from me ever since you came in. You never even shook my hand.

ANDY: I didn't mean anything.

NICK: Let's cut the small talk, kid. Why did you come here?

ANDY: I came because you're sick.

NICK: Performing your corporal works of mercy, huh?

ANDY: Now wait a minute, Nick.

NICK: Wait a minute, Nick. That's great, Nick. Sure, Nick . . . Jesus Christ! You're the writer in this family, aren't you? Why the hell don't you write yourself a few tender things to say. Like, "Hi, Nick, Christ I'm sorry you're going to die . . ."

ANDY: Damn it!

NICK: . . . or "Holy Moley, Captain Marvel, he's a decent kind of chap; we gotta do somethin'". . .

ANDY: I want to do something . . .

NICK: . . . or better yet, "God, Nick, I love you!" (*Bitterly.*) What's the matter, Andy, you don't love your Big Brother anymore?

ANDY: That's not fair!

NICK: What the hell is?

ANDY: I don't know.

NICK: I'm going to die on you, baby brother. Is that fair?

ANDY: Nick!

NICK: Answer me, you son of a bitch, is that fair!

ANDY: No! But that's the way it is, and there's not a goddamned thing I can do about it. What do you want me to say . . . that you're not dying?

NICK: (*A desperate cry.*) Yes! (*Then, more quietly.*) Or tell me why. (*A nervous silence.*) Oh, crap. What are we fighting about, huh? (ANDY *tries to say something, but he cannot.* NICK *takes a pamphlet from the table and hands it to* ANDY.) Here. Take a look at this.

ANDY: What is it?

NICK: Feast your eyes.

ANDY: (*Reading the title.*) "The Terminal Patient's Manual". . . Christ!

NICK: We even get a guidebook. How to die in Five Definite Steps. Well, today you happen to see me right in the thick of Step Three . . . the "Why Me?" step. (*Pensively.*) Why me? Last night I took that little question to the Sacred Heart of Jesus. "Hail, O Sacred Heart," said I. "Why me, huh?" No answer. Then I realized I'd forgotten to plug the damned thing in, so I found the cord, turned on the red bulb, and asked again. "Why me?" (*A pause.*) Ba-ba-boom . . . ba-ba-boom . . . "Why you? *Because . . . you . . . piss . . . me . . . off!*" So much for a stupid question. (*They both laugh self-consciously. Then, three bells are heard.*)

ANDY: What's that?

NICK: Visiting hours are over.

ANDY: Well . . . I guess I'd better go then.

NICK: But not for me.

ANDY: How come?

NICK: We terminal people get extended privileges . . . a little lollipop to sweeten the way.

ANDY: (*Rising to leave.*) You must be getting tired, so . . .

NICK: I'm not tired. I said you could stay longer, unless you want to go.

ANDY: No, it's not that . . .

NICK: You really want to go bad, don't you?

ANDY: That's not true. It's just that I'm . . . well, I'm a bit nervous about the new book, that's all. I've got rewrites to do. I got this goddamned deadline, you know.

NICK: *You've* got a deadline! Jesus Christ, I'm sorry if I interrupted your work schedule. Why the hell did you come here at all!

ANDY: We've been through that. I came to see you.

NICK: Then, Sweet Jesus, see me. I'm here.

ANDY: What do you want from me, Nick? (NICK *is silent.*) I came, didn't I? I mean, what if I hadn't come at all?

NICK: (*Matter-of-factly, changing his tack.*) When did you say your book's coming out?

ANDY: (*Off his guard.*) What? I told you next summer.

NICK: Oh. That's nice.

ANDY: Answer me, Nick. What if I hadn't come at all?

NICK: Hard cover?

ANDY: Yes! Nick, I don't think you ought to . . .

NICK: Good. I really like hard covers.

ANDY: Screw the hard covers! Was I supposed to stay away?

NICK: Oh, no.

ANDY: Then stop blaming me for coming.

NICK: Not at all. In fact, I'm glad you came. I want to wish you every success on your book.

ANDY: To hell with the book.

NICK: Because you're going to need it.

ANDY: What?

NICK: If it's anything like your first book, you're going to need every goddamned good wish you can get.

ANDY: What are you talking about? You liked the first one.

NICK: The hell I did.

ANDY: You said so.

NICK: (*Coolly.*) I lied.

ANDY: I don't believe you.

NICK: You'd better believe me, kid. It was shit.

ANDY: Thanks, big brother. I needed that.

NICK: The man from the *Times* was right, you know.

ANDY: You were ready to kill him when that review came out.

NICK: Mother prayed for his gradual death, but I didn't.

ANDY: Then how come you told everybody to run out and get a copy?

NICK: Figured they'd better get it before it went out of print. I lost a couple of good friends off that piece of crap.

ANDY: Bullshit! If you hated it so much, why did you say you loved it?

NICK: You know how it is. Fraternal obligation and all that.

ANDY: Frater . . . ! Is that the best you can come up with?

NICK: What do you want me to say?

ANDY: Nothing. Forget it! I spent two years of my life on that book and . . .

NICK: Two years, ten years . . . crap is still crap!

ANDY: And when you told me how much you liked it, I really felt, "God, it must have something."

NICK: Was it so important for me to like it?

ANDY: (*Bitterly.*) Yeah. It was.

NICK: Why?

ANDY: I don't know, but it was. And now you tell me you lied about it, and the best you can come up with is . . . fraternal obligation!

NICK: The same thing that brought you here today.

ANDY: The hell it is!

NICK: You came out of goddamned duty!

ANDY: Okay, big brother, you want the truth? I came because I used to love you so goddamned much I couldn't stand it. You remember when Dad died? I was five and your were twenty. You were called home from basic training, and when you walked through the front door with that uniform on . . . Jesus, I could have died for you right on the spot. Or killed any son-of-a-bitching enemy soldier who so much as breathed on you. I just stood there looking up at you, and I forgot all about Dad lying dead in the next room. Death had no meaning for me then. But you were real, and you were home in your uniform. You scooped me up, and you were spinning me over your head once, then twice, and faster and faster until I couldn't help it anymore and I just exploded. I peed all over your army hat and right down your back. Later, I couldn't wait for you to go to bed so I could watch you sleep. I sneaked into your room and sat there on the floor watching you all night. All night. Till dawn. That's why I came today. Are you satisfied?

NICK: (*After a moment.*) Andy, finish the story.

ANDY: I did.

NICK: No. Tell it all.

ANDY: I told it.

NICK: I want you to tell how you did *not* spend all night on that floor watching me sleep.

ANDY: (*Nervously.*) I did!

NICK: How you got into my bed with me . . .

ANDY: That's ridiculous!

NICK: . . . how you put your little five-year-old head down on my big soldier's chest . . .

ANDY: You were sleeping . . .

NICK: . . . and how you tried to whisper so low I wouldn't hear you, "Hold me, Nick; I love you . . ."

ANDY: You were fast asleep . . .

NICK: "Protect me, Nick; I love you!"

ANDY: No! I never said all that.

NICK: What's the matter? Is it so tough for you to admit a little genuine affection. It happened!

ANDY: All right, it happened! But that was a long time ago, Nick. Look, we're fifteen years apart. When I needed you most, you ran off on your own and I hated you for leaving me alone. We didn't have a chance to be brothers the way other guys do . . . but never mind. It's gone. The years got in the way, we grew up . . . people learn to put away the past.

NICK: Usually with the idea that they'll get back to it.

ANDY: But somehow they never do.

NICK: We just did, didn't we? A little? (ANDY *turns away.*) Kid, look at me, will you? I'm going to die. There's still a dream or two, but . . . that's too bad, I guess. (*He feels a strange growing pain.*) Something's happening in me Andy . . . I'm afraid . . . Oh, Jesus! Goddamn you . . . *hold me!* (NICK *grabs at* ANDY *to pull him close, dropping his cane to the floor. He clings to* ANDY, *at the same time pounding him with his fists.*)

ANDY: It's all right, Nick . . .

NICK: Ssssh . . .

ANDY: It's okay now . . . (*They hold each other for a long time.*)

NICK: (*Finally.*) You know what, kid? I think I just got to Step Four . . . good old "Reluctant Acceptance." I hear this one's a killer. (*He tries to laugh.*) Leave a dime on the table. I'll call you when I reach Step Five . . . "Peaceful Submission." Jesus, they got a goddamned poet on the payroll here! (*Three bells.*) Hey, you must be starved. Go on over to the house. Carrie'll have lunch for you.

ANDY: I'm not hungry. I'll just stick around . . .

NICK: Kid?

ANDY: Yeah?

NICK: I got a job for you.

DeAnn Mears (CARRIE) *and Frank Savino* (NICK) *in the Los Angeles Actors' Theatre production.*

ANDY: Sure, what?

NICK: You got to help Carrie. (ANDY *nods.*) Give her a call once in a while. See how she's doing. Maybe even have a cup of coffee with her. She likes to talk over a cup of coffee. (*Hardest of all.*) And tomorrow, or the next day, whenever's best . . . take the boys for a hike, will you? Remember Top o' the World Mountain? Good place; the boys like it there. Take 'em up there, Andy . . . and tell 'em the truth.

ANDY: Nick . . . ?

NICK: Sssh! They got to know. Carrie'll deal with the girls. Think you can tell the boys?

After a long silence, ANDY *nods and goes for his bag. After a moment,* CARRIE *enters in a rage, not seeing* ANDY.

CARRIE: Nick? Nick, what the hell is wrong with that brother of yours anyway? You know I've been down at that bus station waiting, and he never even showed . . . Three damn months you've been in here, and not so much as a card or a call.

NICK: Carrie . . .

CARRIE: One hour I hung around that bus station . . . thought they were going to pick me up for vagrancy . . .

ANDY: Hello, sister-in-law.

CARRIE: (*All smiles.*) Andy, hi . . . nice to see you. Oh, God, if my foot was any bigger I'd choke to death.

ANDY: I . . . didn't take the bus.

CARRIE: I noticed.

NICK: For God's sake, say hello.

ANDY: Hello, Carrie.

CARRIE: Hello, Andy. (*Finally they laugh.*)

NICK: See now? Boy, what the hell would you two do without me? (*A moment.*) Hey, that's a good one . . . you two do without me . . . (NICK *laughs at himself.*)

ANDY: (*Laughing.*) . . . do without you . . .

CARRIE: (*Laughing.*) . . . without you . . . (*The three of them are laughing very hard. Finally the laughter dies away.*)

ANDY: Hey, I'm going to take a look around.

CARRIE: You don't have to go.

ANDY: I won't be long. Just check it out. What's down there?

NICK: East Wing.

ANDY: Think I'll go exploring.

NICK: Who knows? Maybe you'll get an idea for a new book.

ANDY: Who knows? Be right back. (*Goes out.*)

NICK: He's OK, honey.
CARRIE: If you say so.
NICK: Everything's fine. He's going to stick around a few days.
CARRIE: Does he really want to?
NICK: He will. He's going to take the boys for a walk.
CARRIE: You want me to take the girls?
NICK: You better.
CARRIE: Nurse told me about Mr. Kurtz.
NICK: I'll miss him.
CARRIE: I know. You want a back rub?
NICK: Better not.
CARRIE: How come?
NICK: For now, that's how it's got to be. You stay over there. Will you miss me?
CARRIE: (*After a moment.*) Yes.
NICK: What'll you miss most?
CARRIE: (*Thinking a moment.*) Your bridgework in the glass, I think. (*A moment's silence, then they both start laughing.* CARRIE *opens her bag and takes out some papers.*) Honey, you better look this over.
NICK: What is it?
CARRIE: Oh, bank papers, disability forms . . . stuff like that.
NICK: Right to the end, huh?
CARRIE: You have to sign them.
NICK: Now?
CARRIE: No. But soon.
NICK: How soon?
CARRIE: November.
NICK: My birthday. (*Going to the edge of the balcony and calling out.*) I want lemon frosting on my cake, goddamn it. You hear me?
CARRIE: You know what I'm going to miss more than your bridgework in the glass?
NICK: No, what?
CARRIE: The way you smile when they're in the glass. (*They laugh. For a long time they stare at each other across the stage, but they do not approach each other.*) I did the laundry today. I ran it through the dryer twice. I sat on a little bench for an hour and fifteen minutes just watching that laundry dry. Did you ever just sit and watch laundry dry? I saw a red towel spin by, then a yellow sheet, a few pink undies . . . a great big polyester rainbow. And I thought: "My God, it's the most beautiful laundry I've ever had. Why do I hate it so?"

NICK: Stop it, honey . . .

CARRIE: No. You want to know why I hated it? 'Cause none of your whites were there. No work socks. No T-shirts. And not a goddamned pair of jockey shorts in sight. . . . Then your mother called. She's coming down tomorrow and she wants to know if you'd rather have hot sausage or sweet. I told her sweet; so she said no, you have to have hot. It'll clean you out better. . . . Let's see, what else . . . what else . . . nothing. (ANDY *returns.*)

ANDY: Hey, anybody going to feed me?

NICK: You bet. We got an Irish cook in residence. Hey, soldier, get out of here and feed this kid, will you?

CARRIE: Right.

NICK: (*To* ANDY.) Kid, when you come back, could you pick me up some stamps?

ANDY: Here, I've got some in my wallet.

NICK: No . . . when you come back.

ANDY: (*After a moment.*) Yeah.

NICK: On the way, send the nurse up, will you?

CARRIE: You want something?

NICK: Yeah. I vant my shkates.

CARRIE: What?

ANDY: I think he's nuts.

NICK: Go on. Get out of here.

CARRIE: Come on, brother-in-law. I'm going to make you some of my coffee.

ANDY: Aaaagh! (CARRIE *and* ANDY *start to leave.*)

NICK: Hey, kid. That Sacred Heart of Jesus in there . . . unplug it, will you?

CARRIE *and* ANDY *leave,* ANDY'*s arm around* CARRIE. NICK *checks his watch and rushes into his room. He turns on the* TV *and sits on* KURTZ'*s bed. We hear storm-trooper music and crowds shouting: "Sieg Heil," etc.* NURSE *enters.*

NICK: (*Continued.*) Hey, come on . . . It's just starting. Look at Nazis. Look at them broads.

NURSE: God. All in chains. This calls for a celebration. (*She runs out to the wall and gets the wine.*) No point letting this go to waste.

NICK: How'd you know?

NURSE: Quiet. Watch the movie. (*She pours the wine.*)

NICK: (*Caught up in the movie.*) Oh-oh . . . hey, lady, watch it. You're being followed.

NURSE: Run, you damn fool, run . . .

NICK: She can't run . . . look.

NURSE: My god, she's wearing skates . . . Skate, you damn fool, skate . . .

NICK: Here he comes.

NURSE: Who is it?

NICK: Some Nazi. It's . . . mein Gott . . . it's Pop.

NURSE: No.

NICK: Sure, look . . .

NURSE: He's so young.

NICK: That's his forehead. It's Pop.

NURSE: Poor Mr. Kurtz.

NICK: Poor, nothing . . . look at that broad . . . he's got her.

NURSE: Ugly! Strangle her, Mr. Kurtz . . . drag her by the skates.

NICK: Attaboy, Pop . . . give her hell.

NURSE: Chain her, Mr. Kurtz . . . right to the wall.

NICK: Sieg Heil, Pop . . . Sieg Heil, you son of a bitch.

NURSE AND NICK: Sieg Heil. (*They toast, drink, and laugh.*)

Lights out.

Two O'Clock Feeding

Madeline Puccioni

First presented December 7, 1978, at the Magic Theatre, San Francisco. Directed by Suresa Dundes.

LOUISE	Betsy Scott
GEORGE	Binky Goncharoff
PHIL	Gerald Ambinder
MARIE	Stephanie Smith
DR. SILVESTRI	Harry Snyder
DR. SIMMONS	Andrea Yee

Photos courtesy of Magic Theatre

CHARACTERS

LOUISE: About thirty; attractive, overweight.
GEORGE: Louise's husband; about thirty-five, attractive, a resident pediatrician.
KATY: Six-week-old baby.
PHIL: About fifty; George's friend.
MARIE: About forty; Phil's wife.
DR. SIMMONS: About fifty; black woman, staff pediatrician.
DR. SILVESTRI: About fifty; a gynecologist.

SETTING

A simple unit set; clinic doctor's office, left; apartment living room set, center and right. Although the play is "realistic" in mode, a severely simple set, almost surreal, might serve to point up the isolation that closes in on LOUISE throughout the play; such a set would, in effect, enable us to see the world through her terrible fear, sense of failure, and fatigue; she *is* on another planet, and seemingly ordinary objects and events can be unreal and terrifying to her. The telephone is an enemy. The loss of a chance to get out of the house is a life-and-death matter to her sanity. A spilled cup of coffee is a catastrophe, demanding more energy and power of concentration than she has to clean up the mess.

TIME

The present.

Two O'Clock Feeding

Madeline Puccioni

ACT ONE

SCENE ONE

GEORGE *and* LOUISE *are eating breakfast on a coffee table in the living room. They sit on the open hide-a-bed which has become their bed since* KATY *has taken the bedroom as her nursery.*

LOUISE: (*Whispers.*) Two clean bowls, anyway. (*They eat cereal.*)

GEORGE: (*Wipes spoon on hospital coat.*) And a near-perfect spoon.

LOUISE: I may find the sink today. If Katy sleeps more than half an hour at any given time.

GEORGE: Mm. Any more coffee?

LOUISE: In the far corner. Behind the pink and blue bottle warmer Aunt Varinia gave us.

GEORGE: (*Goes to kitchen, returns with coffee. Laughs.*) Bottle warmer. Christ. Didn't we tell them we're breastfeeding?

LOUISE: We can use it as a planter. On the other hand, if this dairy business doesn't get any easier, maybe I can use it.

GEORGE: Oh, no. Throw the damn thing away.

LOUISE: And what about your crib?

GEORGE: Burn it.

LOUISE: You own wittle baby cwib? That yo' mama sent us parcel post fwom Weberville?

GEORGE: Fourteen dollars and thirty-two cents postage due. Fill it with dirty dishes and send it back to her.

LOUISE: I will try to get some dishes done today.

GEORGE: Aw, get some sleep. I can do it tonight.

LOUISE: That's what you said last night. (*Takes his glasses, cleans them.*)

GEORGE: Last night. Last night. Ah, yes. The Perkins baby. Came in late. By the time we got her breathing okay it was too late to come home and then go back for call . . .

LOUISE: I know, I know. (*Sorts through mail.*) Oh, look. City Lights! (*Holds up a letter.*) I've been invited to read my poems in October! Twenty-five dollars!

GEORGE: Hey, congratulations! (*Kisses her.*) Don't spend it all on me!

LOUISE: Are you kidding? I'll be lucky if this pays for books. That Congreve class alone . . .

GEORGE: (*Tries to get glasses back; in a great hurry now.*) Gotta run, honey. Kiss the punkin for me . . .

LOUISE: You should have heard her squeak when I gave her a bath yesterday!

GEORGE: She like it?

LOUISE: She sort of thrashed around, going "Eee! Edee!" I think she liked it.

GEORGE: (*Gets glasses back.*) Gotta go, go. Why don't you call up Marie? She's dying to see Katy. Maybe she'll even babysit so you can get some sleep . . .

LOUISE: Not Marie. I mean, fine, if she wants to come over, but . . .

GEORGE: Phil says she's better. She's stopped drinking . . . Well, get somebody off that list I brought home . . .

LOUISE: Honey, Katy is too young for a sitter. You said you were taking some time off soon . . .

GEORGE: Well, yeah. But the way things are going at the Unit . . .

LOUISE: Ah, the Unit.

GEORGE: We got fifteen new admits yesterday afternoon.

LOUISE: Well, when are you gonna have some time for your own newborn?

GEORGE: Soon—really. I'll get Dorsey to pay me back some of that call time he owes me. I gotta run. See you later. (*Kisses her and dashes out the door.*)

LOUISE: (*Pause.*) Maybe I'll paint her blue and bring her into the goddamn Unit.

Blackout.

SCENE TWO

Two o'clock in the morning. Dark set. KATY'*s screams, of about a minute's duration.* LOUISE *turns up her bedside light, and sits up groggily.*

KATY: Wahhahhah!

LOUISE: Mmf.

GEORGE: Louise.

LOUISE: Mm?

GEORGE: Honey!

LOUISE: All right. (*Gets up, goes to portacrib, picks up* KATY, *puts her on changer, changes her diaper, cleans up the bowel movement, etc.*

KATY *cries throughout.*) Phew! Yuk! Okay! Come on, honeypie, chowtime! (LOUISE *sits in rocker, right, and puts baby to breast.*) AGH! OW! (*In terrific pain throughout nursing.*)

GEORGE: (*Sits up.*) No use trying to get any sleep around here.

LOUISE: Why don't you go to the call room?

GEORGE: Might as well. (*Checks chart above his desk.*) What is that, number four, today?

LOUISE: Number two. To the second power. Yuk.

GEORGE: You've gotta write this stuff down. Color? Consistency?

LOUISE: This isn't the hospital, George.

GEORGE: Honey, this is important.

LOUISE: Peanut butter. Crunchy.

GEORGE: Louise . . .

LOUISE: Why don't I wrap 'em up and save 'em for you in the refrigerator?

GEORGE: I'm afraid I'd get one in my lunch.

LOUISE: Make your own damn lunch.

GEORGE: Hey! She's *gagging!* Hold her head up! (*Pushes* KATY'*s head up.*)

LOUISE: No . . . don't . . . she's just . . .

KATY: Wahhahhahhahhahh!!

LOUISE: Oh, no—she's off!

KATY: Wahhahha!

LOUISE: Get on there! (*Puts* KATY *to her breast.*) AGH!

GEORGE: Here—let me help . . .

LOUISE: Get out of here! I don't want your help!

KATY: Wahhahh!

LOUISE: Ow! There.

GEORGE: You should have toughened up your nipples.

LOUISE: With what? A vise?

GEORGE: They're bleeding. How often do you nurse her?

LOUISE: She cries! She's hungry!

GEORGE: Let her cry! Give her something else to suck on!

LOUISE: I don't have enough milk for her!

GEORGE: You have plenty of milk!

LOUISE: Yes. In the refrigerator. In bottles.

GEORGE: What?

LOUISE: I want to quit breastfeeding.

GEORGE: You can't quit.

LOUISE: I bought bottles yesterday and I . . .

GEORGE: We were going to breastfeed for at least six months!

LOUISE: You have not been doing your share!

GEORGE: Louise . . . Jesus. Do we have to talk about this at two o'clock in the morning?

LOUISE: When do I ever get a chance to talk to you? Should I call Pediatrics and make an appointment?

GEORGE: You're really going to quit?

LOUISE: It hurts! It takes all my energy! I go around leaking like an ol' cow!

GEORGE: You're not giving her that commercial crap . . .

LOUISE: No. I've got it all made up . . .

GEORGE: Why don't you . . . give her a couple bottles a day, let your nipples heal up, then you can go back to nursing her . . .

LOUISE: I want to quit! I hate it! Besides . . . if I don't get some solid sleep I'll go mad. Would you—give her a bottle tomorrow morning? So I can sleep?

GEORGE: I thought you didn't want my help. You don't even let me change her diapers.

LOUISE: You take so long! Washing her with sterile water, for Chrissakes—which I have to boil for you . . .

GEORGE: Well, maybe if you tried some of these things, she wouldn't have this awful rash! She should air-dry for a couple hours!

LOUISE: Air-dry! She'll freeze to death! And pee all over!

GEORGE: See what I mean? Forget it. See you later. (*Starts to get dressed.*)

LOUISE: I'm sorry. Please. Just one feeding. Tomorrow morning. One night's sleep. That's all I need. I'll have everything ready for you. We'll go through it at the afternoon feeding . . .

GEORGE: I get her too excited, or something. Every time I try to burp her, she spits up.

LOUISE: That happens. Please. Tomorrow morning?

GEORGE: The two o'clock feeding?

LOUISE: Just this once. Then I'll be okay.

GEORGE: (*Goes through his schedule.*) I've got so damn much call duty. Wednesday. Thursday. How about Thursday?

LOUISE: Not 'til then?

GEORGE: I'm on call tomorrow and Wednesday.

LOUISE: Write it down. I may live.

GEORGE: You're not the only one who needs sleep. (*Looks at his watch.*) I'd better get to the call room. Seven o'clock is only four hours away.

LOUISE: I know. Katy wakes up at seven. Again.

Binky Goncharoff (GEORGE) *and Betsy Scott* (LOUISE) *in the Magic Theatre production.*

GEORGE: Hey. She's tugging. Isn't it time to change breasts?
LOUISE: Gladly. With anybody.

Blackout.

SCENE THREE

PHIL'*s office;* PHIL *is on the phone.* GEORGE *enters about halfway through the conversation.*

PHIL: Mrs. Sanchez? Dr. Foster. How can I help you? (*Pause.*) Sure it was a dime? Well, watch for choking, breathing distress, but if it's been fifteen minutes with none of those symptoms, chances are you'll have your money back by tomorrow morning. (*Chuckles.*) Not at all. Bye.

GEORGE: What's up?

PHIL: They got the grant.

GEORGE: Federal?

PHIL: And another one from Exxon.

GEORGE: Wheew! Where'd you hear?

PHIL: My little double agent in the steno pool.

GEORGE: The one with the electric T-shirt?

PHIL: Uh-huh. Took a memo from Roberts to the committee this morning, said to read your articles and prepare to interview.

GEORGE: Damn! The fellowship! Who else is getting interviewed?

PHIL: Brewer. Vasquez. But you definitely sound like the front runner. Roberts also mentioned money for the Unit—from the Exxon grant.

GEORGE: How much? Do we get to use the helicopter?

PHIL: (*Chuckles.*) My guess is you'll get space and money for your staff, and maybe for yourself, if you're lucky.

GEORGE: What good's the money if we can't get those kids here in time? Now you know . . .

PHIL: I know—most newborns die on the way to the emergency. Save the lectures for the committee. Oh, and Ervin Hunter's name was mentioned—seems like he's coming here for some guest seminars, he's read your articles and he'd like to help you set up the lab if you get funded . . .

GEORGE: Ervin Hunter's read my articles?

PHIL: The man. So why don't you take your wife out to dinner and tell her the good news?

GEORGE: (*Pause.*) Louise isn't going to like this.

PHIL: Jeez, you'll be making thirteen, fourteen hundred a month . . .

GEORGE: She was counting on the staff job. Nine to five, home for dinner. I don't spend much time at home.

PHIL: Christ, in a couple years, you could be teaching, or full-time research . . .

GEORGE: I'll have to think about it.

PHIL: You can't pass this up. I mean, if you were some hack, or something—but what you do saves lives. (*Pause.*) Well, I got a kid out there, fractured femur. I think his mother helped him fall out of his high chair. See you later.

GEORGE: Thanks, Phil.

PHIL: Don't mention it. To anybody.

Blackout.

SCENE FOUR

That evening. LOUISE *is sorting laundry on the couch.* GEORGE *comes home.*

GEORGE: Hi. Katy asleep?

LOUISE: Sh. Yes.

GEORGE: Anything to eat?

LOUISE: In the oven.

GEORGE: Meatloaf? (*Sniffs.*)

LOUISE: It's in the oven, isn't it?

GEORGE: Definitely. Katy take to her bottle okay?

LOUISE: Yeah.

GEORGE: Yeah, what?

LOUISE: Yeah, she took to her bottle okay.

GEORGE: So did she burp okay, did she have normal stools, did she spit up, did she go for the breast afterward or what?

LOUISE: You want an answer or a case history?

GEORGE: Goddammit, I'm interested! Do I have to cross-examine you to find out about my daughter?

LOUISE: No. You could come home when you said you would and help with the afternoon feeding like you said you would and then you could find out for yourself.

GEORGE: Oh, God. I forgot. I'm sorry. We . . . lost the Perkins baby. I had to stay . . . and explain . . . to her parents.

LOUISE: (*Softly.*) That's too bad, George.

GEORGE: I should be a plumber. I should fix drainpipes.

LOUISE: You do the best you can.

GEORGE: She came in from surgery, all signs stable. Two minutes later her windpipe just collapsed.

LOUISE: I have to get out. We, uh . . . don't have any eggs or milk. (*Starts to go to door.*)

GEORGE: Honey . . .

LOUISE: Sh! I'll try to be back before she wakes up.

GEORGE: Honey—I'm dead. I gotta get some sleep.

LOUISE: I have to get out of here. Keys . . . keys . . .

GEORGE: They got the grant.

LOUISE: Keys! Gotcha!

GEORGE: It looks like I might get that fellowship.

LOUISE: (*Pause.*) Fellowship?

GEORGE: The one I applied for two years ago. And we thought they'd never get the money?

LOUISE: What about it?

GEORGE: Phil says it's damn near mine. If I want it. (*Pause.*) I'd be making good money! We . . . could get a bigger flat. Maybe even a house. (*Pause.*) It means more money for the Unit. Nobody's supposed to know, yet.

LOUISE: How . . . does Phil know?

GEORGE: He has . . .a friend . . . in the steno pool.

LOUISE: No wonder Marie drinks.

GEORGE: Interviews start next week. Ervin Hunter said he'd like to work with me if the Unit gets funded!

LOUISE: But . . . the staff job. The clinic. It was all set.

GEORGE: I don't think . . . we can pass this up.

LOUISE: I took night classes so you could be home with Katy! I'm all registered!

GEORGE: Honey, after I get the lab all set up, and the office, I'll have more time—State will be there spring semester . . .

LOUISE: But the poetry reading! It's only a month away! I only have three poems ready!

GEORGE: Get a good sitter. Where's that list I brought home?

LOUISE: Katy is too little to leave with a sitter! Maybe when her rash clears up . . .

GEORGE: Honey, if it were just the fellowship . . . but there's money for the Unit . . . for Hank and Julie . . . maybe even use of the helicopter . . .

LOUISE: I can't talk. I have to go out.

GEORGE: We've got to talk. This is the big time.

LOUISE: Katy's gonna wake up any second. I have to go.

GEORGE: Okay. (*Sighs.*) Get me some coffee?

LOUISE: Okay. (*From kitchen.*) Big time. Small time. My time. Your time. My time ain't your time, anymore, George . . . I've got *no* time . . . George? (*Returns with cup of coffee.*) George? (GEORGE *has fallen asleep, and is snoring softly.*)

KATY: *Wahhahhahhah!* (LOUISE *puts coffee down, picks up a clean diaper from a stack of laundry on the couch, and goes to the nursery.*)

Blackout.

SCENE FIVE

That night. GEORGE *and* LOUSE *in bed.* GEORGE *puts down his book and turns to* LOUISE. *He rubs her neck.*

GEORGE: (*Pause.*) Feel good?

LOUISE: Yeah.

GEORGE: (*Kisses her neck.*) There's more where that comes from.

LOUISE: Honey, you've got to postpone that fellowship.

GEORGE: (*Pushes away.*) Sorry to bother you.

LOUISE: Like Dorsey? Like Alan Dellafield? I've got to take those classes. *One* class. Something.

GEORGE: Get a good babysitter.

LOUISE: I can't leave her with a babysitter. Not with that rash, and the way she cries . . .

GEORGE: You are not the only person in the world who can take care of a baby. (*Pause.*) I know it's rough for you now, but in a couple months, she'll be sleeping through the night, things will look better . . .

LOUISE: I kicked the dresser this afternoon. I just kept kicking and kicking . . .

GEORGE: All new mothers go through this. You're doing fine.

LOUISE: No. I need you. Katy needs you. You can postpone this thing. They can hold the funds for you. You're hardly ever home now! If you take the fellowship, we'll never see you . . .

GEORGE: Government money's here and gone. (*Winks; pats her bottom.*) If you don't use it, you lose it. Besides, it might be a lot better. I won't have so much call duty.

LOUISE: I *know* you. Articles, papers, conferences—I don't know how long I can hold out! I dream about Katy's diaper rash . . .

GEORGE: Diaper rash, dressers—we used to talk about Lina Wertmüller, tai chi, brewer's yeast—we even used to make love.

LOUISE: You worked, I worked. You studied, I studied. You slept, I slept. Now you've got a one-way ticket on the long train that runs forever, and I . . .

GEORGE: Ah, we've been writing poetry today.

LOUISE: I tried to take a shower today. I took the hair out of the drain, I got the Ajax and put it in the bathtub . . .

GEORGE: Louise, is this your idea of conversation? I think I'd rather sleep.

LOUISE: I got the Ajax and put it in the bathtub. Katy woke up. I burped her. I fed her. I put her in the playpen. Two hours later I got the scrub brush and scrubbed the tub.

GEORGE: Turn out your light. See if you can turn off your mouth.

LOUISE: I scrubbed the tub.

GEORGE: You're repeating yourself.

LOUISE: My days spin around, like laundry in the dryer. I scrubbed the tub. Katy cried. I burped her. I fed her. I changed her. Her rash was worse. I called the clinic. A big mistake.

GEORGE: Who'd you talk to? Not Roberts, I hope?

LOUISE: Makes you look bad, huh?

GEORGE: Louise, we are swamped. You can't call the clinic ten times a day about diaper rash. Who'd you talk to?

LOUISE: This is a shower story. A story about taking a shower.

GEORGE: I had a neat day too, Louise—I got to treat sixteen babies for intestinal flu . . . do you know what a little flu diaper smells like?

LOUISE: You got to take a shower today.

GEORGE: (*Pause.*) We do need some time together.

LOUISE: Just a couple hours a day I can count on . . .

GEORGE: (*Looks at his pocket schedule.*) Well, next week. I'm gonna take some time off. Two . . . three days.

LOUISE: Three . . . days?

GEORGE: Dorsey owes me all that call time and I can get Hank to cover the Unit.

LOUISE: Three days? You're going to take three days off?

GEORGE: Yup.

LOUISE: Three days and three nights?

GEORGE: Don't see why not.

LOUISE: Don't . . . break this promise. Please.

GEORGE: It's not a promise yet—I'll have to check on it. But I'll do my damndest. I can switch call time tomorrow night with Dorsey—how about you and I going out to dinner like we used to?

LOUISE: Not . . . tomorrow night. I'm too tired.

GEORGE: That sounds familiar.

LOUISE: I don't have anything to wear.

GEORGE: Now that's a new one.

LOUISE: We can't afford it. (*Giggles.*)

GEORGE: (*Kisses her.*) I'm easy.

LOUISE: Okay. (*Pause.*) Will you please talk to Roberts about postponing the fellowship?

GEORGE: (*Pause.*) Well—I'll talk to him. (*Settles down to sleep.*) Then we'll sit down to a nice bowl of bouillabaisse and discuss this in a logical, non-poetic manner, hm?

LOUISE: Logic is clickity clack down the track. Poetry is the only answer to cyclones. I do live in a cyclone.

GEORGE: Oh. I almost forgot. I invited Phil and Marie over Friday night. You could roast that chicken . . .

LOUISE: Friday night? For dinner? George, I . . . not with Katy, and the house . . .

GEORGE: They're not fussy. They've been awfully good to us.

LOUISE: Not that good! (*Pause.*) All right. But don't tell Phil to try to talk me into that fellowship . . .

GEORGE: (*Sleepily.*) It'll be *okay!* We can make it work. Get a sitter for tomorrow night, hm?

LOUISE: I won't leave her with a stranger.

GEORGE: Mmhm.

LOUISE: Maybe Helene would do it. She needs the money.

GEORGE: Mm.

LOUISE: Maybe Stella. The landlady's daughter.

GEORGE: (*Snores softly.*)

LOUISE: Maybe King Kong. (*Kisses his hand; addresses it.*) Good night.

Blackout.

SCENE SIX

Next morning. LOUISE *is "walking"* KATY.

LOUISE: (*Softly.*) Well, Stella, the landlady's daughter, is going to babysit for your tonight—she's very nice, she has long hair you can grab . . . Oh! . . . and your famous doctor daddy, you remember him? He is going to stay home next Tuesday, Wednesday, and Thursday! Yeah! You can do your pee-on-the-arm routine for him. (*Pause; looks at watch.*) I don't know what happened to Helene. She's sposta been here an hour ago. You're gonna fall asleep and dumb old Helene ain't gonna get to see your big eyes. (*Mockingly.*) "Oh, call me anytime, Louise—I'll take off work to see that new baby." Sure. (*Puts* KATY *gently into her infant seat. On an impulse, she gets an old doll from the bookcase, and sits down across from* KATY.) Miss Molly, (*Addressing doll.*) this is Katy. Katy, this is Miss Molly. Miss Molly was my first baby. We used to have lots of tea parties.

"MOLLY": (LOUISE *speaks in deep Southern accent.*) And ah am quiet an' polite, an' ah nevah, nevah, poop on people's ahms. You must teach that child some manners, Louise.

LOUISE: I despair, Miss Molly.

MOLLY: All that screamin' an' carryin' on, an' those disgustin' fluids she gives off. You never had none of that with me.

LOUISE: Manners. (*Pause.*) Helene, my dear friend Helene, was supposed to be here an hour ago, and she didn't even call. Now that is unmannerly. People say a lot of things they don't mean, here. Must be the fog. A vagueness in the air.

MOLLY: There is spit comin' out of her mouth. Do something about it, please. It turns mah stomach.

LOUISE: She's just a baby, Molly, an' she's sleepin'.

MOLLY: Good time to put her in her box an' send her back.

LOUISE: I can't do that. (*Giggles.*) She didn't come in a box.

MOLLY: Just put her under that pillow awhile, honey, an' they'll find a box for her, all right.

LOUISE: I think I'll call Helene.

MOLLY: They'll have a fancy name for it—crib death, pulmonary anoxia, some damn thing—you'll look so sad, an' saintly . . . (*Pause.*) Think how quiet it would be, how everlasting quiet . . .

LOUISE: I think I'll take a nap.

MOLLY: Good idea, honey. You are actin' so strange. (LOUISE *settles down on couch; telephone rings; she lurches up, catches it before it rings twice, but* KATY *wakes up, and starts crying.*)

LOUISE: (*Furiously.*) Hello? Yes, I got the flyer, no, I don't want your Children's Encyclopedia. Yes. That's my baby, crying. Babies cry. There is nothing one can do. It could be the telephone, it could be their dreams, their diapers, a twisted colon—C-O-L-O-N. My husband told me about a baby that has one. His mother has to collect his bowel movements in a little plastic bag they attach to his stomach. Now, *he* cries. I mean, how would you like to carry your shit around in front of you like . . . so many Children's Encyclopedias? (*Pause.*) No. I really don't. But I have a friend in Santa Barbara who just had an abortion—maybe she'd go for the condensed version . . . (*Salesperson hangs up.*)

KATY: WAHHAHHAHHAHH!

LOUISE: (*Picks up a book, turn, gets vacuum cleaner and turns it on, then listens, satisfied, then reads, screaming over the noise, to* KATY.) (*From* To the Lighthouse.) "She set her clean canvas firmly upon the easel, as a barrier, frail, she knew, but hoped, sufficiently substantial to ward off Mr. Ramsay"—*listen to me, Katy!*—"and his exactingness"—Here! A bottle! Take it! Take it! Take it! (*Forces bottle hard into* KATY's *mouth, shaking her violently.*) What the hell do you want then? Hah? Well, why not. While you're in a good mood? A poem. Of course. (*Takes paper out of typewriter, reads, screaming over* KATY's *cry.*)

CYCLONE

Cyclone dancing
(LOUISE *begins to whirl.*)
Mindless caterpillar dancing
Through the southwest desert dancing

Shut up, Katy! It gets better! (*Whirls faster.*)

Mindless mouth agape to feed
on fences, windows, cellar doors
Weaving, unweaving, side to side
Leaving behind it papers strewn,
Lawn chairs, boxcars, human dead
Holes in trees
And shredded leaves.

KATY: Wahhahhahh! (*Doorbell rings.*)

LOUISE: Helene! (*Runs to door; offstage.*) Marie!

MARIE: I was on my way down to the Symphony office and I just *had* to see that new baby!

LOUISE: (*Angry; disappointed.*) Come in.

MARIE: Oh! She's precious. May I hold her?

LOUISE: She's sopping, Marie . . .

MARIE: That doesn't scare me—no! (*Takes* KATY *from* LOUISE.) Oh! Her is wet! (*Gives* LOUISE *a brightly wrapped present.*) Here, dear, I've been carrying this around for you . . .

LOUISE: Uh . . . Marie . . . she hasn't finished her bottle yet . . .

MARIE: Well? Aren't you going to open it?

LOUISE: Marie, the phone just woke her up—I think she might go back to sleep if there's no . . . excitement . . .

MARIE: Oh, Louise—she is sopping! A baby can't sleep in a puddle! No! (*Grabs diaper from the stack of laundry on the couch.*) I'll change her, you relax a minute . . .

LOUISE: Marie—I'll do that . . .

MARIE: You do enough of this . . . Good Lord, this rash is awful!

LOUISE: I said I'd do that!

MARIE: Do you wash her every time you change her? Do you let her air-dry?

LOUISE: Goddammit, Marie, what is this, slumming day? I am not one of your social projects! I am not one of your goddamn charities!

MARIE: I was just trying to help!

LOUISE: (*Pause; softly.*) I've been doing everything I know for that rash.

MARIE: You're tired. (*Guides her to couch.*) My Julie was a rashy baby.

LOUISE: You think . . . air-drying helps?

MARIE: Worked for Julie. Of course, you worry less with your fourth.

LOUISE: You want . . . some coffee?

MARIE: No—gotta run. Oh—here's a brochure on the Women's Club Festival—the weekend of the thirtieth. I'm playing a few Chopin pieces . . . (*Indicates her name on brochure.*)

LOUISE: You—play piano?

MARIE: Not like I used to. But I'm . . . brushing up. The old Prince Hotel needs a pianist for the dinner hour. I . . . think I'll give it a try. Phil says I'm stupid—get a bunch of drunks hanging all over the piano, saying "Cancha play Shtardusht?" (*Pause.*) What do you think?

LOUISE: You . . . could give it a try.

MARIE: I think . . . I will. (*Pause; smiles.*) I have got to run. Think about the Festival. Good way to meet other mothers—doctors' wives and widows—though Lord knows, it's hard to tell the difference.

LOUISE: (*Opens gift.*) An . . . electric . . . dogdish.

MARIE: Ha, ha. A cereal bowl. Keeps it hot. I started my kids on cereal when they were about four weeks old. Helps them sleep. (*Telephone rings.*)

LOUISE: Oh—thanks, Marie . . . Bye! (MARIE *exits.*)

KATY: Wahhahhahhahh!

LOUISE: Hello? Oh. Hi. Nothing's wrong. (*Holds receiver over crib.*) Say hi to daddy, Katy. Marie just dropped by. I got a sitter for tonight—Stella Emory. (*Pause.*) But . . . we were going out to dinner tonight. Who? Ervin Hunter? All the way from Des Moines? A week early. Next week. All next week. (*Pause.*) Of course you're sorry. Of course I understand. No! No more of your goddamn promises, George—listen to me—I won't take this. You may not take that fellowship, you hear? I forbid it! You listen to me! You may not go to your precious meetings and conferences next week—tell Roberts you're sorry! Tell Hunter you're sorry! You promised us! Yes! I am irrational! I am mad! Mad is not the word! Mad is the word! *Listen to me!* (GEORGE *has hung up on her.*)

KATY: WAHHAHHAHHAH!

LOUISE: AGHHAHHHHGHGHGHGHGHGHGH! (*Screams and starts toward* KATY *then checks herself, screaming and shaking her fists.*)

Blackout.

ACT TWO

SCENE ONE

DR. SILVESTRI*'s examining room.* LOUISE *clutches white gown around her as she attempts to quiet* KATY. SILVESTRI *enters, on the run.*

SILVESTRI: Louise? Howdy. George said you'd be in. Up on the table, dear—I've got a vicious schedule. And this is Katy! That's okay, dear—I'm used to screaming kids. Got a brand new granddaughter. Feet in the stirrups, that's a girl. You remember.

LOUISE: Once you learn this, you never forget.

SILVESTRI: Scoot down, dear, little closer, that's it. Yessir, I'm a grampa now. (*Puts on gloves.*) Well? That's your cue.

LOUISE: Cue?

SILVESTRI: Yeah, you're supposed to say, "Leo, you don't look old enough to be a grandfather."

LOUISE: Leo, *I* look old enough to be a grandfather. Here. Gray hair!

SILVESTRI: Gray hair! Wait'll your daughter brings home a sailor—brace yourself, dear . . . (*Inserts speculum.*)

LOUISE: *Agh!*

SILVESTRI: It's the ice cubes; everybody asks. . . . Brings home a sailor she picks up at a high-school swim meet. Now what's a sailor doin' at a high-school swim meet? Only eighteen, she's already a mother, an' he's off someplace in the goddamn North Atlantic . . . easy, dear, this'll pinch . . .

LOUISE: *Aaww!*

SILVESTRI: Me an' Rose take care of the kid some nights, or I swear she'd put him down the garbage disposal . . . *Wicked* episiotomy, Louise—they really ripped you open. Uterus still dilated? You stop breastfeeding?

LOUISE: Yeah.

SILVESTRI: Quitter. My mother raised six kids—none of us had a bottle.

LOUISE: It was her or me.

SILVESTRI: Ah, you women nowadays, want everything your way. My daughter, she thought she was gettin' a stuffed toy. I tried to tell her, motherhood ain't easy, even with your own built-in pediatrician, eh, Louise?

LOUISE: I seem to have the portable model.

SILVESTRI: George isn't home much, is he? With the Unit and all.

LOUISE: Even when he's home, he isn't home.

SILVESTRI: Ah, he's a damn genius. Me, I'm a staffer. Nine to four, weekends off. Pap smear, while we're at it?

LOUISE: Okay.

SILVESTRI: Damn shame, dear. Woman like you shouldn't spend her nights alone.

LOUISE: I'm not exactly alone—there's the ten o'clock feeding, and the two o'clock feeding, and . . . *Agh!* that hurt!

SILVESTRI: (*Checking her breasts, caressingly.*) Sorry, dear. Maybe I could come over sometimes, help you out? I've had a lot of experience with little girl bottoms. (*Slaps her bottom.*)

LOUISE: Leo!

SILVESTRI: I mean my granddaughter's, of course. Well, dear, little scar tissue, but it's healing up. Any problems?

LOUISE: Uh . . . well, uh . . . it hurts when . . . George and I try to have intercourse.

SILVESTRI: Well, try it with someone else! Ha, ha. My wacky sense of humor. Up all night with the grandkid, you know?

LOUISE: Are there any woman gynecologists at U.C.?

SILVESTRI: You want some woman slappin' your bottom? ha, ha. Oh, I'm sorry . . . God . . . look at the time. Listen, dear, I gotta run. You're healing up nicely, dear—no problems. You're ready to . . . ah . . . normalize relations any old time. Just get yourself a jar of vaseline.

LOUISE: Put it on your speculum and stick it, Leo.

SILVESTRI: Ha, ha. Just teasing, just teasing. Gimme a call if you need anything. Bye. (*Exits.*)

Blackout.

SCENE TWO

Dark set. GEORGE *and* LOUISE *in bed. Movement.*

LOUISE: Wha—I was *asleep!*

GEORGE: Come here.

LOUISE: Oh, God, I was sound *asleep!*

GEORGE: I want you.

LOUISE: Katy's gonna wake up any minute . . .

GEORGE: Come on, honey . . .

LOUISE: (*Turns on her light.*) I'm supposed to get eight hours' sleep, wasn't that the deal?

GEORGE: (*Throws pillow.*) And if I'm real good, and take care of Katy, and *if* I give up the fellowship, we might make love again, is that the deal, Louise?

LOUISE: I'm dreaming.

GEORGE: It's been over three months since we made love, did you know that? Does it matter? You don't care, you never did really care about that, much, and now you've got your baby and your poetry reading, and no job, who gives a damn about ol' George, as long as he brings home the money every two weeks? (*Paces around, angrily.*) Now if he would only take off work and stay with Katy more, you'd have it all your way . . .

LOUISE: You don't know a damn thing, do you? You haven't been home two waking hours since she was born!

GEORGE: Home? This isn't home. It's a goddamn crazy-house. I don't live here. I don't belong here. I am not wanted here.

LOUISE: Give me some time. Some sleep. I have so much on my mind . . .

GEORGE: I wanted to be on your mind, for a few minutes . . . a few seconds . . .

LOUISE: (*Pause.*) Is that all the time you want with me?

GEORGE: It's the fellowship, isn't it?

LOUISE: Fellowship? We have fellowship. A few minutes, a few seconds, then back to the dryer, back to the train . . .

GEORGE: Talk sense, goddammit!

LOUISE: I will not screw you.

GEORGE: Well. Now we're getting someplace.

LOUISE: Someplace. Anyplace. That George, he's going places. You come rushing in, *en route,* you want dinner ready, shower ready, bed ready, and oh, sometimes . . . me. Ready. Well, this ain't the MacDonald's of love, honey—I don't give instant service.

GEORGE: You don't give *anything!* (*Mockingly.*) "Go to San Francisco, George, go to U.C., you can do it, you can do anything—I'll help you." Sure—as long as it doesn't interfere with your plans, huh? Well, get this, Louise—I did come to S.F., I am going to U.C., and I *can* do just about goddamn anything, and things are speeding up for me right now, and I'm not about to jump off . . .

LOUISE: At least come into the boxcar. Secure the baggage, before coupling.

GEORGE: Are you ever serious?

LOUISE: The faucet is dripping.

GEORGE: We can't talk.

LOUISE: The bathroom faucet is dripping. You forgot to jiggle the spigot.

GEORGE: Maybe you could talk to somebody else. Would you talk to Bernie if I made an appointment?

LOUISE: I can talk. Many women can talk. It is difficult to hear us. We are clattering along behind you, locked in our boxcars with our screaming babies . . . someday we'll all jump track, go spinning into space . . . silver moons in silent orbit . . .

GEORGE: You're a real basket case. You need help.

LOUISE: Yes. Please turn off the bathroom faucet.

GEORGE: I mean professional help.

LOUISE: I'll give you a quarter to turn off the bathroom faucet.

GEORGE: How do you know it's the bathroom faucet?

LOUISE: I know my faucets.

GEORGE: You turn it off. You were in there last.

LOUISE: You brushed your teeth last. You forgot to jiggle the spigot.

GEORGE: Jiggle the spigot.

LOUISE: That's what you do for the bathroom faucet. There's not much one can do for the kitchen faucet. One puts a sponge under it. One accepts what one cannot change.

GEORGE: Jiggle your own spigot. I gotta get some sleep.

LOUISE: You were going to fix the faucets.

GEORGE: You know I haven't had time.

LOUISE: You have time. By the throttle. Full speed ahead, all systems go. *Whoosh!* A blast of hot air. A passing of wind.

GEORGE: Turn out your light.

LOUISE: No. Listen to me. Do your "other mothers" tell you how bad it really is? "I scream at my baby, doctor, I throw things, I kick things, I want to kill my baby, I tried to strangle her today . . ."

GEORGE: Louise . . . don't even joke about that.

LOUISE: No. It's "Yes, doctor, no, doctor, may I kiss your big toe, doctor?"

GEORGE: I rarely get that kind of offer. (*Pause.*) I think this is getting to you. Would you please talk to Bernie?

LOUISE: I cannot talk to a man who dyes his moustache.

GEORGE: Did you see Silvestri? Maybe this is all a low-grade infection.

LOUISE: Silvestri is a sadist. He is a vile, loathsome pervert. According to him, I'm fine.

GEORGE: Silvestri's one of the best GYN's we've got. What'd he say?

LOUISE: He stuck his finger up my twat and asked me for a date.

GEORGE: You're . . . sick, Louise. Paranoid. Everyone's out to get you—Silvestri, Roberts, Phil, and bad, bad George—and don't forget Katy—terrible Katy—she makes you kick dressers and yell at people! Things haven't turned out the way you thought, and you gotta blame somebody! Well, tough shit, Louise—you wanted this baby, and you got her. I want the same things I always wanted, and what do I get? Nothin'! Crazy talk and nothin'! You don't want me, you don't want my help, you don't want my success, you don't want anything I've got to give, anymore, and that's . . .

KATY: WAHHAHHAH!

GEORGE: . . . fine, crazy lady, because . . .

LOUISE: You are the one with brain damage.

GEORGE: . . . I'm ready to move out . . .

LOUISE: A: you cannot hear your daughter crying. B: you have forgotten that you promised to give her this two o'clock feeding.

GEORGE: What?

LOUISE: Surely you recognize her cry? (*Pulls blanket over her head.*)

GEORGE: What the hell are you going to do?

LOUISE: Sleep.

GEORGE: Aw, Christ . . . you're awake—I don't know where anything is!

LOUISE: You were going to come home in time to find out, today.

GEORGE: All right! (*Stomps over to nursery.*) Where are the crib sheets?

LOUISE: I am asleep.

GEORGE: Okay, dammit! Phew! (*Gets close to* KATY.) You've got the wierdest schedule, Katypie! Wow! Louise! Where's the Mycolog?

LOUISE: That stuff is too strong for her skin!

GEORGE: It works on every baby in the nursery! The nurses use cases of it! This rash is terrible! You should go down and put her diapers through an extra rinse! You can stand the exercise!

LOUISE: You can stand . . . on your head . . . in a cow barn.

GEORGE: There is nothing wrong with you, Louise, that a swift kick in your fat ass wouldn't cure.

LOUISE: I might as well take a shower.

GEORGE: Louise! Please help me! She's crying!

LOUISE: (*Turns on shower.*) Oh, she was a lass from the low countree . . .

GEORGE: Come out here!

LOUISE: And he was a lord of high degree . . . What? I'm washing my hair!

GEORGE: About goddamn time! It smells!

LOUISE: What?

GEORGE: I said, you smell, Louise! (*Goes to kitchen; clatter of pots and pans; he gets a bottle, returns, still holding* KATY, *a bottle, a towel, and a rubber duck.*)

KATY: WAHHAHHAHHAHH!

GEORGE: Nice duckie? Katy like duckie?

KATY: Wahhahhahhah!

GEORGE: (*Gives bottle to* KATY.) *Here! Take it!* Oh! Not too fast! There. There. (*Pause.*) Hey, you were hungry! Yes! This is fun! Nothin' to it! I never get the fun stuff like this! I just get the problem kids. Good, good. What's this? A little bruise? Mommy been slugging you again? Louise? She's starving! Maybe we should start her on cereal. Good. Good. Time for a burp? Okay. Here we go. Nice an' easy. (*Gently burps baby over his shoulder.*) Easy now. Oh, God. (*Grabs towel.*) *Louise! Louise!* (*Picks up* KATY *and runs to bathroom.*) She just puked all over me! Let me in! I gotta get this shirt off!

LOUISE: Da-da-da-da-da-da *da-da-da-da-da-da-da,* the good ol' motherhood ra-a-g!

GEORGE: *Louise* get your fat ass out of there! (*Gives* KATY *to* LOUISE.)

LOUISE: (*Emerges wearing her bathrobe and a towel on her head, sits on the bed and feeds* KATY.) A real mommy would wear that shirt until she could get her baby fed and comforted and asleep in its own little bed.

GEORGE: You want blood, don't you?

LOUISE: All I wanted was one good night's sleep.

GEORGE: I'm going to the call room.

LOUISE: Run, don't walk. Keep moving, George. Don't stop now.

GEORGE: I'll call you later.

LOUISE: Don't call me, I'll call you.

GEORGE: Always the smart-ass remark, eh, Louise?

LOUISE: I mean it. The phone wakes up Katy.

GEORGE: Don't leave it off the hook! Tried to call you three times yesterday! She'll get used to it. (*Gets his coat, clipboard, etc.*) I'll see you tomorrow, Louise. Or Friday. Or Saturday. Or maybe next week?

LOUISE: Why come home at all? You have a nice bed and a hot shower and good food and the pretty thin nursies call you *Doctor* Collins—get a couch like Phil has, right under the baby pictures in your office, and you'll never have to come home at all . . .

GEORGE: Don't think the idea hasn't occurred to me. I work around a lot of attractive women and I can't help comparing. (*Opens door.*)

LOUISE: Why not shop around? (*Screams.*) Take their showers and their nursies and their fellowship—I said, take their goddamn fellowship, George, and stick it! It's the only kind you understand! (GEORGE *slams door, leaving.*) It's all right, Katy. Everything's all right.

Blackout.

SCENE THREE

Friday night. PHIL *and* MARIE *are seated on the couch.* LOUISE *sits in rocker, feeding* KATY. GEORGE *pours drinks.*

PHIL: Thanks, fella, I can use this.

GEORGE: Rough day?

PHIL: The usual. At least it's over.

GEORGE: Beats pumping gas in Weberville.

MARIE: None for me, dear, I'm driving.

GEORGE: Honey, another drink?

LOUISE: Yes. Set it on the table.

GEORGE: And one for Papa Bear. Ever see such a beautiful kid?

PHIL: Twenty of them. This afternoon.

MARIE: She is beautiful. May I hold her?

LOUISE: (*Hands* KATY *to* MARIE.) Watch out. She goes for earrings.

MARIE: Look at those toes. Babies have such cute toes! How's her rash?

LOUISE: Better. I've been air-drying her bottom. Seven out of ten pediatricians at U.C. agree that air-drying . . .

GEORGE: Louise is taking a survey. Next she's gonna call St. Luke's and talk to all their pediatricians, twice a day, then S.F. General, then, who knows? New York, the Mayo Clinic, then—ah, why not? Lourdes. Right. After two thousand and thirteen medical opinions and a voice in a whirlwind saying: "AIR DRY HER BOTTOM," she might believe ol' George . . .

PHIL: Ha, ha. Don't bet on it. Marie never listens to me. She's gonna try for a job in some piano-bar tomorrow . . .

MARIE: It's not a piano-bar.

PHIL: Whatever. But I must admit, with four kids, she probably knows as much about babies as I do—you just have to learn for yourself, Louise. Don't let us pediatricians boss you around.

LOUISE: Oh, pediatricians are great—on the phone. Only way to talk to them. Patient, thoughtful, kind—real long distance lovers.

GEORGE: That's the only kind you're interested in, isn't it?

LOUISE: Why do you think I call the clinic so often?

MARIE: Uh . . . (*Feeding* KATY.) Katy really takes to this bottle, doesn't she?

LOUISE: Yeah. Dr. Collins' nursing program wasn't working out. At home, anyway.

PHIL: Well, next baby, you'll know what's right for you.

LOUISE: There won't be a next baby, if I know what's right for me.

PHIL: You want a little boy, don't you? Gotta have a lawyer in the family to handle all George's malpractice suits.

LOUISE: Katy can be a lawyer. I know several woman who are lawyers.

GEORGE: You know one. Marsha.

LOUISE: Judy was admitted to Hastings. And Helene has applied.

GEORGE: That doesn't make them lawyers. And Helene just wants to meet men.

LOUISE: I have decided to become a lawyer.

GEORGE: You? Since when?

LOUISE: This afternoon.

GEORGE: Ha, ha. Are you serious? You gonna write your briefs in lunatic iambic pentameter?

LOUISE: I will knock off my husband and kid and confess. After the initial barrage of psychiatric tests, on which I will register bonkers, having had some experience, I will become the model prisoner, also having had some experience. I will be . . . California's living proof of prison rehabilitation. I will be the San Quentin Poster Girl. I will study law in the prison library, and then I'll work for women in prisons everywhere, until we are all free of boxcars, husbands, babies . . .

PHIL: (*Pause.*) You . . . uh . . . really want to put us guys out of business, don't you?

KATY: WAHHAHHAHHAHH!

LOUISE: It's too late. (*Rises to take* KATY *to nursery.*)

GEORGE: Need some help?

LOUISE: Sure. Might as well start sometime, George. (*They exit to nursery.* PHIL *and* MARIE *exchange uncomfortable glances.*)

GEORGE: (*Stage whisper.*) Knock it off! We didn't ask them over to listen to weird talk and watch us fight!

LOUISE: Then they shouldn't come when both of us are in the same room. (*They return to the living room.*)

PHIL: Uh . . . ready for the interview next week, George?

GEORGE: Ready as I'll ever be.

LOUISE: Interview?

GEORGE: For the fellowship. As I recall, your parting advice this morning was for me to "take" the fellowship?

PHIL: Uh . . . lot depends on the interview—but with Roberts and Hunter pulling for you, I don't think you'll have any trouble.

MARIE: There's a chance George won't get the fellowship?

PHIL: Three other guys have their applications in. But, barring natural disaster, George has the inside track.

LOUISE: He's off an' running.

PHIL: I'd have given a lot for a chance like this when I was a resident. George is lucky. And . . . gifted. He's somebody who can make a difference.

MARIE: Unlike a wife. And family.

PHIL: That's a laugh. I could have gone for a fellowship in prenatal neurology, but I had four little mouths to feed. George could be teaching in a couple years, Louise. Eight to four, home for dinner, no call duty. Me, I'm just a lousy staffer. I spend nights just catching up on my files and correspondence.

LOUISE: I've heard that.

GEORGE: People all over the country write to Phil about their kids' birth defects. He's considered an expert in his field.

LOUISE: I've heard that, too. The hostess at the Red Lion, the "little friend" in the steno pool, they'll tell the world that Phil's an expert in his field.

GEORGE: Louise!

LOUISE: Doctors work around a lot of attractive women and they can't help comparing. Right, George?

PHIL: But none can compare with my little wife, or yours either, eh, George?

MARIE: Wife? "A doctor is married to his prctice." We're all just . . . "other women," Louise. Haven't you heard?

PHIL: No matter what you've heard, Louise, George has an incredible chance, here, an' you can't hold him back.

LOUISE: What can I do, Phil? I hate the taste of gin.

PHIL: Try rum. Marie mixes it with the kids' orange juice. (*Telephone rings.*)

GEORGE: Hello? Speaking. Oh, God. Turn up the oxygen. Check the blood gases. I'll be right there. Don't take your eyes off her. (*Hangs up.*) Dorsey. I've got to go.

PHIL: Doctor's dilemma. Louise, let's make this another time? You don't need anybody to wait on right now. Marie?

LOUISE: Marie—I'm sorry.

MARIE: Call me tomorrow. We can talk. (PHIL *and* MARIE *exit.*)

GEORGE: (*Getting coat, etc.*) Well, that was all time.

LOUISE: Are you going to be late?

GEORGE: I don't know. I'll call you. (*Exits.*)

LOUISE: (*Quiets* KATY.) It's all right. Everything's all right.

Blackout.

SCENE FOUR

LOUISE *is asleep on the couch.* KATY *is asleep in the crib. Telephone rings, wakes up* KATY, *then* LOUISE, *who lurches to phone.*

KATY: Wahhahhah!

LOUISE: Hello! George! Katy was asleep! So was I. (*Pause.*) You won't be home tonight? So what else is new? (*Pause.*) *Worried* about you? (GEORGE *hangs up on* LOUISE.)

KATY: WAHHAHHAH!

LOUISE: (*Throws phone against the wall, pulls books off shelves and flings them around, throws laundry, papers, everything she can grab, around and around, screaming animally.*) AAAAGHGHHGHHGHH-GHHGHHGHGHGHGHGH!

KATY: WAHHAHHAH!

LOUISE: (*Grabs the screaming* KATY *and throttles her; then puts her down in her crib and draws back, aghast. Silence.*) Katy? (*Pause.*) Katy? (*Pause.*) Please, God! Katy! (*Picks* KATY *up, breathes into*

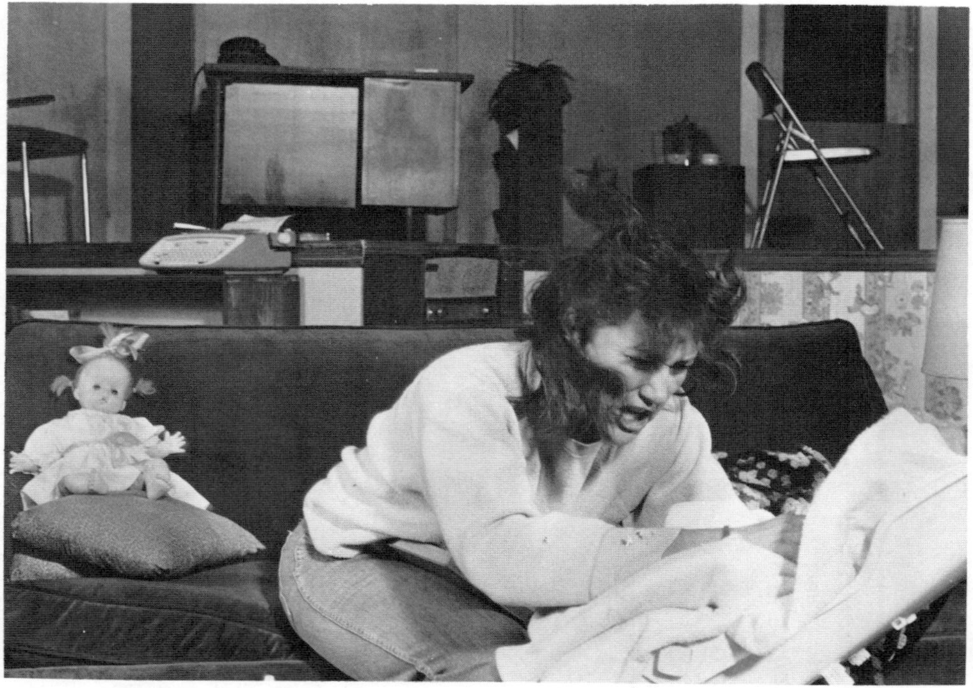

Betsy Scott (LOUISE) *in the Magic Theatre production.*

her mouth, haphazardly, distractedly, then goes to telephone and dials, holding KATY *against her shoulder.*)

KATY: (*Softly.*) Wahh!

LOUISE: *Katy!* Oh, Katy! (*Replaces receiver. Stares at the telephone for a moment; then decides to dial for help.*) Hello? Pediatric Advice, please. Yes. I'll hold. (*Pause.*) Hello! Yes. I . . . um. I . . . um. (*Starts to replace receiver, then forces herself to continue.*) I . . . just tried to . . . I just hurt my baby. Yes. She's . . . I think she's okay. No. What? I don't have a car. Wait. There is someone. Yes. About twenty minutes. Dr. Simmons. Um. Louise. Collins. (*Hangs up; re-dials.*) Hello? Marie?

SCENE FIVE

DR. SIMMONS'*s office.* LOUISE *enters, holding* KATY. SIMMONS *is seated at her desk.*

SIMMONS: Mrs. Collins?

LOUISE: Yes.

SIMMONS: This must be Katy. (*Rises, takes* KATY *to a small table and examines her.*) Let's have a look. Hm. Bruised thorax, some swelling. Possible . . . internal bleeding. Hm. Breathing okay, though.

LOUISE: How bad . . .

SIMMONS: We'll need some x-rays. It doesn't look too serious. (*Returns* KATY *to* LOUISE.) Have a seat.

LOUISE: Hardly anybody here tonight. I brought Katy in once for, well, her diaper rash, there were hundreds of people. (*Pause.*) I never noticed how nice they keep the floors polished here. Tonight, if you had the right socks on, you could run, slide two hundred feet, not bump into anybody. I come from a small town. You could put Weberville and half of Baker's Flat in that hall, and they could all slide two hundred feet without bumpin' into anybody . . .

SIMMONS: (*Gently.*) Louise, what happened tonight?

LOUISE: I . . . um . . . was asleep. My . . . husband . . . George . . . called. The phone woke up the baby. I've told him not to call. I've told him it wakes her up, but he says her aural nerves aren't that well developed, or she'll get used to it, or something . . . He doesn't believe me.

SIMMONS: And then what happened?

LOUISE: Hm. Um . . . I . . . was . . . throwing things around . . . ah . . . laundry, books, all my books, God . . . all over . . . and I heard this . . . screaming . . . it was me, and Katy, screaming . . . she screams a lot, I don't know why . . . I've heard some babies just eat and sleep, and never cry, but not Katy.

SIMMONS: And after you were screaming and throwing things?

LOUISE: I . . . um . . . she was screaming . . . and she wouldn't stop . . . and my . . . hands were on . . . her neck, and I was . . . um . . . I was . . . choking her.

KATY: Wahhahhah!

SIMMONS: (*Chuckles.*) You weren't too successful. (*Pause.*) You stopped choking her?

LOUISE: I . . . saw my hands. (*Weeps.*)

SIMMONS: Well, Louise, you've got a lot going for you. You didn't seriously hurt Katy, and you did call for help. Many parents never call for help, never admit, even to themselves, that they hurt their children. Did you call George? He's working tonight.

LOUISE: No. I called Pediatrics Advice. I always call Pediatrics Advice.

SIMMONS: George works very hard. Young residents don't have much time to spend with their families.

LOUISE: He's up for a fellowship, and there's the Unit, you know, he started that—he has to spend a lot of time there. Uh . . . I was thinking, I was thinking, one of those classes on infant care might really help me—it doesn't come naturally, like in the Pampers commercials.

SIMMONS: (*Chuckles.*) No, it doesn't. A class would be a good idea. We have several programs that can help you.

LOUISE: Classes. Fine. Good. I'll call you tomorrow and we can discuss it. (*Rises to go.*)

SIMMONS: Louise, you can't go. Katy has to have x-rays. There may be spinal damage. She'll spend one, maybe two nights in the nursery, while we make sure she's all right.

LOUISE: Oh, no.

SIMMONS: There are some papers for you to fill out. And a couple of officers from the CES are on their way over.

LOUISE: Officers. Police?

SIMMONS: They're plainclothes officers, specially trained for this. We are required by law to notify them in these cases.

LOUISE: These . . . cases.

SIMMONS: They'll ask a few questions, help us decide what's the best way to help you and Katy—and George. No one here has to know, except George, of course, and Roberts.

LOUISE: Oh, God—not Roberts.

SIMMONS: He's our chief of staff.

LOUISE: You didn't have to call the police! I didn't really hurt Katy!

SIMMONS: Louise—has this sort of thing happened before?

LOUISE: (*Pause*) Yes.

SIMMONS: What might happen the next time? (LOUISE *reflects; nods.*) Next week there'll be a private hearing in court. I'll be there. I can tell you right now that I'm going to recommend . . .

LOUISE: My God! Court! Police!

SIMMONS: We are required by law to call the police. George would have to call them, if . . .

LOUISE: George . . . wouldn't call anybody. He wouldn't believe me. He's never home. (*Pause.*) Maybe that's why I didn't call him.

SIMMONS: Did you think you could make him stay home?

LOUISE: I don't know. (*Buzzer sounds;* SIMMONS *answers it.*)

SIMMONS: Yes? Fine. We'll meet them down in x-ray. And page George Collins on Five. Ask him to meet us there. Emergency.

Blackout.

SCENE SIX

LOUISE *and* MARIE *enter living room, without* KATY.

LOUISE: Can you stay a minute?

MARIE: If you like.

LOUISE: You want some coffee?

MARIE: No. Thanks.

LOUISE: You think she'll be warm enough in that room?

MARIE: She'll be fine.

LOUISE: She was so quiet.

MARIE: She was almost asleep when we left.

LOUISE: I was going to kill her.

MARIE: But you didn't.

LOUISE: Her little neck . . . so soft . . . so strong.

MARIE: Take the sedatives Dr. Simmons gave you.

LOUISE: No.

MARIE: Take care of yourself, Louise. If you learn nothing else from this. (*Gives her paper cup with pills in it.*) You need sleep.

LOUISE: (*Takes pills.*) She was breathing okay. They said she was breathing okay.

MARIE: She was breathing fine.

LOUISE: George didn't say much.

MARIE: He was shaken.

LOUISE: I'm glad Phil was there.

MARIE: I found him—in the cafeteria. With Shirley Harris. Drinking coffee. Laughing.

LOUISE: (*Pause.*) How can you stand it?

MARIE: Sometimes I can, sometimes I can't. I . . . drink. I'm sure you've heard. Not often. Never in front of the children. (*Pause.*) Babies . . . don't always bring you closer together. Sometimes they just fill up the space between. (*Pause.*) It helps . . . to talk. Would you . . . like to come over next week? Mindy'd love to take care of Katy. We could talk.

LOUISE: Will you play "Stardust" for me?

MARIE: (*Tucks blanket around* LOUISE.) Sure. (*Hugs her.*) Bye.

Blackout.

SCENE SEVEN

GEORGE *comes home, later that day.* LOUISE *is asleep on the couch. She wakes up.*

GEORGE: Place looks like a cyclone hit it.

LOUISE: I took a nap.

GEORGE: I gave Katy a bottle about an hour ago. She took it pretty well. There's a lot of swelling.

LOUISE: (*Looks at her watch.*) They'll let me see her at two.

GEORGE: We can bring her home tomorrow. X-ray didn't find any spinal damage.

LOUISE: Thank God.

GEORGE: Had a talk with Roberts.

LOUISE: Oh?

GEORGE: Told him . . . I want to withdraw my application for the fellowship. He was nice. Said to take a few days off. Think about it. (*Pause.*) Hunter was there. He said I could have a job in Des Moines. Try for a fellowship there.

LOUISE: That was nice.

GEORGE: Yes. Nice. Hunter, Roberts, the nurses, the reception- the janitors—everyone's been very nice. (*Whispers.*) "There goes Collins—great pediatrician, but . . ."

LOUISE: His wife's a child-abuser.

GEORGE: You see Roberta Sherwood today?

LOUISE: Yes.

GEORGE: Was she nice?

LOUISE: Very—clinical psychologist.

GEORGE: And Marie? That was nice of her to take you to the hospital. And Dr. Simmons? She was nice, and the cops from CES—they were nice . . .

LOUISE: Stop it!

GEORGE: (*Pause.*) Did . . . Roberta take you through the Family Center?

LOUISE: Yes. I met some of the parents, a couple of teachers.

GEORGE: Were they . . . nice?

LOUISE: Very . . . sympathetic.

GEORGE: Did you ask them what they did to their children? I mean, it must be a topic of conversation there. Cigarette burns? That's a common one. Blows to the body, where no one can see? We get a lot of that. Razor cuts? Twisted ankles and wrists? Little bones pulled out of their sockets? That's so easy. Poison? I've seen what Lysol can do to a six-month-old stomach. It isn't nice. Did you tell them you tried to strangle our baby? Hm? That wasn't nice, Louise. *That wasn't nice!*

LOUISE: (*Pause.*) We have to be in court Monday at ten.

GEORGE: Court. Then what?

LOUISE: They decide if . . . Katy's safe with us.

GEORGE: Oh, God.

LOUISE: Dr. Simmons will be there. She's going to recommend that we join the Family Center.

GEORGE: Simmons—of all the inflexible . . . why the hell didn't you call me, Louise?

LOUISE: I didn't think you'd believe me.

GEORGE: (*Pause.*) Did you ever hurt Katy before?

LOUISE: Yes.

GEORGE: Why didn't you tell me then?

LOUISE: I tried.

GEORGE: Some . . . wild poetry? Crazy talk?

LOUISE: (*Pause.*) Yes.

GEORGE: Oh, but you could talk straight enough to Dorothy Simmons and the cops and the social workers and now you have a Family Center, and day-care center, and groupie-helpie meetings, and a police record—is that what you wanted?

LOUISE: I wanted help. I've got it, now.

GEORGE: Lord, yes—the whole goddamn hospital.

LOUISE: You're just worried about your precious reputation, aren't you, doctor?

GEORGE: What about your reputation? Louise Collins, published poet, authority on Virginia Woolf and whole-grain breads, has botched it as a mother—*failed failed failed!*

LOUISE: And you're such a great success as a father, you . . .

GEORGE: Katy's life was in danger, and you didn't have the guts to tell me! Or even admit it to yourself! All that crap about silver moons, and orbits—running away into crazy fantasy!

LOUISE: Where was all this fatherly concern when I was begging you for one night's sleep?

GEORGE: You wanted this baby! I thought you knew what to expect!

LOUISE: I wanted this baby! What did you want? Baby pictures for your office? You could have borrowed some old ones from Phil! You could have sent for some from the Pediatrics Supply Catalogue!

GEORGE: I didn't think we were ready for a baby—but you were so happy about it! You saw a way out of that dead-end job of yours and you grabbed it!

LOUISE: Hell, yes, I wanted out of that dead-end job—I supported your career for six goddamn dead-end years, and you were finished with your residency and it was *my* turn!

GEORGE: What . . . did Katy mean to you? What is she now? An irritation? An inconvenience? Something you wish you'd flushed away while there was still time?

LOUISE: That was your idea. Go see Silvestri. If you're not sure, you'd better not have it.

GEORGE: And . . . this is better? Bruises on her throat? Black and yellow bruises? Hm? And red skin burns, where you *twisted* . . .

LOUISE: You put them there, too, George. Your hands and mine. You think you can walk out on this one? (*Grabs his hand.*) Look at your well-scrubbed hands, George—*we* gave her life. And *we*—almost killed her.

GEORGE: (*Long pause, softly.*) It was noisy here. Messy. It smelled bad. Wet diapers. Puke. You were noisy. You didn't listen to me. The important people were outside, in the real world. (*Pause.*) Oh, Louise.

LOUISE: She was supposed to make me happy. Keep you home nights. She wasn't doing her job. (*Pause.*) Oh, God, she must hurt. So frightened, and hurt. Angry.

GEORGE: (*Takes off his glasses; rubbing his eyes.*) You were so capable; so possessive. I just didn't know. Didn't . . . want to know.

LOUISE: (*Takes his glasses; cleans them.*) I was doing fine. All new mothers scream and kick dressers.

GEORGE: You didn't want my advice, my help . . .

LOUISE: I didn't need help. I was the perfect mother. (*Pause.*) All I needed was one night's sleep. (*Laughs mirthlessly.*) Well . . . I have help, now. Groupie-helpie meetings, day-care center, Dr. Simmons. (*Pause.*) What I'm saying is, you can go to Des Moines, or the call room, and not come back.

GEORGE: Is that what you want?

LOUISE: I want . . . time. For myself. For Katy. I can have it now. Without you.

GEORGE: You want me to go?

LOUISE: I won't live with a locomotive anymore. I get angry. I take it out on Katy. So . . . if you can't give us that kind of time, we are better off without you.

GEORGE: I see. (*Pause.*) They . . . don't need me at the Unit as much as I . . . like to think. Hank can handle the routine stuff. Dorsey can take on the emergency schedule two, maybe three, nights a week. He's doing it for the next five days. I am . . . taking off until next Thursday.

LOUISE: (*Warily.*) They said I could see her at two. She'll be hungry. I'll get a bottle ready for her.

GEORGE: I can get it.

LOUISE: (*Pause.*) I'll get her blanket. It's cold in that room.

GEORGE: (*Gets bottle.*)They have a bottle warmer in the nursery.

LOUISE: Oh, her bear. (*Gets a little stuffed bear from crib.*)

GEORGE: (*Pulls out two coupons with red-haired clown on them.*) How about dinner afterward?

LOUISE: Double cheeseburger? The other night you were going to take me to Sabella's. (*Looks at watch.*) Oh, God—now we've got to hurry.

GEORGE: We'll get there. (*Embraces her.*) We'll get there.

FINAL BLACKOUT

Earth Worms

Albert Innaurato

Produced at the Berkeley Stage Company, January 1978. Directed by Robert W. Goldsby.

BERNARD	Drew Eshelman
ARNOLD	Scott Paulin
MARY	Judith Weston
EDITH	Angela Paton
BUCKY	Michael O'Connor
SCODGE	Matthew Gottlieb
MICHAEL	John Vickery
BOY	Robert E. Goldsby
MARGE	Linda Dobb
NUNS	D'Alan Moss
	Kathy Leavelle
	Ruth Coopersmith

Photos by Jerald Morse

CHARACTERS

BERNARD: Is seventy, heavy, though not obese. He is large-framed, tall, slightly stooped but in good health and very robust. He has a grand manner, a booming, deep voice, and is inclined to be rhetorical.

MARY: A young Southern girl; accent is heavy at first; in the course of the play it is modified.

ARNOLD: From South Philadelphia.

EDITH: His aunt. She only crawls, never walks, is blind.

MICHAEL: Flamboyant drag queen, but very tough.

BUCKY: Of the neighborhood; twenty-three.

SCODGE: Of the neighborhood; twenty-three.

MARGE: Of the neighborhood; twenty-six.

A BOY: Fourteen; of the neighborhood.

THREE NUNS: In old-fashioned habits: long black gowns, wimples, black gloves, over-sized weapon-like rosaries. Their faces are never visible.

PLACE

The play opens in Virginia, but most of the scenes occur in the Italian section of South Philadelphia.

SETTING

The stage is meant to be bare. If possible there should be two levels connected by a rough stairway. There should be entrances on both levels. Different locations should be suggested by lighting, and the set should be very flexible, able to embrace a variety of locations, in some cases simultaneously.

A number of the scenes occur in a row house in South Philadelphia. The house is meant to be without furniture except for a large desk down right, and a small, dirty kitchen area far left. There can be a small, old-fashioned stove and sink in the kitchen. The balcony or second level, in those scenes, represents the house's second floor.

Certain other sections occur in a small bar, which can occupy the kitchen section with a small table or bar dragged on. There should never be more than a small attempt to suggest any location.

TIME

The mid-nineteen-fifties.

Earth Worms

Albert Innaurato

ACT ONE

SCENE ONE

In a spot, BERNARD *appears. He acts as though looking in a mirror. He adjusts on his head a lady's bonnet and wears an elaborate shawl. Both look as though they were made in the 1890s.*

A light comes up down right. The sound of a stream is heard.

MARY *is lying face down, weeping. She is barefoot and in a rough dress. Her light builds as* BERNARD *starts to speak.*

BERNARD: (*Calling in different tones, now sad, now angry, now pleading.*) Ellen Mac Jones! Ellen Mac Jones! Here, Ellen, Ellen, Ellen! Ellen Mac Jones Aberdeen! Ellen! Miss Mac Jones! Please, Ellen, Why do you make me call you and call you? Ellen Mac Jones Aberdeen! Ellen!

His light goes out.

ARNOLD *enters slowly. He wears an army uniform which is muddy and torn. He is obviously lost and has been wandering, trying to find his way. He sees* MARY *who is still crying, her head buried in her arms. He approaches shyly and listens to her. Suddenly she speaks without looking up or around. She continues to sob.*

MARY: (*Heavy Southern accent.*) Oh, I know you're there. Don't want to hear nothin' from you. You're evil, evil! I bet you think I'm lyin' here just awaitin' for you. Well you're wrong! (ARNOLD, *startled, looks around.*) Oh, I know you're lookin' around just to see if anyone can hear me. A girl callin' her own daddy evil and him a Baptist deacon. It'ud be a scandal. Well, I don't care. You are a prime example of the devourin' parent. I read all about you in that book you ripped away from me.

ARNOLD: (*Urban accent.*) Look, I'm sorry, but I think you're makin' a mistake . . .

MARY: (*Whips around.*) Who are you? (ARNOLD *shifts.*) Who are you?

ARNOLD: (*Hesitating.*) Arnold Longese.

MARY: Why'd you hesitate?

ARNOLD: Well, people around here, well, they ain't used to names like that. You know, they look at me, well, funny.

MARY: Ain't that an Italian name?

ARNOLD: Why, yeah, Longese, that's Italian. (*Embarrassed.*) Them Wop names, you know.

MARY: Don't you like bein' Italian?

ARNOLD: Who's Italian?

MARY: Why you just said . . .

ARNOLD: Nah! I'm American. Red-blooded. Got this Italian handle because my pop came over with his sisters, you know, from Italy, when they was kids. But, nah, I'm raised over here, in South Philly.

MARY: South Philly . . . you mean, Philadelphia?

ARNOLD: City of Brotherly Love! Where I come from everybody's gotta name like mine.

MARY: That true?

ARNOLD: Sure! I mean, Longese, that's my name, that's common. Then there's, let me see, well, Gambone, Mastroangelo, De Felice . . .

MARY: De Felice . . .

ARNOLD: Yeah. Means "Of Happiness." Boy, was he weird. Then there's Squatarelli . . .

MARY: Beautiful names.

ARNOLD: (*Looking at her.*) Well, lotta beautiful things in this world. (*A pause.*)

MARY: You at the base?

ARNOLD: Medical orderly.

MARY: Longese, that right?

ARNOLD: You can call me Arn.

MARY: Arn? Don't you read the funny papers?

ARNOLD: Me? Nah!

MARY: Why, Prince Arn, he's Prince Valiant's son. Oh, he's a handsome old boy. Don't know how old. You can't never tell in them funny papers. Some days he looks fourteen, some days he looks twenty. Some of us girls, well, we used to spend time a-seein' if we could find us a bulge. Well, you know where. He wears tights, you see . . .

ARNOLD: You mean them tight things? (*Pulls pants up.*) Up here? In the funny papers?

MARY: Why, yes. But they's never a bulge. Never a bulge on anybody. I looked at Superman, Tarzan, and Lothar, too. Prince Arn . . . he's brave, got curly hair, looks like you . . .

ARNOLD: Aw, I don' look like nothin'!

MARY: You do too look like him. Or, I guess, he looks like you, bein' he's in the funny papers and you—you're real. He has brown eyes too and this nice nose, just like yours. (*Touches his nose. He is startled.*) Oh, I'm sorry, I didn't mean to touch it. But I ain't never been this close to a nose like that.

ARNOLD: (*Pause. He shifts.*) Boy, it's hot. That water sounds nice.

MARY: Water is a symbol. That's what Jung (*Mispronounced.*) says. If that's how you say his name. I think that's what he says, somethin' about Anima . . .

ARNOLD: Yeah, animea, that's where you ain't got no blood . . .

MARY: No, this is somethin' different.

ARNOLD: No it ain't, my mother died from it . . .

MARY: No, this is about sex. (*Stops, shocked at what she has said.*) I didn't mean that, I mean with the idea of sex. Oh, I better shut up. I worked in the university library after school . . .

ARNOLD: You go to college . . .

MARY: Why, no. My daddy'd never let me. No, I just this summer graduated high school. This teacher, he taught history, Mr. Shingles? Well, he got me this job end of soph'more year in exchange for me lettin' him rub up against me in his Chevy. I think the pursuit of knowledge justifies anything, don't you? So, I'd work there in the afternoons and steal the books—just until I had them read. That's what happened today. Daddy came in early and found me in my room with Jung and got his switch out after me. We're Baptist, you know. Well, he caught me today, let me tell you. He gave me this. (*Shows him her lip, which is cut.*)

ARNOLD: Yeah, I seen that. Looks bad. Have you cleaned it?

MARY: Why, no. Well, he hit on me with that switch. A prime example of hysteria, to judge from Dr. Freud (*Mispronounced.*) Of course, I ran off a-weepin'. That's what little girls is supposed to do and to him I'm still a little girl even though I'm a full-growed seventeen and don't crowd me so much.

ARNOLD: You ought to wash that cut. Let's go swimmin'.

MARY: Swimmin'? (*A pause; she muses.*) I ain't supposed to go swimmin' with boys. I mean, I go with my brother but he ain't a boy in the sense I mean.

ARNOLD: I think you should go swimmin' for medical reasons, that cut after all—

MARY: How old are you?

ARNOLD: Nineteen. Wanted a be sent to Korea. Wound up here. My luck. Let's go swimmin'.

MARY: You start undressin'. (*He takes his shirt off.*) Why, you don't have much hair up here at all. Can I take a hair? Just for me. (*Takes a hair. He giggles. She puts the hair in a pocket.*)

ARNOLD: You take somethin' off.

MARY: Near the river. They's a bush there. (*They get up.*) You won't do nothin' to me?

ARNOLD: Me? Nah! I got lost and have been stumblin' around, tryin' to get back, I'm lost.

MARY: Well, I'm puttin' myself at your mercy, Prince Arn.

ARNOLD: What's your name?

MARY: Why, Mary.

A pause. Shyly, he takes her hand; they start off. As they exit, the lights brighten and become very harsh. The entire stage is lit. A street in the Italian section of South Philadelphia is represented.

SCODGE *and* BUCKY *run on wildly, playing basketball. They are in their mid-twenties, husky going to fat.* MARGE *appears, twenty-nine, heavy, tough.*

MARGE: (*Hearty, mocking.*) Gee, guys, can I play wit you?

SCODGE: Hiya, Marge! (*Throws the ball at her; she screams but gets it.*)

MARGE: Bastids!

BUCKY: What's the number, Marge?

MARGE: Nine-oh-three.

SCODGE: Shit! And I bet nine-oh-four.

MARGE: You guys and the numbers!

MARGE *dribbles. The men get the ball away from* MARGE *and play.*

MICHAEL DE FELICE *makes a flashy entrance in full drag. He is wildly effeminate but with more than a hint of toughness underneath. The men greet him with whistles. He flounces all the more.*

MICHAEL: Keep them balls bouncin', boys!

BUCKY: Hiya, Michael, what's the name today?

MICHAEL: Madame Bovary.

MARGE: Madame Overy? What the hell kinda name is that?

MICHAEL: Don't judge it, bitch!

SCODGE: Hey, you, show some respect!

Three NUNS *enter. They are in old-fashioned habits as would befit the fifties. Their faces are covered. One plays a funereal rhythm on a tambourine, the others carry a large crucifix between them. It is a garish crucifix with Christ's wounds alarmingly clear. They march slowly across the stage. Everyone looks away except* MICHAEL *who stares at them.*

After the NUNS *exit, the game starts up again. The fourteen-year-old* BOY *runs on;* MICHAEL *grabs him.*

MICHAEL: Hello, Liu.

BOY: Cut it out. Who?

MICHAEL: That's the victim from the opera *Turandot.*

BOY: Christ, you're weird.

MICHAEL: You think about my offer?

BOY: Up yours.

The BOY *starts off.* BERNARD *enters wearing the shawl and stares at the* BOY *with obvious interest.* MICHAEL *notices this. The* BOY, *confused, starts off.* MICHAEL *calls out to him as he exits.*

MICHAEL: (*To* BOY.) Remember, that's something I know how to do. (BOY *runs out.* BERNARD, *acting oblivious, passes* MICHAEL.) Hiya, Turandot.

BERNARD: (*Neither stopping nor looking up.*) I despise Puccini.

Blackout.

SCENE TWO

One of the NUNS *enters with a chair; she places it in a dim spot. The two others lead* ARNOLD *into the spot. He is wearing undershorts but nothing else; his hands are bound behind him. The* NUNS *seat him and tie him to the chair.* ARNOLD *is terrified.*

FIRST NUN: (*Showing him a picture.*) Look at this picture.

ARNOLD: I didn't mean to do it. I'm sorry. I'm ignorant even if I did go to high school. (*Tries to look away.*)

SECOND NUN: Hold his head, force his eyes, make him look!

FIRST NUN: (*Showing another picture.*) Look at this one! (NUNS *cluck,* ARNOLD *groans.*)

THIRD NUN: That is not merely a sin of commission but in the end of emission too.

ARNOLD: Please don' show me no more. I'm sorry. Oh, my God, I am heartily sorry for having offended thee and . . .

SECOND NUN: (*Clamps her hand over his mouth.*) No! Can't repent. You haven't atoned enough.

FIRST NUN: The pursuit of happiness is the filthiest pursuit!

SECOND AND THIRD NUNS: The pursuit of happiness is the filthiest pursuit!

The NUNS *make a jingle of this line and dance in a circle around* ARNOLD. *They build until they are shrieking, then they freeze. After a pause, they unbind* ARNOLD *mechanically and kneel. They cross themselves and pray, whining very softly.*

ARNOLD *stands up, very shaken. He walks right.*

A light comes up far right. MARY *is asleep on a cot.* ARNOLD'*s clothes are piled near the cot. He dresses, still very upset. When he is dressed he stares at* MARY. *The* NUNS' *whining increases for a moment.*

MICHAEL *and the* BOY *come on, far left. They settle in a spot and start to play cards.*

ARNOLD *kisses* MARY, *who awakens.*

MARY: You goin'?

ARNOLD: Had this awful dream.

MARY: Tell me, I read Dr. Freud (*Mispronounced.*) on dreams.

ARNOLD: No.

MICHAEL *has dealt cards. The* BOY *looks at the back of his cards curiously.*

BOY: Hey, Michael, what's this onna back of these cards?

MICHAEL: They're pictures, hon, play.

BOY: I know they're pictures. Whataya think, I'm ignorant? I go a high school. Who they pictures of?

MICHAEL: You think about my offer? You bring it up wit you brother? Stop starin' for Christ sake! It's Arnold Longese.

ARNOLD *has tried to leave* MARY *who has hung on him.*

ARNOLD: See you.

He starts to leave. Impulsively, MARY *hugs him.*

BOY *laughs, looks more closely at the pictures.*

BOY: No kiddin, that Arnold? He's got his face covered in this one—yeah, yeah, I guess it's him. Look at what he's doin' wit you on this one! Can't be him, he was a he-man.

MICHAEL: That's for sure. And nobody knows it better than me!

They play cards.

MARY: (*Kisses* ARNOLD. *He is uncomfortable.*) Arnold, baby, when you goin'—well, you know, with me?

ARNOLD: (*Disengaging himself.*) This ain't the time.

MARY: It's been three weeks, I mean, I enjoy the kissin' and the spendin' the nights, but that's all we done . . .

ARNOLD: Not now.

MARY: When you comin' back?

ARNOLD: Look, Mary, I been thinkin' I . . . (*Looks at her. She smiles. He can't bring himself to say it.*) Thursday, I'll be covered.

MARY: We'll go to a special place I know. A Magic Place. We'll go at a magic time, I have your hair . . .

ARNOLD: I'll come. Look, Mary, remember what I asked you, before? Abour shavin' . . . down there?

MARY: I'll shave, Prince Arn.

They kiss. ARNOLD *gently gets away from* MARY *and goes.*

The BOY *and* MICHAEL *play a new hand.*

During their dialogue MARY *rips the sheet from the bed and begins a dance with it. It is a ritual dance. She presses it to her breasts, embraces it, treats it as though it had a human shape.*

BOY: But how'd you get him to pose? I wouldn't.

MICHAEL: I begged and wept as only I know how. I sang: "Deh, non credea mirarti!" from *Sonnambula,* into his ear. No luck. So's I knocked over a nigger liquor store and paid him three hundred dollars. I had the cards made up. I love him!

MARY *has finished her dance. She wakes herself as though she were in a trance and exits. The* NUNS *rise and take the chair off stage.*

BOY: Aw, guys don' love other guys!

MICHAEL: You think about my offer?

BOY: Gin!

Blackout.

SCENE THREE

BERNARD *enters wearing an expensive-looking mantilla from the 1890s. A bus goes by, car horns are heard, a thumping is heard, as though a ball were bounced against the wall of the house.*

The scene is the row house in South Philadelphia. The house is meant to be empty except for a desk and desk chair down right and a small kitchen area stage left. In the kitchen there can be a small old-fashioned stove and sink. The desk is old and very battered but large.

BERNARD *waves his mantilla about, caresses it, treats it as though it had a human shape. He clears his throat. A thump is heard.* BERNARD *goes off, clearing his throat, and returns with a large yellow envelope. He clears his throat. He removes a manuscript from the envelope, along with a letter. He reads the letter in a fury, then crumples it.*

BERNARD: Only editors have names like that!

He puts the manuscript on the desk, clears his throat, rips the letter up and pads into the kitchen. He passes what appears to be a bundle of old rags near the stove on the floor. He spits in the sink.

The bundle of rags starts up violently. This is EDITH. *She is in a rage. She is blind.*

EDITH: That's right! Spit inna sink! You fat lousy creep! Go 'head, spit inna sink like a pig, and while you're at it, why don' you stick them hairy fingers down your throat and throw up, hanh? And then, why don' you drape that fat ass over the sink and shit in it? Fuckin' fruity Wasp nurd! Why the hell you gotta spit inna sink all the time? Ain't hygienic! All that education and never learned where to spit. Inna toilet! That's where, like a human being. That's the way we do it in Civilization. (*Tries to find* BERNARD *by waving her arms about.*) Where are you, creep, where are you? (*Finds his leg and bites it.*) That'll teach you, you bum!

BERNARD *yanks his leg away with a cry;* EDITH *collapses. He kicks her repeatedly.*

BERNARD: And another thing, you blind odoriferous legacy of a fetid past, there wasn't even a postcard from Arnold. He's forgotten his old Aunt Edith. (*Runs out calling.*) Ellen Mac Jones, here Ellen, Ellen! Ellen Mac Jones Aberdeen!

Blackout.

SCENE FOUR

A graveyard. The three NUNS *stand like a monument. One of them is holding the heavy crucifix upright.*

A small light goes on. MARY *has lit a small lantern. She has the sheet from the cot laid out on the ground near the* NUNS. *She and* ARNOLD *are sitting on it.*

MARY: (*To* ARNOLD, *whispering.*) Watch 'em now, watch 'em, they'll inch out . . .

ARNOLD: Forget the worms for Christ sake!

MARY: Lookit, there's one . . .

ARNOLD: We shouldn't have drunk so much of that stuff . . . you said it was magic . . . (MARY *picks up a worm.*) Put that worm down!

MARY: You afraid of a worm?

ARNOLD: Look, Mary, I been thinkin' . . . will you put that down? Jesus Christ, this ain't the place. A graveyard, it gives me the willies. An' these worms . . .

MARY: Do you love me, Arnold? I ain't never felt loved . . .

ARNOLD: I'm cold. I think I'm gettin' a chill. Hold me? (*She puts her arms around him.*) Hey, what is that all over your hands? Jesus Christ, it's worm blood! (*She puts her hand on his crotch; he leaps up with a cry.*) Jesus Christ in Heaven, you got my pants dirty. How's that gonna look when I get back to base? (*Takes a handkerchief out, spits in it, starts to work at his pants.*)

MARY: It's time for us to do it, Arnold. To make it hold. The moon is full. I buried your chest hair here, and my hair that I shaved. I buried them here the very instant the cock crowed. I marked the spot. And I'm ripe for love. So we have to do it here, tonight . . .

ARNOLD: (*Still working at his pants.*) It ain't comin' off. Shit, I run outa spit. Here, spit in this, would you? (*She spits in the handkerchief; he works.*)

BERNARD *becomes visible in a dim spot, moving his lips but inaudible.*

MARY: Forget that!

ARNOLD: Let's go!

MARY: Why?

ARNOLD: How'm I gonna screw you wit worm blood all over you, hanh?

MARY: But that's why I brought us here. We must do it on the earth, crushin' worms as we roll. We must do it on the ground with the dead all around.

ARNOLD: (*Frightened.*) Mary! What did I get into with you?

BERNARD *becomes audible.* MARY *puts up her hand.*

MARY: Listen!

BERNARD: (*Sadly.*) Ellen! Ellen Mac Jones! Ellen Mac Jones! Ellen!

MARY: I hear somethin'.

ARNOLD: Mary!

MARY: It's sayin' this place is right for us. Won't be right anywhere's else. Won't be good. What has to come of it won't come right anywhere else.

ARNOLD: Please, Mary, for me, I'm cold. I'm scared . . .

MARY: The earth is our mother. She will warm you. Lie back, feel our mother. (*She pushes him back gently.*) You are here, Arnold, your hair is here. Take your shirt off. (*Unbuttons his shirt.*) I'll turn this light off. (*Lantern off.*) Now, take off the rest, Arnold. (*It is very dark save for the dim spot on* BERNARD *and another even dimmer on the* NUNS.) Oh, Arnold, the worms, the worms . . .

BERNARD: (*Making a crescendo.*) Ellen Mac Jones! Ellen Mac Jones! Ellen Mac Jones! Ellen! Ellen!

Blackout.

SCENE FIVE

The row house. BERNARD *sits at his desk, writing.* EDITH *is killing roaches in the kitchen.*

EDITH: Hey, fat Wasp creep? I thought I heard weepin' last night. Was it you? (*Kills a roach.*) Gotcha!

BERNARD: (*Reading what he has written.*) "Is Reality a Dream of God's? Then we are fragments in the Divine Nightmare. Thus thought Mark as he drove alone in his yellow Volkswagen through the swamp."

EDITH: I asked you a question, fuck face.

BERNARD: Please, Edith, I'm working.

EDITH: (*Imitating.*) Please, Edith, I'm working. (*Kills roach.*) Gotcha!

BERNARD: Must you kill roaches while I work?

EDITH: Only thing I'm good for anymore. Even though I can't see 'em, I can hear 'em. I locate 'em through sensin' them. Lissin', I hear another one comin'. This one's a giant, madonna me, a giant. He's thinkin', aw, that Edith, she's blind, she ain't gonna notice me. But I heard his roach feet patterin' onna floor. Why, this bevone! He's made a bet he can get by old Edith, the Blindie—that's what them roaches call me, so like the braggart jerk-off he is, he's comin' closer a me. I hear you, roach bastid, and I'm gonna get you. Gotta pray first, this is the big match. (*Crosses herself.*) Oh, Virgine, you who was the biggest Mother of them all, help me for once, hanh? I got him located exact. Now: uno, due, e tre . . . (*Lurches, misses.*)

BERNARD: You missed, Edith.

EDITH: I'll get him this time. (*Lurches, misses.*)

BERNARD: Missed again.

EDITH: Defeated! I massacre a hundred tomorrow. Then when he come back, I can brag a Arnold.

BERNARD: Really, Edith, you haven't heard from that moron in close on three years. He was gone when I arrived and in my time here you have had exactly three postcards from him all in execrable taste and none of which you could even see.

EDITH: He don' know I'm blind. Happened after Benny left. Three years, hanh? Yeah, yeah, I guess Benny's been gone that long. Tell me, Bernard, did he say where he was goin'? Benny, I mean. Did he say anything about me? (*A silence.*) Yeah, how many times I asked you, hanh? But that wasn't like Benny. Sure he was a bum, he played around, wit my own sister if you believe them stories, but he always come back. And he loved Arnold. Hell, they was gonna put Arnold inna home and it was Benny's idea . . . (*Kills roach.*) Gotcha! I think I got him that time, Bernard. Wasn't like Benny. But Arnold, he'll come back, he's gonna rescue me. And he's gonna beat you up, fat Bernard, he's gonna get you. I won't be alone and helpless forever. He's gonna save me! (*Crawls into the kitchen, curls up in her old rags near the stove.*) He'll be back. Then we'll see who's boss. Time to go sleep.

BERNARD: (*Reading his work.*) "Is Reality a Dream of God's . . . ?" I wonder should Mark drive a Porsche? "Thus thought Mark as he drove his Porsche through the swamp . . ." (*Considers, puts down pen.*) Arnold, indeed!

A knock at the door. BERNARD *goes off to answer it. A pause.* BERNARD *comes in again, trailed unwillingly by the fourteen-year-old* BOY.

BERNARD: Come in, my brave young man, come in. (*He peeks into the kitchen to see if* EDITH *is asleep.*) Tell me about those magazines.

BOY: Coulda told you at the door.

BERNARD: It's more comfortable in here.

BOY: It is? Don' see no furniture.

BERNARD: Disappeared.

BOY: Oh. Bookie?

BERNARD: Oh, my, no.

BOY: That crazy old lady, she lives here, don' she? She your daughter?

BERNARD: Good Heavens!

BOY: (*Fast mumbled.*) All right, I'm sellin' these magazines to get me through high school, Bishop Neumann. From the commission on the order you sign I can not only put myself through but buy myself a few extras such as a growin' boy needs.

BERNARD: You certainly are a growing boy.

BOY: Yeah. Well, for forty-nine fifty at a saving of twenty-five seventy-nine, you can have the following: *Vogue, Good Housekeeping, House and Garden* and *Ladies' Home Journal.* Sign here.

BERNARD: Why don't you sit down?

BOY: Where?

BERNARD: On the floor. (*Sits.*)

BOY: Why would I wanna sit down wit you onna floor?

BERNARD: (*Pats floor.* BOY *sits, unwilling.*) We've met, you know. Oh, we haven't exchanged words. Perhaps we were close in a past life. Teacher and pupil, perhaps, father and son. It was a recognition I felt when first I saw you and since then I've been a witness to your spectacular ball playing at Johnson Field. I've sat there in the autumn sun and memorized you, you modern Achilles. And I know you've noticed me watching you like an ancient sage. And you see, my handsome young man, I know good ballplaying. My days go back to Ty Cobb and the Great Ruth.

BOY: You wanna suck my cock?

Street noises. A ball is thrown against the side of the house making a thumping noise. EDITH *stirs and wakes.*

EDITH: Damn kids, always thumpin', get the hell away . . .

BOY: Well, what gives, you was leadin' up to that?

EDITH: Damn kids . . .! (*Stretches.*)

BOY: I'll tell you what, you buy the magazines and I'll lay here for a bit. Don't guarantee nothin' though . . .

BERNARD: You whore, you filthy whore, get out!

EDITH: (*Crawling into living room.*) Tell them kids to go thump against their own walls. You hear me, Bernard, I says . . . Wait, there's somebody here, ain't there? Who is it? Arnold? You come back? Benny?

BOY: Jesus Christ!

EDITH: Whoever you are, get the hell outta my house.

BOY: Aw, shut your mouth, you friggin' old lady.

EDITH: You fuckin' jerk-off, where's your respect!

BOY: It's right here, you witch!

Kicks EDITH. *She grabs his leg. They struggle.* EDITH *fights like a tigress.*

EDITH: Hey, Bernard! Help me, for Christ sake! This bastid's tryin' to kill me!

BERNARD *runs into the kitchen, gets a knife, returns, brandishing it at the* BOY.

BERNARD: Get out!

BOY: Hey! You gonna come at me wit a knife? You fat fuckin' corpse? You gonna come at me? Well, come on, old man, come on, faggot. (*Starts dodging and teasing* BERNARD.) It's like runnin' them bases, like who—Ty Cobb?

EDITH: Bernard! You slit that mother's throat.

BOY: (*Making a game of dodging* BERNARD.) Hey, hey, hey! I'm the Great Ruth! Come on, faggot, come on, old man!

BERNARD *rushes the boy, knocks into him and knocks him off balance. The* BOY *grabs him for support.* EDITH *finds them and trips the* BOY. *He falls. She starts to beat him ferociously.* BERNARD, *out of breath, drops the knife. The* BOY, *frightened and hurt, gets away from* EDITH *and runs out, yelling.*

BOY: Hey, they're tryin' to kill me!

BERNARD *stares after the boy, gasping for breath. Suddenly, he starts to cry.*

BERNARD: Gone . . .

EDITH: Hanh? Bernard? I didn't hear you. You breathin' awful heavy, Bernard. Why do you do it hanh? You're an old man, why you gotta run out afta kids for, hanh? An' if you gotta screw around, pick up somebody of age, for Christ sake! (*A pause.*) Hey, you cryin', Bernard? Yeah, what you gonna do. You cry and you cry . . . Don' cry, Bernard, don' mean so much. Sex! Who cares! Them kids, they're mean by nature and we old people, well, we got nothin' for them, can't expect nothin' back from them . . .

BERNARD: Oh, Edith, what am I going to do?

EDITH: You could start by acting your age.

BERNARD: And what is acting my age? Dying? (*Exits.*)

EDITH: Povero vecchio, non acetta nulla. (*A sudden loud pounding at the street door.*) They come to lynch you, Bernard, better make a act of contrition. (*More pounding.*) God damn that kid. All right, I'm comin'. (*Crawls to street exit, admits* BUCKY *and* SCODGE *with the* BOY.) Who is it?

BUCKY: (*Looking around, shocked.*) Hiya, Edith, how you been?

EDITH: Who's 'at? 'At you Bucky? I recognize you voice.

BUCKY: Yeah, Edith. Scodge is here, too.

EDITH: Hiya, Scodge.

SCODGE: (*Also shocked.*) Hiya, Edith. (*A pause. The* BOY *pulls at* SCODGE, *who hits him.*)

EDITH: Ain't seen you guys in years, not since Benny . . .

BUCKY: Yeah, Edith . . .

EDITH: And Arnold . . .

SCODGE: Yeah, yeah, Edith . . . .

EDITH: Youse never came around no more afta they . . .

SCODGE: Well, we had it hard gettin' outta the army . . .

BUCKY: Draft board wouldn't take no for an answer. Now Arnold . . .

SCODGE: He wanted a go . . .

EDITH: Well, sit down and talk.

BUCKY: Well, Edith, to tell you the truth, that is, I don' see nothin' to . . . well, you know . . .

SCODGE: To sit down on.

BUCKY: Yeah, Edith, like Scodge here says, I don' see nothin' . . .

SCODGE: To sit down on.

BUCKY: Yeah.

EDITH: (*Pretending to be hurt deeply.*) You guys, you guys! Why 'ja hafta go an' say somethin' like that, hanh? Can't you see I'm blind? I can't tell if you sit or not. So's what youse shoulda said was: sure, Edith, thanks. And then you stands right where you is. That way you don' hurt a poor old blind lady's feelin's. Oh, you guys!

BUCKY: (*Taken aback.*) Jeez, Edith, I didn't think of it that way . . .

EDITH: First you guys come here and hurt me by bringin' back the good old days, them days when . . . Benny . . . (*Fakes a sob.*) Than, you hurt me by commentin' on the barrenness of my house . . . Shit, guys! (*Pretends to break down sobbing.*)

BUCKY: Jeez, Edith, I'm sorry. Didn't mean nothin' by it. Didn't think of it that way. You, Scodge?

SCODGE: Tell you the truth, Bucky, I didn't think of it that way.

BUCKY: Well, Edith, we'll sit right here onna the floor.

SCODGE: That's a good idea, Bucky, we'll sit right here, onna the floor.

BOY: (*Not taken in by* EDITH.) I thought you guys . . .

SCODGE: Shut up, kid, and respect you elders. (BUCKY *sits;* SCODGE *sits and forces the* BOY *to sit.*)

BUCKY: Hey, what is this shit? Sorry, Edith, but there's somethin' . . .

SCODGE: Sticky . . .

BUCKY: Yeah, somethin' sticky and well . . . smelly, onna floor.

EDITH: Dried dog food.

BUCKY: Oh, that explains it, Scodge. Dried dog food.

SCODGE: Yeah, Bucky, that's what I thought it was. Dried dog food. (*An uncomfortable pause. The* BOY *squirms.*)

BUCKY: What's dried dog food doin' onna the floor, if I can ask, Edith?

EDITH: Bernard leaves it out for his dead dog.

SCODGE: Well, Edith, now that you mention this . . . this . . .

BUCKY: Bernard . . .

BOY: Wanted a blow me, then tried to kill me wit a knife!

SCODGE: (*Raises a hand, threatening.*) Shut you mouth, kid, we'll take care of this.

EDITH: What about Bernard?

SCODGE: Well, Edith, you know this is a good, clean neighborhood. Catholic. Good Catholic.

BUCKY: No Irish.

SCODGE: Then, all of a sudden, this old guy is here. Right afta Arnie goes away. Never seen him before, ain't related to youse. Then, before we know it, Benny's gone. This old guy ain't Italian, never seen him in church . . .

BUCKY: We was onna corner, shootin' the breeze when this kid come outta you house, yellin' . . .

EDITH: You believe that kid?

BOY: You bitch . . . .

SCODGE: (*Raises a hand.*) Shut you mouth, you!

EDITH: Bernard is a seventy-year-old man. He ain't got it up for years.

BOY: Don't make no difference, queers do other things.

EDITH: Like what, little boy?

BOY: Well, other things . . .

EDITH: How do you know, you queer?

BOY: Hey, who you shittin'!

EDITH: You out for money, is that it, hanh? I heard, I heard you little bum. That poor man, he's lonely, he's got nothin' inna whole world and this little creep comes a the door. Hey, mista, I heard him say, I'll let you blow me for a quarter.

BUCKY: Nah, in the neighborhood?

SCODGE: That's for uptown.

EDITH: I heard him say it!

BOY: She's lyin'! (SCODGE *hits him.*) Owww!

EDITH: Well, naturally, Bernard is shocked. Remember, you guys, he was a college professor, he ain't used to reality. He can't believe his seventy-old-ears. When he says no, this kid starts to holler. Then he runs inna house, runs over to me and starts to kick me. Bernard goes for the knife, then this kid runs out inna street!

BUCKY: I thought there was somethin' fishy in this story.

SCODGE: Yeah, a seventy-year-old Irish man . . .

BUCKY: They can't get it up when they're forty!

SCODGE: All them potatoes.

BOY: But she's lyin'!

EDITH: And ain't he kinda old, this kid, hanh? Ain't he fourteen or so? He can't take care of himself around a seventy-year-old man and a blind old lady?

SCODGE: Well, Edith, you gotta point.

BUCKY: Come on, Scodge. (*Slaps* BOY.) That's for you, shittin' us.

BOY: Hey, but lissin' . . .

SCODGE: Show some respect! (*Hits boy.*) Sorry to bother you, Edith.

EDITH: Aw, it was a pleasure seein' you guys again, I mean, it woulda been a pleasure seein' youse if I could see . . .

BUCKY: Let's go. See ya, Edith. (SCODGE, BOY, *and* BUCKY *leave.*)

EDITH: Friggin' good for nothin' bums! Who the hell are you to come around here—to do what? (*Crawls toward kitchen.*) Jeez, Bernard, you're a bundle. Jeez! (*Kills a roach.*) Gotcha! The things a person's gotta put up wit in their own house. (*Curls up in quilt near the stove.*) Time to go bye-bye. Grow up, Bernard! Sleepy, hope Arnold comes soon. Mio piccolo, my Arnie. I'm ready for him.

BERNARD *sweeps out onto the stage. He is wearing an elaborate ball gown from the 1890s. It is a full gown with a long train.* BERNARD *acts as though he were making an entrance at a Grand Ball. He uses a large fan coquettishly and hums a slow waltz. A bus goes by. Car horns are heard.* BERNARD *waltzes about and waves at other guests.*

A spot on MARY. *She is in a hospital bed attended by the three* NUNS. *They are faceless.* MARY *is in labor with* ARNOLD*'s child. She is in great pain.*

MARY: How much longer, sister? (*Silence.*) Why don't you never talk? How much longer? Why ain't Arnold here? Have you really called him? Surely it is my time. This pain has gone on and on . . .

FIRST NUN: Remember, this is the wages of sin!

SECOND NUN: Next time the flesh calls, remember this agony. (MARY *screams.*)

BERNARD: (*As though speaking to someone at the ball.*) Why, thank you, kind sir. Yes, it is a lovely gown, isn't it? I had it made specially, at Maude's on Fifth Avenue. Oh, you fresh thing! I'd love to. (*Whirls about as though dancing with uninhibited partner.*)

MARY: Why do they have to be so long? Why does bein' born mean so much pain? Baby? Baby? Are you feelin' it too? Your father ain't been around. That bastard! (*Gasps.*) I'm sorry, baby, I didn't mean to curse your daddy. I'll be good. Just don't twist in me so much.

BERNARD: (*Using his fan as though slapping someone's wrist.*) Fresh! Hands to yourself. I'll thank you, sir, to respect me as you ought. I am a young woman worthy of your deference. My, but you do dance well. (*Whirls about again.*)

MARY: Baby, I promise to try and love you but please, please don't stab me like you have a knife . . . (*Screams.*) God damn you, you monster child!

THIRD NUN: (*Slaps her.*) Cursing is God's business.

MARY: Why does God use women this way?

BERNARD: (*Spreading his fan.*) If you wish, you may kiss me behind my fan. (*Hides his face, giggles.*)

MARY: Why ain't your daddy here, baby?

BERNARD: (*Deep curtsey.*) Why, thank you, kind sir.

MARY: (*Screams in agony.*)

Blackout.

SCENE SIX

The BOY *enters walking. Suddenly* MICHAEL DE FELICE *appears, dressed up like an Indian maiden. He jumps on the* BOY *and wrestles him to the ground.*

BOY: Hey, Michael, what the hell!

MICHAEL *stuffs a gag in his mouth and ties him up.*

MICHAEL: (*Very swishy and camping wildly.*) Oh John, John Standish, come to your Pocahontas! She's all wet for you and the stream is so far and cold on my Indian maiden skin!

MICHAEL *circles the* BOY *who is quite frightened. Caresses him, circles him again and whips out an ax. The* BOY *screams in terror through his gag.* MICHAEL, *without warning, jumps into a vaudeville routine, using the ax as part of his dance. He directs his dance to the* BOY.

MICHAEL: (*Singing and dancing.*)

I wanna be loved by you
And nobody else will do
Boo boo dee oop!

MICHAEL *sings under the following.*

MARY *enters into a spot on the other side of the stage. Her face is set, her manner hostile.* ARNOLD *follows, despondent.*

ARNOLD: Mary, come on, don' run away. Don' carry on like that, hanh? Okay, tell me I'm a worthless bum, 'cause I am. I shoulda been there, come on, hit me, right here, on the jaw. Oh, please, I'm sorry, it was all my fault. I was guilty but forgive me . . .

MARY: It's done now.

ARNOLD: No, it ain't. Nothin's done. It's just startin'. We made that baby together. I got inna bed wit you and we made that baby . . .

MARY: Was the graveyard.

ARNOLD: Look, I got drunk, and them nuns, they told me they don' want the father around. Ain't hygienic or somethin' . . .

MARY: It's dead. All that pain for nothin' and you nowhere to be found. It's like I'm a-livin' under some curse. I did all that I could, found the right spot, did the dance, buried your hair and my hair and it was all for nothin'. And I thought you big city boys, after all, them city Jezebels, my daddy talks like he knows . . .

ARNOLD: Your daddy don' know nothin' . . .

MARY: I left my daddy for you, he'd never take me back. I bore your child. Had to get married at the last minute like two criminals and it was all for nothin'. Oh, you were so handsome in your uniform and you were lost and I felt like you were some prince, like you might be the one to magic me away. And where did you magic me? Into a big, cold, white room where they strapped me up like some animal and where they dug out from in me a dead thing. And you did it to me!

ARNOLD: I'm sorry, I'm sorry, it's so ugly, stop it. I'll make it up to you!

MARY: I can't stay here, I have to run away!

ARNOLD: Come with me. I'm gonna be discharged soon. Come with me.

MARY: Where? Is there a hell beyond hell?

ARNOLD: To South Philly. My Aunt Edith's there. She'll love you, she's good people and, after all, you are my wife, you're family now. There you can read. We have huge libraries, you won't have to steal the books. And I'll go to work—you can go to school. It was my fault, let me make it up to you, come back wit me . . .

MARY: One more trap!

ARNOLD: Trap? What trap? Oh, the city's a beauty. There's so much to do. People ain't stupid, ain't backwards like they is here. People are kind. You see, there are these men on the corners, you know, sellin' pretzels, it's like, I don' know, I can't explain it . . .

MARY: Do you know what I need, Arnold?

ARNOLD: Some love, like me, we're lonely kids . . .

MARY: Look at what my life has been. It ain't easy for me, born like I was. I wanted to know, and to be free. Sounds real simple, real natural. For a boy, a city boy, it is. But for me it was impossible. Every part of me was chained, held fast by steel and iron. When I first saw that library, why I almost died. There was all these people, they had dresses and suits, they was readin' and oh, it was so quiet! And everywhere, books, like stars in the night sky. Well, you can't reach the real stars, they just twinkle and twinkle and come mornin' they're gone. But books, why, they're always there, all it took was some kind of magic that everybody seemed to know. I wanted it, I wanted to be free of this big ditch I'm stuck in. But learnin' that magic takes teachers, real teachers, not them prissy old maids. Then, I met you and thought you might could rescue me and . . .

ARNOLD: Come wit me, then. You'll find a teacher, I'm sure. We'll start all over.

MARY: Well . . .

ARNOLD: I owe it to you, let me make it up to you.

MARY: (*After a hesitation takes his hand.*) All right, Arnold.

They walk off hand in hand.

MICHAEL *finishes his routine with a flourish. He removes the boy's gag and tries to kiss him. The* BOY *turns his face away.*

BOY: God damn you, I'm too fuckin' old for cowboys and Indians!

MICHAEL *laughs. The three* NUNS *cross the back of the stage with a large baby doll impaled on their crucifix.*

Blackout.

SCENE SEVEN

The row house. BERNARD *enters with a large plate of dog food. He puts it up center on the floor, then exits.*

BERNARD: (*Going off, whispering.*) Ellen! Ellen Mac Jones! Ellen Mac Jones Aberdeen! Here, Ellen!

EDITH *crawls on, stopping occasionally to kill roaches.*

EDITH: Gotcha! Eighteenth today. Almost a record. Smell somethin' weird. Hey, Bernard! You didn't shit inna middle of the floor, did you? Bernard? Well, maybe the bastid went out. He don' talk a me as much as he usda. Aspett'—there's this big roach. I sense him. (*She is near the plate of dog food.*) He's enormous. He's the cock of the walk roach. An' he's just sittin' there waitin'. He's sayin': She won't get me, this old blind lady. Well, I'm gonna get you, roach bastid. Gotta pray first, this is the big match. Holy Virgin, help me massacre this roach and I'll hold my breath for a count of sixty tomorrow. Sometimes I think that Holy Virgin got shit in Her ears. I pray and pray and does somethin' good happen? Nah! Not once in fifty years. Hanh? This roach is makin' fun of me. He's sayin' I don' know my ass from a rancid pimple. Don' think there's much difference sometimes . . . oh, he's laughin'. That Edith, she's funny. She's gotta sense of humor. Blind, filthy, lonely, ugly and horny and what does she do? She makes jokes! Well, just for sayin' that, I'm gonna smash you. 'Cause it ain't no joke. I got nothin' and I know it and jokin' don' drown out no pain! Uno . . . due . . . e tre . . . (*Thinking it is a roach, she heaves herself into the dog food. She screams.*) Jesus, Mary and Joseph! I got shit on me. That no good bastid shit inna middle of the floor . . . (ARNOLD *comes in in a new suit and big smile. He stops shocked at the state of the house.* EDITH *thinks he is Bernard.*) That you, Bernard? God damn you! (*Hurls herself on* ARNOLD. *He leaps away.*)

ARNOLD: Get off me!

EDITH: Who are you and how'd you get in?

ARNOLD: You ruined my suit and it's fuckin' new.

EDITH: Answer me, who the hell are you?

ARNOLD: (*Working at his suit.*) It's me, Arnold. Whatsa matter, you blind?

EDITH: Arnold?

ARNOLD: (*Working at his suit.*) Shit! Sixty-four bucks down the drain. Oh, Christ, you are blind!

EDITH: Arnold? Bello, bello, is that really you? (*Starts to cry.*) I waited and waited so long and thought you wan't comin' back. You ain't pretendin' a me? Please don' pretend a me. I'm blind, you see, an'—you're here at last! Arnold! Look, look, I'm cryin'. Didn't know I could do that no more . . .

ARNOLD: What happened, hanh? Where is everything? Ain't there no furniture no more. Where's Uncle Benny . . .

EDITH: . . . Kiss your old aunt . . .

BERNARD *enters with a large piece of paper.*

ARNOLD: Who are you?

BERNARD: (*Holds paper out.*) Your landlord. (ARNOLD *stares, shocked.*) I realize that Italian ghetto schools are ineptly run, usually by sexually frustrated primitives who style themselves "sisters"; but I thought they taught two things with minimal efficiency. One: to understand English; and two, to read it accurately, however slowly. You appear to contradict that impression. Read the lease, boy! I own this house, and everything in it, including your aunt. She is my vassal.

ARNOLD: (*To* EDITH, *not comprehending.*) Aunt, what the hell . . .?

EDITH: Let me feel you face, hanh, Arnold? They say that works when you blind and I ain't seen you in three years. Squat down.

ARNOLD: But what the hell is this? There ain't nothin' here and Uncle Benny . . .

EDITH: Squat down, you bastid! (*He does. She feels his face.*) Big nose. I wonder if it's the biggest thing you got, hanh? Feel them cheeks, smooth. He's got all his sufferin' before him. (*She shoves a finger in his eye. He falls back, howling. She crawls to him and whispers.*) Arnie, you mine, you mine. I'm inna this trap and you gotta get me out. You gotta save me. I did that to show you it ain't gonna be easy . . .

BUCKY: (*Off.*) Hey! Getta load of that package on Edith's stoop.

SCODGE: (*Off.*) What you doin' honey?

ARNOLD: (*To* EDITH.) I ain't alone. I mean, I'm . . . oh, shit. I guess I better . . . Oh, Christ . . . (*Goes out.*)

EDITH: Hey, Bernard, you meet my nephew?

BUCKY AND SCODGE: (*Off, crying out.*) Hey! Hey! It's Arnie Lungs! He's back, he's back!

MICHAEL: (*Further off, shrieks.*) What's that I hear? Arnie's back?

BERNARD: He's popular.

ARNOLD *enters with* MARY. *She is exhausted. She is shocked by the state of the house.* ARNOLD *is frightened.*

ARNOLD: Here goes. Aunt . . . (*Cannot continue.*)
EDITH: What is it?
BERNARD: (*After a pause.*) There is a young lady on your threshold looking wide-eyed and exhausted. Were I to reduce this to cliché, which is all you are capable of understanding, I would say the young lady had traveled a while without sleep and was a wife.
ARNOLD: Oh, I gotta headache. You got any asperin, Aunt Edith? I'll go look and see. Jeez, I oughta change. Aunt Edith, this is my wife, Mary and oh, the bags is outside. I'll get 'em . . .

ARNOLD *runs out.* MARY *stares about her.* BERNARD *peers at* MARY. EDITH *is working to grasp the situation.*

BUCKY: (*Off.*) Hey, Arnie Lungs, let's get drunk!
ARNOLD: (*Off.*) Ain't a bad idea, Buck. Say, you got fat.
BUCKY: (*Off.*) I don't got a cute chippy like that to work it off.
MICHAEL: (*Off but closer.*) Where is my Arnie?
ARNOLD: (*Enters with the suitcases.*) I'll drop the suitcases here. Where'd you say the asperin was? (*Goes into kitchen and looks around.*)
EDITH: You married, hanh?
ARNOLD: I met Mary near the base.
EDITH: She was smart, got pregnant, then forced you to marry her.
MARY: That ain't true at all.
EDITH: Holy Jesus in Heaven, it's a hilly billy. A fuckin' farm girl! Jesus Christ, he married a turd of cow dung!
ARNOLD: Now, Aunt, she's family. (*Pointing to his stained suit, to* MARY.) Had a accident, Mary, better change. (*Opens a suitcase.*) My clothes in this one? Shit! Why'd you have to put my clothes onna bottom? All these friggin' books! (*Throws some books on the floor.* BERNARD *notices them with interest.*) She's ya niece, aunt, you'll learn to love her. (*Rifles suitcase, sets about changing.*)
EDITH: She's my niece, I'll learn to love her. You hear that, Bernard? You hear what my nephew and godson says the first thing afta leaving me alone for three years, you hear that? You'll learn to love her. That Edith always was a patsy. Well, come on niece, I'm gonna learn to love you. Come on, little girlie, come on little niecie, here niecie, niecie, niecie . . .
ARNOLD: (*To* MARY.) Go on for Christ sake!
EDITH: Here niecie, niecie, niecie . . .
MARY: I hear you and I'm comin'.
EDITH: (*Imitating.*) I hear you and I'm comin'. Isn't she adorable? Isn't this farm girl hilly billy from the pig pen and the outhouse all sweet and cuddly?

ARNOLD: (*Changing.*) Where the fuck's my checker tie? Oh, I found it.

EDITH: (MARY *is close to her.*) This you leg, little hilly billy? (*Feels* MARY'*s leg.*) Feels nice, this leg. I bet you're real pretty. I was never pretty, never had a nice leg. Mine was fat and thick, you could hold the meat away from the bone. Can't do that wit yours. Bernard, is she pretty?

BERNARD: Beautiful . . .

ARNOLD: (*Still dressing.*) Oh, my God, is Uncle Benny dead?

BERNARD: Ran off with good reason.

EDITH: I bet this hilly billy's got soft white skin and pretty boobies.

BERNARD: Exactly, Edith.

EDITH: Ahhh! Maledetta! (*Bites* MARY'*s leg.* MARY *screams and tries to get away, but* EDITH *hangs on.* ARNOLD, *half dressed, hovers on the periphery of the fight unsure how to stop it.* BERNARD *is amused.*)

MARGE: (*Off.*) Hey, that was a scream in there!

BUCKY: (*Off.*) You all right in there? (*Bangs on door.*)

MARY: (*Kicks* EDITH, *who screams.*) You animal, I'll tear your head off!

ARNOLD: Yo, Mary, show some respect! (*Gets pushed out of the fight; the banging on the door continues.* ARNOLD *after hesitating a moment runs out and admits* SCODGE, MARGE *and* BUCKY.)

EDITH: (*Being kicked by* MARY.) I'm hurt, I'm hurt!

MARY: It's just beginnin' for you, you ugly bitch, I'll kill you. (*Pummels* EDITH *ferociously.* EDITH *defends herself, screaming.* BUCKY *and* SCODGE *hang back, admiring* MARY. MARGE *plunges in trying to separate the two.*)

MARGE: Come on, you two. (EDITH *is howling but still fighting.* MARGE *looks to* BUCKY *and* SCODGE.) Help me get them apart.

BUCKY: You do it, Marge, we're printers, we need our hands for work.

MARGE: Edith, for God's sake! (*Pulls* EDITH *aside.* MARY *is panting.* MICHAEL *runs in in full but hurriedly assembled drag. The* BOY *is with him.*)

MICHAEL: Where is this Arnie that's back? Where? (*Sees him.*) Arnie Sweets! (*Throws his arms around* ARNOLD *and kisses him long and passionately.*)

EDITH: She hurt me, she hurt me . . .

MARY: You're lucky I didn't kill you!

MARGE: (*To* MARY.) That's enough, show some respect.

BUCKY: (*To* SCODGE, *about* MARY.) Look at her, Scodge.

SCODGE: I'm lookin', Buck! (ARNOLD *struggles in* MICHAEL'*s grasp, gets away and is confronted by* MARY *in a rage.*)

MARY: And you're a man? To bring me to this? Two days on the train and you starin' off? This is the mud hole you dragged me into? There's nothin' here, nothin'! After two days and no sleep there's nothin'! Barren, barren, barren!

MICHAEL: Sing it, baby! (*Mocks her in operatic falsetto.*)

MARY: I'm lost!

MICHAEL: Well, honey, these men'll do it every time!

EDITH: She hurt me, she hurt me.

MARGE: (*Looking her over.*) You don't look hurt, nothin's broken . . . (BERNARD *has been staring at the* BOY. MICHAEL *approaches.*)

MICHAEL: (*To* BERNARD.) Ten-fifty.

BERNARD: Seven even.

MICHAEL: In advance. (BERNARD *pays.* MICHAEL *turns to the* BOY.) Go on up wit him and relax. I'll give you half and it's just startin'. (BOY *exits with* BERNARD. ARNOLD *has finished dressing.* MARY *is crying.*)

EDITH: I usda cook him tripe and spare ribs and baccala, mio piccolo, and pig's feet in the gravy, that was his favorite. And I have to live and see him come home wit a cow girl . . .

MARGE: All right, Edith, relax.

MARY: (*To* ARNOLD.) Stop racin' around.

ARNOLD: Gotta finish gettin' ready. Goin' out.

MARY: No, you ain't. You ain't gonna leave me. (*Grabs him.*)

MICHAEL: Ding! The Friday Night Fight is on the air.

MARGE: Jesus, not another one! Somebody better call the cops. (MARY *and* ARNOLD *tussle.* SCODGE *and* BUCKY, anxious to get their hands on MARY, *try to pull them apart.*)

SCODGE: She's strong.

MARY: (*Kicks him.*) Don't you touch me.

MARGE: (*Thrusting herself in.*) Here! Get over here and quiet down. They're men, honey, and if you don' wan' that pretty face smashed up, give in. (MARY *tries to get away from her.* MARGE *grabs her.*) Stay over here, I says, and relax. (*Gets her across the room.*) Shit! You think this is the worst that can happen or you're the first it happened to?

ARNOLD: Need a mirror. Got a compact, Marge?

MICHAEL: Take mine. (*Pulls compact out of his purse.* ARNOLD *takes, it, brushes his hair.* MICHAEL *feels his muscles.*)

BUCKY: (*Approaching* MARY.) Don' you mind Arnie Lungs, he's a regular guy. (MARY *is about to hit* BUCKY. MARGE *grabs her hand.*)

MARGE: Hold it!

EDITH: (*Has crawled into the kitchen.*) Gotta sleep, sleep . . .

SCODGE: Boy, this place is a mess.

ARNOLD: Okay, I'm ready, let's get loaded.

BUCKY: Bring your wife, Arn.

MICHAEL: He can't. (*Takes* ARNOLD*'s arm.*) She's a wife, what he needs is a woman.

MARGE: Maybe Michael's gotta point. (*To* MARY.) Look, girlie, you stay here, put things away, clean up, wash your face, get some sleep, you been cryin' a lot, take some asperin. That way, there won't be no trouble. It's better that way.

ARNOLD: (*Not looking at* MARY.) Yeah, Mar', you get some sleep. Pick this stuff up, make up wit Aunt Edith, she's family, you know . . .

MICHAEL: I got some ups.

BUCKY: Let's pick up a pizza . . . (*They go off.* MARY *sinks down near the desk, sobbing.*)

EDITH: (*In the kitchen near the stove.*) Benny? Benny? Shut up, Edith, ain't no Benny. Didn't make no difference when there was a Benny. Oh, Virgine, make me die, make me die, this instant; or send me back to when the pain wasn't so big and I could manage it. Shut up, Edith, they'll think you're a crazy, blind, old lady. Chilly. Sleep. Everything ends. I hoped so much. Arnie . . . And now I lost him, I know, I know I lost him. Got nobody . . . Arnie, piccolo mio, bambino mio . . . (*Cries quietly, tries to sleep.*)

The BOY *comes out, peers at* MARY *curiously, then runs out. The room is a shambles. There are books, papers, clothes all over the floor. The suitcases are open. After a moment,* BERNARD *enters. Slowly, he picks up the books. He avoids* MARY*'s glance. He looks through some of the books, puts them on the desk.*

BERNARD: Would you like to hear a joke? A man of seventy meets a young woman of twenty on the subway. She invites him to have sexual congress with her. He does. A week later and the old man is in agony and there is a terrible swelling. After a week there is no end to the pain. His doctor says wait a week and see if it goes down and the pain ends. It gets worse. He sees the doctor again. Have you had sex recently? asks the doctor. Why, yes, answers the man, three weeks ago. Well, don't get excited, says the doctor, and it may take a week or two, but you are about to come. (*He looks at* MARY *and laughs. She is puzzled by the joke but smiles politely.* BERNARD *continues picking up the books.*) I'm sorry, I couldn't help myself. It's disgusting, isn't it? Not just the joke, everything. That thing in there is named Edith. I am Bernard. I gather your name is Mary. How do you do. I take it these books are yours? Jung, Karen Horney, Freud. Why do you read them?

MARY: I don't mean no harm.

BERNARD: Please! I don't mean *any* harm. Repeat, please.

MARY: I don' mean *any* harm.

BERNARD: Why are you afraid? It's wonderful that you read. A girl from your class; I'd say it was remarkable.

MARY: Maybe you are a teacher.

BERNARD: Why, yes, for many years, I was.

MARY: (*Stands up, very shy.*) I guess I better . . .

BERNARD: I'll help you. (*Together they pick up the suitcases and clothes.*) You know, I could put you out. This house is mine now. Do you keep a diary?

MARY: Why, no.

BERNARD: I'll teach you. For I've decided, quite on the spur of the moment, you'll be happy to know, to take you in hand. Why are you still crying—gratitude . . .

MARY: He hasn't wanted to touch me in weeks . . .

BERNARD: I shouldn't want to be touched by him. These Wops are an unclean crew, even if the young ones are, well, you know what they are . . .

MARY: Oh, I bet you don't understand about husbands and wives.

BERNARD: Don't I indeed? But see here, you've had a bad liaison with one man, whom in your Southern aristocratic naïveté you thought attractive because he was greasy and had a lot of hair.

MARY: Arnold don't have a lot of hair.

BERNARD: Then he is a mutant and you're lucky to be rid of him. How old are you?

MARY: Why, nineteen.

BERNARD: And beautiful. When I was nineteen I was fat and had pimples everywhere—do you hear? Everywhere! I was be-pimpled in the land of the bronzed complexion, smelly in the land of the deodorant, overweight in the country that invented the crash diet and clumsy in the land of the athletic supporter. And look at me now I am seventy! Seventy! I am a failure by every standard. Look at how I am living. I write but no one wants what I write. What hope is left me?

MARY: Why there is always . . .

BERNARD: It was rhetorical, my dear.

MARY: Rhe— what?

BERNARD: You're right, there is no hope! (MARY *starts to interrupt.*) Pray don't interrupt the flow of my narrative. I was dreadfully alone, dreadfully. But I wasn't without optimism of a sort. So I thought: In the years to come, Bernard . . . and didn't fill in the blank, just let it settle around me like a hot bath. What came? More misery! I have been cursed with a long life. My funds ran out, friends died, and to be frank, I never had many, it was the state nursing home or this! And thus it happens I am a seventy-year-old wreck and worse, that I have spent my life in bondage. I was never loved. I always paid for what I got, either through the nose, or more subtly. I was robbed countless times, I was violated and disappointed and all for boys! For rotten, stupid, worthless automatons with penises. But I am strong. I have stopped identifying with Virginia Woolf. I no longer look longingly toward fast-flowing streams and I am going to educate you. Latin tomorrow and our first trip to the library. The museum next, soon German. The works of Shakespeare—I am an expert on Shakespeare, my book—never mind!

MARY: Hold off a minute! I just got here, he ran off and I don't . . .

BERNARD: I have so many secrets to impart. Do you like pretty dresses? Do the Gay Nineties appeal to you? I'll turn this pathetic hovel into a finishing school! Miss Bernard's! You'll learn Romantic Poetry, Leopardi for the truth, Rilke for pretty affectation.

MARY: But so much has happened. You don't understand, you don't know the half of it. I'm alone here, a stranger, I don't know if I can do it.

BERNARD: Nonsense! You must say one hundred times a day: I shall survive!

MARY: I shall survive!

BERNARD: No, no no! Not in that accent. Try to say it like me. (*Booms, oratorically.*) I shall survive!

MARY: (*Booms in imitation.*) I shall survive!

BERNARD: Closer, you have a good ear.

MARY: I like singin'.

BERNARD: Now, repeat after me: I . . .

MARY: (*Repeating.*) I . . .

BERNARD: Good. Shall . . .

MARY: Shall . . .

BERNARD: Survive!

MARY: Survive!

BERNARD: I shall survive!

MARY: I shall survive!

BERNARD *prances about, strikes a pose and booms I shall survive.* MARY *strikes the same pose and booms I shall survive. The poses become more grandiose, their voices louder, both are nearly yelling. At one point,* MARY *giggles and falls into* BERNARD*'s arms. He embraces her. Both become conscious of this, react embarrassed and are silent for a moment. Suddenly* MARY *booms: I shall survive.* BERNARD *takes it up and they march around the room yelling it again.*

EDITH *has been awakened by the noise. At first she is frightened, then pulls herself together and crawls into the living room.*

EDITH: Hey! What the hell is this, hanh? You wanna scare me to death makin' all that noise? Two grown up people screamin' like niggers prancin' naked inna desert?

BERNARD: Jungle, you cripple, and I shall survive!

EDITH: Youse is both crazy. Well, go on, make some more noise!

BERNARD: Mary and I are survivors both!

MARY: We shall survive!

EDITH: All right! (*Screams.*) Ellen Mac Jones! Here, Ellen! Ellen Mac Jones Aberdeen! (*The thumping against the side of the house is heard; car horns are heard.*)

MARY: I shall survive!

BERNARD: I shall survive!

EDITH: Ellen Mac Jones! Ellen Mac Jones Aberdeen!

This builds to an immense noise. Blackout.

ACT TWO

SCENE ONE

In a dimly lit area the three NUNS *appear. They have a paper cutter and a box of cheap dolls. They decapitate the dolls in the paper cutter as the lights build.*

NUNS: (*In chorus.*) Amo, amas, amat! (*A doll is decapitated. One* NUN *sprinkles ketchup over the doll as though it were holy water.*) Amo, amas, amat! (*As above.*)

Lights build in the row house. A small area to one side is set apart to serve as a street.

The house looks cleaner; a chair has been added near the desk. A kitchen table has been added in the kitchen.

BERNARD *is in the kitchen finishing breakfast.* EDITH *is eating out of a plate set on the floor.*

A month has passed since MARY*'s arrival.*

BERNARD: (*Calling.*) Mary! Come! Come!

EDITH: He calls her like she was his dog. Well, she is a bitch. Oughta be put asleep!

BERNARD: Be quiet, Edith! Mary!

EDITH: She likes to sleep, she likes to sleep alone. That's why he ain't come back. This is his home, but he don' wanna share it with her. (*The* NUNS *hover on the periphery of the scene, well to the back. Eventually they wait in the street area.*) This bacon's too well done. I like it soggy. And you put too much black pepper in the eggs. When you lie on the floor alla time like me, black pepper sets you to sneezin', and that's no picnic!

BERNARD: Mary!

MARY: (*Off.*) I'm comin'. (BERNARD *goes to his desk and opens a notebook.*)

EDITH: (*Still in the kitchen.*) Why don' you talk a me no more, hanh? Always wit her, always gigglin', readin' a her. Never offered to read to me. Thought I was ignorant even though I went a high school. Benny thought I was dumb too, didn't think I caught on about where he picked up them fancy smells . . . (*Calls.*) Mary! He's waitin'! (*To* BERNARD *whom she thinks is still in the kitchen*) Tell her to get a job. She oughta go a the convent and get a job, that would suit her, workin' for them nuns. I wouldn't touch a dollar a nun handled, you don' know where it's been before. The hand or the dollar. Them nuns got weird ideas.

BERNARD: (*Calling.*) Dress warmly, Mary, there is still a steely spike in the morning air.

EDITH: I remember my brother tellin' me when we was kids. He knew this nun, see, who kept her rosaries up her ass as a penance. Nah, I'm serious. My brother never lied, too dumb, he was Arnold's father, you know, like father like . . . (*Thinks for a moment*) Arnold. Well, he had this nun in school, see, and this one day she wanted a award this particular kid for doin' somethin' special, see. Don' know what it was. Maybe he shit without makin' any noise. That's an art. Least it was in them days, the way we usda eat. Well, that was durin' the Great Depression. Well, anyways, you listenin'? She wan's a award this kid, so she reaches back inna her ass, pulls out the rosary and reaches it to the kid, sayin' this is for you, you sweet little boy. And the kid takes it, see, and says, thank you, sister, and kisses it! Yeah, I'm serious. That's what my brother told me, he saw it wit his one good eye, God rest his soul. So this cow girl should go to work for them nuns . . .

BERNARD: (*Ironic.*) Don't you realize, Edith, we are all working for the nuns? God is a nun. I was about to say, a nun belonging to the Immaculate Conception Order, save that, A, there is no order in the universe, and B, God is hardly an Immaculate Conception. (*Chuckles.*) I think I'll put that in my novel. (*Calls.*) Mary!

MARY: (*Off.*) I'll be there.

BERNARD: (*Having found his manuscript, makes a note.*) "Is Reality a Dream of God's? Then we are all fragments in the Divine Nightmare being dreamed by a nun. Thus thought Mark driving through the . . ." (MARY *enters. She is wearing an attractive old-fashioned dress with a cloak.*) Mary!

MARY: (*Speaks more carefully than she did.*) Good morning, Bernard. (*Goes into kitchen, pours herself coffee.*)

EDITH: (*Sarcastic.*) Good morning, niece.

MARY: Good morning, Aunt Edith. (*Drinks coffee.*)

EDITH: Ain't she sweet? I guess they didn't teach her much about fuckin' in that pig pen she comes from, that's why he ain't come back.

MARY: If you don't want hot coffee poured over you, shut up.

EDITH: God damn bully! Gotcha! Shit, was an ant!

MARY: Why don't you eat at the table. That's why there are so many of them roaches.

BERNARD: It was good of you, Mary, to clean up for us.

EDITH: Bitch! Takin' away my work!

BERNARD: Don't worry, Edith. Where you are there are sure to be roaches. Come, Mary, we must away, matutinal instruction calls. (MARY *is pensive.*) What's the matter, pray? Does something dissatisfy you?

MARY: How could he have just left me? (*She and* BERNARD *go into the living room.* BERNARD *sets about getting ready to leave, including the donning of a heavy but expensive-looking and old-fashioned ladies' cloak.*)

MARY: I miss him. I like our trips to the library and all but I remember the way he used to be, at night, beside me, sleeping. I had power then. It was like magic. Him open to me, tender . . . that's gone for good.

BERNARD: (*Disturbed.*) Perhaps . . . perhaps not for good. Perhaps there will be others, maybe not so young as he, no, nor so beautiful.

MARY: That isn't the point, old man.

BERNARD: Then, what is the point, young lady? Do you want to be chained to some cretin's marital bed, squeezing out of you one rancid pimple after another, naming one after you, and one after him, and one after your mother?

MARY: You talking about children?

BERNARD: Is that what you want? I can't think of anyone less fitted for the bearing of children than you. You have a mind. And what is the venting of those rubber mouths we call babies after all? A simple reflex. One becomes full of an unmentionable substance, it grows, tumor-like, in one, then comes a day of agony pressing it out!

MARY: You only talk that way because you never fathered a child.

BERNARD: Didn't I indeed? I married, and my wife bore me two sons.

MARY: Bernard! Didn't you say you was homo-sexual, like that, that Italian painter, and that—what was it, Russian composer . . .?

BERNARD: What difference does that make? I slept with my wife enough to make two children, boys both, and I thought quite handsome boys.

MARY: But what happened?

BERNARD: It is time to go to the library. And did you remember your Latin text? Today is the fifth declension. Soon we start on German. (*She tries to interrupt.*) I may write a monograph about you. You are a living refutation of Hume. He felt that one's environment was everything. That were a child to be locked into a dark room for twenty years, seeing no one, hearing nothing, he'd never have a thought. I used to believe that. So passionate was I you might have called me a Hume-sexual.

MARY: But your wife!

BERNARD: I must call Ellen Mac Jones Aberdeen. (*Calls.*) Ellen! Ellen! Ellen Mac Jones!

MARY: Haven't you realized that dog is dead?

BERNARD: Of course. I saw her smashed-up corpse near the baseball diamond at Johnson Field. But I call her and put out dog food for her in commemoration.

MARY: Commemoration?

BERNARD: Certainly. If a congregation of idiots can eat bread and drink wine in commemoration of a crucified charlatan who has been dead two thousand years, I can do this in commemoration of the best friend I ever had.

MARY: I want to hear about your wife and sons.

BERNARD: What sort of freak are you? Do you want to hear a seventy-year-old wreck neutered by adversity muse on his wife? It should be enough I am a wreck.

MARY: You aren't a wreck.

BERNARD: Then come with me this instant to the library. (*Calls.*) Good day, Edith, you have your water . . .

EDITH: If you see Arnold . . .

BERNARD: Goodbye! (*They enter the side street. The* NUNS *surround them.*)

FIRST NUN: Taxi?

BERNARD: We'll bus, thank you.

SECOND NUN: Help our convent! (*The* FIRST *and* SECOND NUNS *intercept* BERNARD. *The* THIRD NUN *takes* MARY *aside and whispers to her.*)

MARY: (*To* THIRD NUN.) You know where he is? Where? (THIRD NUN *whispers.*)

BERNARD: (*Realizing he has been separated from* MARY.) Away, you harpies!

MARY: (*To* THIRD NUN.) I'll come . . . (*Runs off with* THIRD NUN. *Other* NUNS *stop* BERNARD *from following.*)

BERNARD: Mary! Why, Mary . . . What's . . . (*The two remaining* NUNS *buffet* BERNARD, *rip off his cloak.*) My cloak! Stop! (*The* NUNS *push him, until he runs into the house.*) Mary!

EDITH: Is she dead?

The two NUNS *laugh, drape the cloak over both of them and trot off.* BERNARD *collapses at his desk.*

Blackout.

SCENE TWO

The THIRD NUN *joins the other two in a rock and roll dance from the fifties, done without music. Their routine includes the typical hand gestures and body movements associated with certain rock groups. They are describing eternal torment and damnation.*

As lights build, the THIRD NUN *leaves the other two, who, far to the back, in shadow, watch the scene.*

The scene is a bar, the hangout of MICHAEL DE FELICE. There is *little change in the set; another table, or a small bar can be added. The atmosphere is shady.* ARNOLD *slumped at a table,* MICHAEL *watchful.*

ARNOLD: Something in my head . . . veils . . .

understand a little better now. But you have to do what's right, you're my husband . . .

ARNOLD: How did you find this place?

MARY: Come back with me.

MICHAEL: (*Contemptuous.*) Go 'head, Arnie, go 'head. (BUCKY *and* SCODGE *enter.*)

BUCKY: Yo, Michael!

SCODGE: Yo, Mich . . . (*Sees* MARY.) Hey, getta load, Buck.

ARNOLD: (*To* MARY.) Not now. Get your hands off me.

MARY: I'm beggin' you, don't pay no mind to these people . . .

ARNOLD: They don't like outsiders like you.

SCODGE: Yes, we do, baby.

MICHAEL: (*To* SCODGE.) Shut up!

MARY: I ain't no outsider.

ARNOLD: You're a fuckin' hilly billy. Go on! Get out!

MARY: I won't have you callin' me names.

ARNOLD: You won't have, you won't have! Who the hell are you to talk, hanh? Just like a fuckin' woman, fuckin', fuckin' woman! Always readin' them stupid books, stupid! Hilly Billy! There's no teacher around here for you to rub up against. Get out. Get out!

MARY: You're a coward, a fool!

ARNOLD: Fuckin' Southern idiot! And another thing, you don' even fuck good! (BOY *giggles and applauds.* MICHAEL *hits him.*)

MARY: I don't fuck good? I don't fuck good! Why, who done it all, Superman? I just about had to rape you in that graveyard. And before that, the hints I dropped, God Almighty! And when I first met, I just about put your hand up me; innocent Prince Arn, he didn't know what was happenin'!

BUCKY: Oh, ho, I'd a known baby . . . (MICHAEL *silences him.*)

MARY: "You won't do nothin' to me," and, "I'm puttin' myself at your mercy, Prince Arn"! Shit!

MARGE: What's this Prince Arn crap?

MARY: A grown man from the city, no less. And when I finally did get you to do it, I had to put you on top of me like you was a toy and guide you in. (SCODGE, BUCKY *and* BOY *much amused by this.* ARNOLD *in an agony of embarrassment.*)

ARNOLD: God damn you for this, God damn you, I'd like to rip them filthy tits off . . .

MARY: Go ahead! Then I'll be more like a man and you can love me! (MARY *runs out.* BUCKY *and* SCODGE *look after her.*)

MARGE: Well, that was better than TV.

MICHAEL: You need some two hundred proof. Kills hangovers. (*Pours.*)

ARNOLD: (*Drinks, coughs.*) Kills more than hangovers.

MICHAEL: Come to! I wanna go to the shore today. Construction workers' convention. You'll do well wit them. You're their type. Straight actin' and stiff. I also gotta blue movie laid out . . .

ARNOLD: Stop it, I ain't one of them . . .

MICHAEL: We been through it before. I'm gettin' bored wit it. I asked you if you wanted a go back to her. Nah, nah, a week later, you wanna go back to her? Nah, nah. It's a month now. Make up your mind: me or her. Also, you gotta start earnin' your keep. (*The* BOY *runs on.*)

BOY: What's hot?

MICHAEL: We are. I talked a Father Gambone inna the confessional. You're to go to him at two this afternoon. He'll need you until three. So be prepared to be patient. If you plays your cards right, there's a bishops' conference in town next month. We'll hit the big time. (*The* THIRD NUN *leads* MARY *into the bar, disappears.*)

BOY: (*Seeing* MARY.) Holy shit!

MICHAEL: (*To* MARY.) I'm sorry, but we don't cater to fish!

MARY: (*Approaching* ARNOLD.) Arnold . . .

ARNOLD: What you doin' here? You come to embarrass me?

MARY: Why, no . . .

ARNOLD: Where'd you get them funny clothes . . .

MARY: Why, Bernard, he's been helpin' me—

ARNOLD: Get out of here. (MARGE *enters.*)

MARGE: Yo, Michael!

MICHAEL: (*To* MARGE.) How much?

MARGE: Three scores. Sixty-five fifty. (*Sees* MARY.) Jesus Christ!

MICHAEL: Count it out.

MARGE: (*Keeping an eye on* MARY, *counts her money.*) Ten . . . fifteen . . .

MARY: Come back with me, Arnie baby, I miss you . . .

ARNOLD: Not here.

MICHAEL: (*To* MARGE.) Your share, and a bonus.

MARGE: (*Watching* MARY *and* ARNOLD.) Thanks.

MARY: Where else then? You don't come back to me. You left me alone, a stranger here, in this city. I waited for you, by the window I waited, I looked for you, in the streets, everywhere. That first night there wasn't even a mattress for me, or a sofa to lay on. I had no money, but I waited. I've been patient. Maybe I

MICHAEL: (*Camping.*) Nothing is better than TV . . .

BOY: He means transvestite.

MARGE: Lissin' a that vocabulary! (*Embarrassed for* ARNOLD, *but also cruel, they ignore him.*)

BUCKY: (*To* MARGE, *joking.*) Come on, baby, let's make some hay . . .

MARGE: You ain't got enough to feed you kids and I don' go on credit.

BUCKY: Well, maybe we'll make a bundle today.

SCODGE: Goin' a the track.

MARGE: Don' you guys ever go to work?

SCODGE: (*False heartiness.*) Ho, Arnie Lungs!

BUCKY: Ho, Arnie!

MARGE: Prince Arn! (*They laugh.*)

ARNOLD: (*To* MICHAEL; *voice breaks.*) Give me a scotch!

MICHAEL: What, Sweets?

ARNOLD: Scotch! (MICHAEL *pours,* ARNOLD *gulps it.*) Another! (*Gulps again.*)

MARGE: (*To* ARNOLD.) Tryin' to put hair on yer chest?

SCODGE: Maybe he's tryin' to put titties there.

BUCKY: That would make it a dyke affair. (*They laugh.*)

ARNOLD: (*Hurls his glass at* BUCKY, *barely misses. To* MICHAEL.) Broke that glass, give me another . . . (MICHAEL *pours.*)

BUCKY: (*To* ARNOLD.) You throw that glass at me, mother fuck?

MARGE: (*Seeing* ARNOLD *gulp another drink.*) Whoa, horsey, gonna get snowed.

ARNOLD: Yep.

MARGE: Why?

ARNOLD: Because I need! (*Suddenly grabs and kisses her violently.*)

MARGE: (*Gets away.*) What's that prove?

BUCKY: (*To* ARNOLD.) You buy me a drink and I'll forget about the glass.

ARNOLD: Sure. Hey, Michael, go piss inna glass and give it to my friend here, wit my compliments . . .

BUCKY: You're really spoilin' for it, ain't you? If I wasn't a printer I'd come afta you, but I need my hands for work.

ARNOLD: Why? You don' go in much!

SCODGE: (*Stopping the angry* BUCKY *from attacking* ARNOLD.) Come on, you guys, quiet down. (*Pulls* BUCKY *aside. They go over racing forms. Suddenly* ARNOLD *again takes* MARGE *roughly in his arms.*)

MARGE: Arnie! Whatsa matter you?

ARNOLD: You a whore, ain't you?

BOY: Give it a her, Arnie.

MARGE: Fuck you! (*Tries to get away but* ARNOLD *holds her. They struggle.*)

BOY: Oh, oh, that's the way to go. Oh, oh!

MICHAEL: (*To* BOY.) Come over here, you. I wanna tell you exactly how to act wit Father Gambone. Always remember the bishops . . .

MARGE: (*Fighting with* ARNOLD.) Get away from me, Arnie, I'm warnin' you, don' start no trouble. Michael, call him off!

MICHAEL: Look afta youself, bitch!

MARGE: (*Still fighting.*) Come on, Arnie, I was always nice to you, never said nothin' nasty. You got somethin' a prove, you go afta somebody else. Come on, Arnie . . . (*He hits her. She punches him. The fight becomes furious.*)

BUCKY: (*Watching.*) If only I didn't need my hands for work.

SCODGE: Marge can take care of herself. I think we oughta put a deuce on Turandot in the fourth. That's what Tony Putty says.

BUCKY: Oh yeah? (*They consult the racing forms.*)

MARGE: You're hurtin' me, Arnie, stop it, please . . .

MICHAEL: (*To* BOY, *ignoring* MARGE.) You take a shower before Father Gambone, too, don' wan' them big feet smellin'.

BUCKY: (*Consulting racing form.*) Scooter the Dwarf told me Golden Glue was a sure thing inna the third . . .

SCODGE: Italian owned, that's for sure . . .

MARGE: (*Kicks* ARNOLD *in the groin. He cries out and falls.*) You rotten queer, you think you can take me just like that, hanh?

SCODGE: No need to use your hands now, Buck.

BUCKY: That so, Scodge?

SCODGE: That's so. (*They start kicking* ARNOLD.)

ARNOLD: Hey, you guys, hey!

BOY: (*To* MICHAEL *about* ARNOLD.) Hey, Michael, look—ain't you gonna stop them?

MICHAEL: I'll give you a free lesson, princess, he's gotta call me. Now, when Father Gambone . . .

ARNOLD: You're fuckin' killin' me . . . Michael! Help!

MICHAEL: (*To* BUCKY *and* SCODGE.) Stop it, you guys!

SCODGE: Hey, look who's commandin'.

BUCKY: Hey, look who's commandin'.

MARGE: She's Arnie's man.

MICHAEL: Get off him.

SCODGE: You fuckin' pervert, I've been meanin' to . . . (MICHAEL *removes a gun from his purse.*)

MICHAEL: One more sound and your wife's a hairy chested widow. You! (*To* BOY *who takes out a switchblade.*) Now, you lissin' a me. Arnie's mine, he's my territory, you mess wit him, you messin' wit me, and I don' take no shit from nobody. Now, you all kneel down and beg Arnie's pardon, just like he was the Virgin. Go on. (*They don't move. To* MARGE.) You first, cunt. (*She doesn't move.*) All right, I'm gonna start countin'. When I get to three, I'm shootin' a tit off, when I get to six I'm goin' for the other tit. Got that?

MARGE: (*Kneels.*) I'm sorry, Arnie, I didn't mean to kick you.

SCODGE: (*Kneels.*) I'm sorry, Arnie, I didn't mean to kick you.

BUCKY: (*Stands.*) Yeah.

MICHAEL: Kneel and say it all!

BUCKY: (*Kneels.*) I'm sorry, Arnie, I didn't mean to kick you.

MICHAEL: Now, get the fuck out! (*They run out. To the* BOY.) You! Go steal a car, I wanna get him to the hospital. (BOY *runs out;* MICHAEL *kneels beside* ARNOLD.) Now, just you remember, Prince Arn, you're mine now, you're my baby, and I'm gonna take care of you. (*Embraces him.*)

Blackout.

SCENE THREE

The row house. BERNARD *is at his desk, head in his hands. It is very dark.* EDITH *is in the kitchen.*

EDITH: Geez, it's a hot night. Hey! Bernard! You didn't leave any dog food out did you? You should have, that hilly billy bitch'll be hungry when she comes back. Gotcha! (*Kills a roach.*) Shit, I don' hear him. (*Crawls about.*) Gotta be careful, don' wanna get into dog food. Dog food is just like shit; smells the same, sticks to you the same, feels the same and don' nobody wonder out loud how comes I know so much about shit. I lived in it for years, that's how I know. Fifty-eight years, come February. Yeah, I was born under the sign of La Pesce, the Cold Fish, like Benny usda say. He called me that because I couldn't get with child. We tried, Madon', how we tried. Only thing I hadda show from it was some bruises, only thing he hadda show was some bites. How I bit him! Well, he run off. Hey, Bernard? You know anything about it? Why'd he run off? Shut up, Edith, Bernard ain't here. And now, Arnie . . . (*Kills a roach.*) Gotcha! I'm a fuckin' survivor, at least. One of these days I'll get up and walk again, I'm just savin' my strength. It ain't easy to be over fifty and blind. But, one of these days I'm gonna get up and go lookin' for that Arnie. And I'm gonna say get the hell home with your aunt, where you belong. Why ain't he come home? Maybe it's because he's queer and thinks I don' know. Christ, it's obvious. Look at that slit he came home wit. Only a queer would go afta her, look at the old man. But Arnie, who gives a shit? What's wrong wit bein' queer? He could use a pineapple for all I care. Ain't like havin' a big blotch on you face, ain't like havin' no arms. Ain't no excuse to leave me. You tell my Arnie his Aunt Edith says there ain't nothin' wrong wit bein' queer and for him to come and see her once in a while. Oh, why has he left me wit nothin'—you ask him that. I've ended up wit nothin', that's so hard, no eyes, no legs, no future. Don' think I'm garbage because I got nothin', I still got feelin's, I still got needs. Just because I don' got nothin' to give don' mean I don't wan' nothin'. Oh, Edith, pull yourself together. You're goin' crazy. Old and blind and horny and now crazy. Geez, you can't win! Sleep, gotta sleep. Gotcha! (*Kills a roach.*) How 'bout that, two of them! (*Curls up near the stove in her rags.* MARY *enters.*)

BERNARD: Mary. I've waited for you. I've been reading Hopkins. Remember who he is? I dozed off. We'ver read him. "I wake and feel the fell of dark not day, What hours, oh what black hours you have spent this night . . ." We've read it often.

MARY: Where can I go, Bernard? I have no home, no money, no husband.

BERNARD: You saw that moron.

MARY: I walked around and around wanting to lose myself. Where can I go? How?

BERNARD: But, Mary, there is no reason for you to leave here.

MARY: I'll have to get a job. That's the first thing.

BERNARD: Listen to me . . . (*Touches her.*)

MARY: Please don't touch me.

BERNARD: We must stay together, you and I. I feel it. It is right. We have known each other in a past life; teacher and pupil, perhaps, father and son. And when you are educated, perhaps there will be a way we can get away, together . . .

MARY: I wanted so much . . . I can't say it now. I wanted to be free of the mud I was stuck in and here there is more mud and more mud and more—let me hold your hand, I'm sorry I pushed you away.

BERNARD: You mustn' let that fool . . .

MARY: No more about him. Did you go through the same thing with your wife? Is that why you turned against women?

BERNARD: I haven't turned against women.

MARY: How did you meet her?

BERNARD: Well, she wrote, I wrote. I was teaching. I had my book published: *King Lear and the Norns* it was called. Shakespeare criticism from the practical point of view. What practical point of view! I directed an all-girls *Macbeth* at a summer camp once. It was peculiar. That was virtually the extent of my acquaintance with the Bard. She came to me with her first novel, a fictionalized treatment of Catherine the Great. I was struck by her elegant prose, her well-turned adverbial phrases, her shapely handling of form. I advised her—Moira, that was her name, it's Gaelic for Fate; actually, its true meaning is Fart which is what she turned out to be. Drop dead, Moira, if you haven't already! Well, I advised her. The book was published, favorably received, and I became her mentor. She began a book on Dante Gabriel Rossetti. Then, one evening, with nothing better to do, I brushed her upswept breasts. She outlined her second chapter: Dante Gabriel's adolescence, and then, with barely one word spoken, she moved in. We slept together, my first time. I remember kissing her breasts, they were very soft, as yours must be. One night, I said to myself, Bernard, you must be honest with her. You must confess. Confess! She was researching Dante Gabriel's drug addiction. Moira, my fate, I said, drunk, weeping, on my knees, in fact; forehead wrinkled, fourth scotch balanced too carefully on the threadbare rug; Moira, my Fate, I'm queer. Well, since we had slept together not altogether unsuccessfully, and because I was spending more time with her than anyone, she naturally thought this a drunken eccentricity, or better, a sort of personal metaphor. She even used it in her fifth novel. Can you imagine how painful that scene was for me and then, to see it on page seventy-two of a ninety-five-cent paperback twenty-two years later? But then, what excuse did I have? I was hardly truly young at the time. And when had I ever been young? I was born skulking about hiding my premature pot belly, hiding precocious bald spots, covering festering pimples with fluttering hands. There was no excuse for me. Well, Moira was not bothered by my confession. I fascinated her. It's all so dreary! She was overly attached to her father and whom do you think I reminded her of? We wed. (*Musing.*) Moira, I'm queer.

MARY: Well, that's hard for a woman to hear. I never knew anybody like that down home, leastwise, anybody who was open about it. I've got to leave here, leave this city. I have to be free of this. Bernard, I'm going to pack . . .

BERNARD: Our lessons . . .

MARY: I can't let you support me. I can't stay here with him two blocks away in the arms of that . . .

BERNARD: Don't throw this chance away, Mary, I can give you so much; don't let a silly pride . . .

MARY: Pride? When did I have pride? I was born a beggar. Beggars have no pride. Oh, how I begged, from the time I was two months: love me, teach me, hold me I begged, if I'd been just a mite crazier I'd have begged the trees and bushes. If you had seen me throw myself on that boy when he found me a-weepin' . . . Pride? I did everything. I went to the old women and worked out a spell step by step. I trapped him, I trapped myself and for what?

BERNARD: I've been so alone. Don't you want to hear about my children? The rest of my life?

MARY: Won't make any difference . . .

BERNARD: Listen, please, where was I? Moira, I'm queer. Oh, yes, I have it here in my diary, volume sixty-eight. (*Rummages through drawers in the desk, comes up with a volume.*) I'll run my eye over it, don't be impatient, Mary, it's very interesting. Some day it will make a novel, like all the best things in anyone's life. (*Continues his narrative.*) Our marriage after eight uneasy months had sustained more cracks than the Parthenon in age. A child was considered the solution. A boy was born, then, for the same reasons, a year later, another boy.

MARY: You as a father . . . ? (*Laughs.*)

BERNARD: I have reserves of tenderness. And pay attention. They loved their mother, she adored them. By this time she was working on the Brontës. She loved the children in the room with her where she worked. The three of them communed, surrounded by copies of her book on Dante Gabriel Rossetti, an enormous success. They'd giggle and make faces at one another, it was a foreign language. The *Atlantic Monthly* accepted three stories from her. How I grew to hate them, those boys, those boys and their noise, their silly babble, their incessant messing. And I hated to hear her cooing over them, whether they'd mouthed their first inanity or had diarrhea. Oh, I tried to conjure up feeling from within me somewhere, how to love these little monsters, these sucking, filthy, little monsters, their god damned souls are rotting somewhere I hope! And yet, what a hideous monster I was, caught in this quicksand of misery and confusion. I didn't know what I truly felt or where I stood with these three strangers: two messy midgets and their full-grown female trainer. By the time the eldest was eleven they were both emphatically mama's boys. Emphatically. Moira was working on her second novel, an updated version of Saint Teresa, the Little Flower. No, I thought, for one summer they shall be truly away from both of us, in a summer camp. I sent them off, over her violent protestations. There was even an excruciating operatic scene between us at the train station. I think she had a bit of the Wop in her. But I held firm, I sent them off, they had to go. One night, in mid-July, they decided, against the rules, to go swimming. The younger had cramps, began to sink, his brother dove in to save him, they both drowned. I thought: Obviously, I've killed them. I was addicted at that time to the greatest fiction writer of the century, Sigmund Freud, and thought that unconsciously I had willed the whole thing. Their mother was prostrate, needless to say. A divorce. She has had considerable success with her books and how have I ended? Look about you.

MARY: (*Touched.*) You haven't ended yet.

BERNARD: My boys drowned in lake water and I've drowned in mediocrity, in illusions, in foolish fantasies about myself, about other people. I have been a victim of optimism, an unwillingness to die, to end my life . . .

MARY: (*Takes him in her arms.*) I never thought you was one of them, you hear? (*Kisses him.*)

BERNARD: (*Starts to cry, stifles it.*) Self pity. I'm so old . . .

MARY: Hush. (*They kiss. He allows his hand to brush against her breasts.*)

BERNARD: (*After a pause.*) Come, let's dress up. (*She looks surprised.*) I have an extensive wardrobe. (*Runs upstairs and drags a large wardrobe on stage.*)

MARY: You want me to help you?

BERNARD: (*Rushes off and returns with elaborate dresses.*) No, I don't need any. (*Shows her the dresses, opens the trunk.*) Voilà, madame. (MARY *is stunned by the beauty and obvious expense of the dresses.*) Yes, I know, they're miracles of design.

MARY: Where did you get them?

BERNARD: Oh, the museum of art, various collections. I've stolen them all. Remember when I told you that dress you're wearing was one of Edith's old ones? I was lying! This piece of trash was a practice theft. Yes, I've stolen them all. It's very easy once you conquer the inevitable stage fright. I was caught only once and succeeded in passing myself off as a harmless old eccentric. They took the dress in question, it was this one, back politely and said: Mustn't do that. I stole the same dress two weeks later wearing a false mustache and wig.

MARY: I have never seen the like . . .

BERNARD: (*Displaying another dress.*) This one is a ball gown first worn circa 1895. I stole it from the La Modeste Collection. (*Displaying another with particular pride.*) This! This one is 1898, first worn by Josephine DuPont, at her coming-out party. She was a beauty. I've seen pictures. Look how thin she was—you take this one. You shall be Josephine DuPont and I shall be your duenna, Madeleine.

MARY: My what?

BERNARD: Your teacher. I'll get into this one . . .

MARY: You gonna put that dress on you?

BERNARD: Don't worry, it'll fit, I've had it on before. I've been good since you've been here but, why not?

MARY: A big old man like you in a dress like that?

BERNARD: Come, for me, put it on. I want to see you dressed up.

MARY: Well, how?

BERNARD: Here are the bloomers, and the petticoats. First you put on the bloomers, then over them, the petticoats, then the gown. Here are stockings, and a corset, just in case. Then these earrings should do nicely, and try these rings, also this necklace . . .

MARY: Are they real?

BERNARD: Of course not, my dear. But I'm an old hand at high-class paste. I wrote some, remember?

MARY: Oh, Bernard, I don't even think I can play at what you're askin'.

BERNARD: Do it for me. (*She goes upstairs.* BERNARD *dons his dress and jewelry, all the while behaving like a grande dame who has entered a ballroom and is watching a ball in progress.*) Oh, my goodness, how full our ballroom is. (*As though to a butler.*) Jenkins, Miss Josephine will be down shortly. (*As though watching those present.*) Why, there are the Astors, and there, the Carnegies. All here for little Josie. All this grandeur for her and I can remember when she'd throw up at the drop of a pin. I'm the duenna. (*Primps himself, waltzes.*) Oh, and the intoxication of music. And the beaux, oh, the beaux. So handsome and virile, and yes, young. Not yet mowed down by the First World War.

Oh, were it only 1917 instead of 1897. I'd like to see all this male beauty mangled, blown to bits, all dead, these handsome young boys, all dead! (*Curtseys as though greeting someone who has spoken to him.*) Why, thank you, sir, but I don't dance with hypocrites. (*Fans himself, watches this imaginary interlocutor leave.*) Really! Coming and asking me to dance, just so he'd have Josie's ear through me. I'd never put in a syllable for him. I'm suspicious of that cologne. Only the most virile for Josie! (*Starts to sway to an imagined waltz.*) Oh, that music, that music. (*Calls.*) Josephine, hurry! (*Waltzing.*) I'm dancing, yes, dancing alone. What does it matter? Those young men were never for me, they ignored me and slunk away at my approach. They wilted, these young flowers, when I cast my rapacious black eyes on them. Well, so be it! Some are beauties, and some turn men to stone. (*Calls.*) Josephine, hurry! You keep them waiting too long. Necks crane in anticipation, the best-bred necks in New York are twisting themselves to see your sweeping entrance. And these mouths, these mouths sweet from having kissed and sucked the lips of the greatest beauties are all whispering: Where is she? Where is she? Josephine, it's time! Josephine! (MARY *appears at the top of the stairs, very beautiful, radiant in the dress. She stops, embarrassed and uncomfortable.* BERNARD *stares up at her, stunned by the completeness of the transformation. The* NUNS *flicker and swirl at the back of the stage, always in shadow.*) No, it can't be you. (*He is himself now, not acting Madeleine.*) You know, I didn't really think it would be so . . . total . . .

MARY: (*Whispers.*) Bernard . . . (*Starts to walk down.*)

BERNARD: No, still, still as stone . . .

MARY: (*Whispers.*) Don't make me stand here, Bernard, the prisoner of your eyes. Don't make me stand here imprisoned in this dress. You've caged me in. You've worked a spell. Stop staring at me. Every second you stare you are stealing me from me . . .

BERNARD: Wait, I'll bring you down. (*Runs up the stairs, trips on his gown, falls.*) No, don't move. Pretend I'm prostrate, laid low by your beauty. (*He rises, takes her hand, escorts her down.*) Now, curtsey. Imagine the applause, the march played by the band, the overpowering scent of the flowers, the most costly perfumes. Curtsey again, and again curtsey. The waltz! They've struck up. Magic. Sway! (*He forces her to sway to his imagined waltz.*)

MARY: (*Swaying.*) Something . . . familiar . . . dressed like this. Swaying in this hole. (*The* NUNS *are swaying also, always in shadow.*) It's as if I'm a corpse laid in earth, new buried. It's like a graveyard filled with turning worms. That's the music, that's the spinning. No! (*Stops swaying.*) Yet it is in the air, that smell, it is in the earth, and it's the eternal earth trapping us and we must dance to the humming of those worms. I've heard them humming and turning and we must dance. Dance . . . we must dance . . . (BERNARD *takes her and kisses her passionately. They sway together,* BERNARD *kissing her, running his hands over her body. The* NUNS *continue their swirling.*)

BERNARD: You are the most beautiful creature I've ever seen. More beautiful than a woman can be, a creature, a writhing, soaring, asexual creature. You are the most beautiful thing I've ever held. Don't slip away from me, Mary, don't slip away . . .

MARY: Too tight. It's too tight. Don't crush me. Oh, please, don't suck on my skin. (*Breaks away from him.*) Vampire! Vampire! Don't take what little I have. I don't want to die.

BERNARD: To die into freedom! (*Takes her roughly in his arms, rips her bodice, kisses her breasts. She struggles momentarily, then goes limp.*) You are mine, now. I can taste myself on your skin. I can smell myself in your hair. I can feel my saliva running along your body. Come with me. Truly, you are my clay, and my wanting you has brought you a new life. Come on! (*Drags her off. From the* NUNS *emerges a loud, high keening. They swirl about the stage wildly.* EDITH *wakes, shakes her head.*)

EDITH: What's that noise? Arnold, you back? That you? You makin' that bitch whimper and scream like the animal she is? (*One* NUN *makes baby noises. For a moment all make loud baby noises, particularly of crying.*) I hear a baby. Bambino. Arnold. As a baby . . . ? What's that noise? Somebody kill that kid, its mother doesn't want it. Oh, Jesus, Mary and Joseph, it's so ugly, it's always been so ugly. I see these swirlin' things . . . (*She tries to see, and listens intently. The* NUNS *whine, make distorted animal noises, pant, their swirling continues, wild and fast, their noises are loud.*) Benny? Benny? That you? You come home afta all these years? You fuckin' that hilly billy slut, hanh? Oh, I know, Benny, I know you played around, you couldn't get enough. But you must be old now, ain't you tired? Why don't you come back to me? I need you, she don' need you, she can have her choice. I ain't so awful. I don' care if you do it to her, but then, when you through, come to me, hanh? You god damn bastid, why did you desert me. Let's make up like we did in the old days. Maybe, if I work at it, I can make some pigs' feet, or some spare ribs in the gravy and we can eat and laugh and get the sauce all over each other like we usda. I remember you drippin' red sauce on me and sayin' I looked like a Red Indian. An' me sayin' it was blood. Love blood. You tongue won't rot off, if you kiss me. Talk to me at least, talk to me, I been dry for years, these tits is dry, my insides is dry, everything, everything is dry except my eyes and I can't see outta them. Benny . . . (*The* NUNS *swirl about her, almost touching her but not quite.*) That you, Benny? (*Crawls out of the kitchen. The* NUNS *seem to be leading her toward the stairs.*) You touchin' me? I'm comin' afta you. Like a game . . . (*Laughs.*) Hide and seek. I can kill a dozen roaches just by sensin' them. Touch me again, Benny. I'm comin'. Benny, I can almost see you . . . Hello, Benny, hello, how you been, hanh? Almost . . . (*On the stairs.*) I tell you what, I'll get up—yes? I'll get up, I know I can . . . I ain't walked in a long time, age you know how it is, gets to all of us, what you gonna do, la vecchaia, can't see, can't walk, old Edith, the Blindie, them roaches, I'll get up— (*With great difficulty gets up.*) I'm standin', Benny, I can come to you, I love you, I love you just like the old days, I love . . . (*Loses her balance, tries to grab onto something, can't. Falls, dies. The* NUNS *laugh and shriek, hurl themselves about the stage.*)

Blackout.

SCENE FOUR

The beach at Wildwood. The upper level represents a section of the boardwalk. The ocean is in front. There is a broken-down bench on the boardwalk.

The BOY *lounges on the boardwalk in tight shorts and shirt.* MICHAEL *and* ARNOLD *are walking up and down the boardwalk,* MICHAEL *forcing* ARNOLD *to walk arm in arm with him.* MICHAEL *is in cheerful beach drag. Eventually they sit on the bench.* MICHAEL *keeps an eye on the* BOY.

MARGE *walks by in a tight summer dress, waves at* MICHAEL. *Occasionally, she walks through the scene.* BUCKY *and* SCODGE, *very uncomfortable in tight clothes, also walk through on occasion.*

MARY *and* BERNARD *are on the lower level, which represents a section of the beach. Both are dressed in* BERNARD'*s costumes.* BERNARD *has on an old woman's beach costume from the 1890s.* MARY *is dressed in beautiful flowing white. They are sitting, facing front, on a cheerful beach blanket with a picnic basket nearby.*

It is fall and everyone is chilly in the summer attire. A month and a half have passed since the preceding scene.

The three NUNS *walk across the boardwalk. Their habits are tucked up; they wear large beach hats over their wimples. They are turning into cockroaches. They eye the* BOY *as they pass him and giggle.*

MICHAEL: (*To* ARNOLD.) Sit still, Arnie babes, I wanna watch him.

ARNOLD: Look . . .

MICHAEL: Don't say it, super sweets, just don't say it. (*Eyes the* BOY.) Look at him, he's a beauty. (*Blows* BOY *a kiss.*) We'll go to the outdoor opera in Rittenhouse Square next week. *Turandot,* it's one of my favorites. (*Croons in falsetto.*) "In questa reggia, or son mille anni e mille . . ." That's where the frozen fish, Princess Turandotty, sings of her desire to avenge her frozen but be-raped ancestress fish, Principessa Lu-Ling . . .

MARY: (*To* BERNARD.) Do you see them, Bernard?

BERNARD: Certainly. Not altogether fortunate, but it will be a test of your ability to withstand that fool who traduced you. (MICHAEL *tries to neck with* ARNOLD.)

ARNOLD: Cut that out!

MICHAEL: Why? Don' you love me?

ARNOLD: No, for Christ sake, no!

MICHAEL: That makes it more fun! (*Kisses him.*)

MARY: (*To* BERNARD.) He's with that man dressed up as a woman.

BERNARD: So it seems, though that man is very good at it.

MARY: He's not! I could tell right away.

BERNARD: (*Offers her cheese from the picnic basket.*) Brie?

MARY: Bernard! You've already eaten a whole one.

BERNARD: I no longer worry about my weight, thank goodness. (ARNOLD *has risen from the bench and paces.*)

MICHAEL: Stop pacin', Arnie princess, you're callin' attention to us.

ARNOLD: *I'm* calling attention to us, Jesus Christ, *I'm* calling attention . . .

MICHAEL: Whatsa matter, Arnie hom?

ARNOLD: She's here wit that old man.

MICHAEL: I seen them. He's weird. I mean, I like his style, but he's sloppy. He looks like a fat teddy bear in somethin' frilly.

ARNOLD: Let's go, hanh? I know she's seen me. Let's go!

MICHAEL: But why, Arnie hon, you don' love her?

ARNOLD: That ain't the point, God damn it!

MICHAEL: What is the point?

ARNOLD: Don' look right for my wife to see me here wit you!

MICHAEL: So who's lookin'?

Boardwalk scene in the Berkeley Stage Co. production.

ARNOLD: Jesus! (*A man walks on and past the* BOY. *This "man" is obviously one of the* NUNS. *The* NUN, *however, has tucked her habit up and wears a fedora and a fake beard and smokes a cigar. The* NUN *stops and eyes the* BOY, *then starts a conversation. To* MICHAEL.) It's one of them nuns.

MICHAEL: So? They got needs too. So long as they pay . . . (BOY *and* NUN *go off in the same direction as the other* NUNS.)

BERNARD: (*To a nervous* MARY.) Be still.

ARNOLD: Shit! Shit! I got nothin', I got nobody, Aunt Edith . . .

MICHAEL: I showed her respect. All the flowers I sent, I had every male hustler on Market Street send her a rose. But I've been thinkin', I need a house, a place to ply my trade so to speak. Your house would do fine, we just gotta get rid of the old queen and the young fish . . .

ARNOLD: My aunt's house!

MICHAEL: Sweetheart, your aunt's house is Holy Cross Graveyard now. I need to diversify my activity, wit you and that kid, Marge, and now Bucky and Scodge, I'm gonna need a nerve center.

ARNOLD: I gotta get away, you're killin' me!

MICHAEL: I'm feedin' you, I'm puttin' you up, I'm givin' you pocket change, who else is gonna do that, hanh? I'm your whole world!

ARNOLD: Mary! Mary! (*Runs down to* MARY.) You gotta help me. You're all I got. He don' mean nothin' to me.

MICHAEL: (*On the edge of the boardwalk; sings in ugly falsetto.*) "In questa reggia or son mille anni e mille, un grido disperato risonno . . . (*Continues singing under the scene.*)

BERNARD: (*To* MARY, *ignoring* ARNOLD.) Josephine, I hope you like the cheese . . .

MARY: (*Ignoring* ARNOLD.) I do, Madeleine . . .

ARNOLD: (*To* MARY.) Ain't you gonna answer me?

BERNARD: It's cold for early fall, Josephine, and here on the beach the wind has an icy edge.

MARY: The wind is icy, Madeleine, as though it wasn't fall at all.

BERNARD: As though it weren't fall; subjunctive, too . . .

ARNOLD: (*To* MARY.) Aw, come on, Mary, come on. I know you're angry at me and you got every right. I ain't denyin' that. I'm a pig. You can hit me, if you like, right here in the kisser. I know I did wrong. I'll tell you what, you help me now and we'll try again. When I get myself set up somewheres away from here, we'll try again, we'll have kids, you can go to school . . .

BERNARD: Tangerine, Josephine?

MARY: Better a peach, Madeleine.

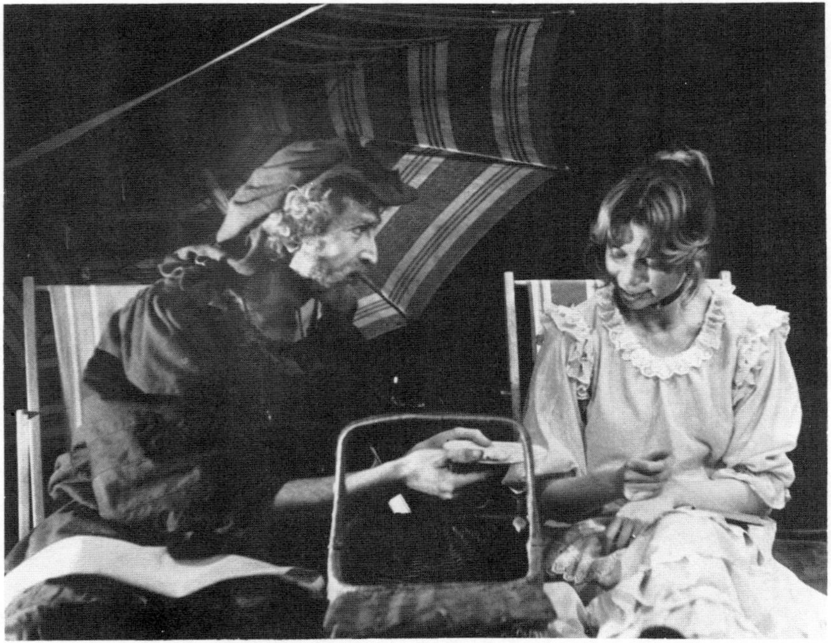

Drew Eshleman (BERNARD) and Judith Weston (MARY) in the beach scene in the Berkeley Stage Co. production.

BERNARD: It's too late for peaches.

ARNOLD: All right, Mary, all right. I got confused. I shouldn't have married you. I wasn't ready to get married. But you trapped me, you know, you chained me up. Maybe I played along wit you a little, but hell, that's what guys do wit broads and the other broads don' take it so serious . . . oh, please, God, I don' know what I'm sayin'. Look, my nose. (*Takes her hand, forces her to feel his nose.*) You remember? You said: I'm sorry, I didn't mean to touch it, I ain't never been this close to a nose like that. That's what you said. And you looked at my chest, you took a hair, remember? You said I had a boy's body. But I was a boy, don' you understand? Why won't you help me, for old times' sake. I did the best I could, wasn't good I know but—you see, he trapped me, I gotta get out. Do you have some . . . well, you know . . . that I could . . . well . . . you know . . . borrow . . . I gotta run, understand me, I need, I need, please, I need . . . (*A silence.*)

MICHAEL: (*Finishes his aria in grand style.*) Brava, brava! She don't know who you are, sugarwafer. She's in a different century. I'm bored wit this game, we both got work to do.

ARNOLD: Mary? (*Watching her, he backs up slowly to the edge of the boardwalk.* MICHAEL *grabs him, pulls him off stage.*)

BERNARD: (*Kisses* MARY.) Brava, brava! You were wonderful. It brought a tear to my eye. You were the very picture of a beauty scorned. Henry James would have loved you. (*Rumbles in a Jamesian manner.*) And she sat there, beached as it were, bleached by the merciless sun, her face, hard as stone, white as the sand shifting listlessly about her . . .

MARY: Shut up, Bernard!

BERNARD: Well, naturally, you're upset. What you did isn't easy.

MARY: Do you think it's hard to be cruel?

BERNARD: Melodramatic stuff. How grand you were, how like a queen . . .

MARY: You're the queen, Bernard, not me . . .

BERNARD: You dropped the cheese. It's all sandy and that's the last of the brie. Let's read the Hopkins. (*Finds the right page in a book, reads.*)

> I wake and feel the fell of dark, not day.
> What hours, O what black hours we have spent
> This night! what sights you, heart, saw; ways you went!
> And more must, in yet longer light's delay.

What does that mean to you, Josephine?

MARY: It means that everything is one long night and an endless nightmare, maybe God's nightmare. That waking I am twisted, and dreaming I am twisted more. It means there is no end and every cry for help just echoes back, distorted. You know, Bernard, there was a time when I went to sleep and felt my spirit crawl out of my skin and fly. You'll call me silly. Then I'd wake up and feel trapped. And now I don't even dream freedom.

BERNARD: Well, that's a reasonable paraphrase of those lines. Now for this: (*Reads.*)

> I am gall, I am heartburn. God's most deep decree
> Bitter would have me taste . . .

MARY: I want to stop now, Bernard, I want to stop. And I want to go back to the city. I want to change these clothes, they aren't mine. No, don't say anything. No man ever pleaded with me like that, you know? Not even to get into me. I was pretty but I didn't have enough to give. And some instinct, some male instinct sensed that and went elsewhere. Only Arnold, a half man, couldn't sense it and stayed to play along with me, then to plead with me. And the worst part of it is I was part of his deception. I played maiden in distress by a stream, and I got him to play rescuing prince; and it ended on this beach, cold in the fall with that heaving, indifferent ocean out there, indifferent like the earth . . . so I knew all along how false it was, I played too. What right do I have to act like a beauty scorned?

BERNARD: Josephine!

MARY: Mary is me. I'm not a rag doll you can dress up!

BERNARD: But what's happened to you? We were happy!

MARY: You were happy. You are not a teacher, just a girl man who plays dress up.

BERNARD: Oh, stop it, please. You are all I want, dear Mary, immortal beloved. You are my Diana, my Artemis. I know today has been a strain on you, the long bus ride, this cold beach, a picnic in the fall, it was an idiot's idea, my fault, and then, that cretin, Arnold . . . (*Embraces her.*)

MARY: Get away! (*Pushes him away.*)

BERNARD: Oh, but I loved you, don't you realize? I'm not comely, I know that, I'm somewhat overweight, I'm perhaps, well, slightly, all right, I'll be honest, very much past my best. But it's been more than a month, every night in your arms, I can't imagine . . . No, no, a mood; Moira had them too, it will pass. Monsoons pass, tidal waves pass, earthquakes are forgotten, volcanic eruptions become legend, thus will it be with my Mary's moods. Now, kiss me, hold me, my Mary, eternally soft, infinitely sweet, return to me. I won't fail you again. That's it, isn't it. It's because I failed you last night . . .

MARY: It's because of all the nights you didn't fail. What do you think it was like lying under you and having your whale's carcass heaving over me? There's nothing in Jung about that. All that sweat! And your seventy-year-old breath! Where does that occur in Freud?

BERNARD: You are condemning yourself to ignorance, you stupid, Southern . . . No, I didn't mean that. You are my pupil. I can teach you . . .

MARY: How to fake an orgasm? From my father to Arnold to you; one trap to the next, all sucking on me, like I was some dangerous candy to lick then lock up for tomorrow!

BERNARD: Don't leave me!

MARY: I want to go back to Philadelphia alone. Give me the money! (BERNARD *fumbles in his purse, crying.*)

BERNARD: I will die, don't you understand? (*She takes the money.*) I'm so old. I won't live long. How much longer, a few years? Stay with me until then, you'll still be young. And, Mary, listen, when I die there is money. Edith's husband, when he left, hid money in the house. I found it. He was killed by the Mafia. It isn't all that much but I've been keeping it, living poor, hoping to use it if ever I got sick or when I'm certain I'm about to die. I still hoped for royalties, a benefactor, I'm a stupid optimist, but there's money, under the first drawer in the desk, the wood is loose, in there. You can have it. I'll will it to you if you stay with me, or we can spend it now . . .

MARY: I'll never touch you again, never kiss or smell you again. It's finished. Goodbye! (*Runs off.*)

BERNARD: Mary! (*Calls.*) Ellen Mac Jones, Ellen Mac Jones! What? What? Alone! Not after all those nights of love. Oh, I knew I'd be punished for using that word. I'll chase after her. (*Makes to leave the stage, stops.*) Ugly, she said? Rotten breath? (*Breathes into his palm.*) That's not rotten, it smells like brie. My teeth are in good shape. See? I can grind them. (*Grinds teeth.*) I inherited that from my father. When he took me to the dentist, the dentist after examining me complimented my teeth, he said I had successful teeth, I'd be the factory manager or the construction boss, never merely a worker . . . Is all hope gone? Into the sea with me! (*Rushes downstage as though toward the ocean.*) No! I am not

Virginia Woolf. I shall survive! Ellen Mac Jones! Ellen Mac Jones! Here, Ellen! Oh, Mary, and she smelled so good. (*Calling off.*) I hope the bus crashes with you in it! No, I don't mean that. (*Looks down.*) Oh, a good omen. She didn't ruin it for me. That wasn't the last of the brie. (*Takes a bite of the brie, starts folding the blanket sadly. The* NUNS *cross the boardwalk carrying the* BOY *bound like an animal to a pole.*)

Blackout.

SCENE FIVE

The row house. MARY, *in regular clothes, comes down the stairs with a small suitcase. She goes to the desk, opens the drawer and removes the money. She runs out.*

The three NUNS *enter on the upper level. With them* ARNOLD, *hands bound behind him. Very slowly, they bind him to a chair as they did in Act One.* ARNOLD *wears a look of utter defeat.*

BERNARD *runs in carrying a picnic basket, bonnet askew.*

BERNARD: (*Calling.*) Mary! Mary! (*Races upstairs, returns caressing the dress* MARY *wore on the beach. He comes down stairs, collapses in grief.*) Gone! (*He weeps into the dress.* MICHAEL, SCODGE, BUCKY, MARGE *and the* BOY *materialize very slowly out of the shadows.* MICHAEL *stares at* BERNARD, *then goes upstairs to assure himself the house is empty.* SCODGE *goes through the desk,* MARGE *goes through the kitchen, the* BOY *stares at* BERNARD, BUCKY *stands by the street exit as though on guard.*)

ARNOLD: (*With the* NUNS; *the others do not see him.*) Yes, I'm guilty, guilty of everything. Always guilty, eternally guilty, uniformly guilty. (*The* NUNS *swarm over him like cockroaches.* MICHAEL *returns.*)

MICHAEL: This should do very well. Yes, we'll overhaul it, deck the girls out in his dresses. Whataya think, Marge?

MARGE: Sounds cool a me, Michael.

ARNOLD: Guilty, I am guilty, Arnold Longese, black hair guilty, brown eyes guilty . . .

MICHAEL: (*To* BERNARD.) Hey you! Get out! You hear me?

ARNOLD: (*With the* NUNS.) Male, guilty, female, guilty, long nose, guilty, dusky skin, guilty, well built, guilty . . . (*The* NUNS *swarm over him.*)

MICHAEL: (*More threatening, to* BERNARD.) Get out or die, it's one and the same to me.

ARNOLD: (*With* NUNS.) About five-nine, guilty, big feet, guilty, stupid, guilty, big hands, guilty . . .

BERNARD: (*Pulls himself together.*) No, no. Let me change. I'll leave . . . (*Very sadly, goes upstairs to change.*)

ARNOLD: (*With* NUNS.) . . . queer, guilty, formerly strong, guilty, formerly promising, guilty, now wasted, guilty, too much a dreamer, guilty, wop, guilty, greasy, guilty, not very hairy, guilty, scar on right thigh, guilty, scar on left palm, guilty, circular birth mark on right shoulder, guilty, second toe longer than big toe, guilty, unmanly, guilty, weak, guilty, a faggot, guilty, non-sexual, guilty, worthless, guilty, unfeeling, guilty, a braggart, guilty, a phoney, guilty, stubborn, guilty, and guiltless, guilty, guilty, guilty! (*With a wild cry the* NUNS *swarm over him covering him completely with their black habits, wimples, and black-gloved, claw-like hands.* BERNARD *comes down stairs, having changed. He is in a very old-fashioned, slightly too small suit. He carries a worn small suitcase. He goes to the desk, opens drawers.* MICHAEL *stops him, angry.*)

BERNARD: I won't give up. I want my manuscripts. I've still a novel or two in me, maybe a book of reflections . . . (*Takes his manuscripts, put them in a valise.*) And Mary . . . out there, if I hurry perhaps, no, certainly, I can find her.

MICHAEL: (*Throws some money at* BERNARD.) Car fare.

BERNARD: (*Hesitates but takes it.*) Thank you, young man.

MICHAEL: Don't mention it, Turandot.

BERNARD: That's right, once, long ago, you referred to me in the streets as Turandot. Do you like that opera? I saw Eva Turner sing it with Martinelli in London many years ago. It's an exciting opera when well sung but not one of my favorites. You can keep the dresses. I have my favorite in here. (*Lifts suitcase.*) They're worth thousands, perhaps hundreds of thousands. I've stolen them all from famous collections. The jewels you'll find are paste, that means fake. (*Nears the door, turns, surveys the house.*) Thus I leave all this behind. This house, poor dear dead Ellen Mac Jones Aberdeen, she had a long life, fifteen, I think. I wonder if I shall like the Salvation Army. I shall go there first, then Goodwill Missions, then a hospital. I'll fake a complaint, how skeptical can they be? A man off the street at my age with a dress in his suitcase. The least I'd get would be a month in the mental ward. So long as they have a library it won't be so bad. Who knows? Perhaps they'd have *King Lear and the Norns* in their library—I wrote that, you know. In any case, farewell, Sweet South Philadelphia.

MARGE: Poor old man, why don' you let him stay, hanh, Michael? He could dress up for the clients, add some class . . .

BERNARD: No, no, my good woman, that is very kind of you. But I'll be off. An artist it seems must steel himself, or herself, as the case may be, to be alone if necessary. I only became an artist a few years ago. Before that I was a failure. You may not think there is a difference, but there is, a small one . . . (*Leaves the house.*)

MICHAEL: All right, let's get busy . . .

MARGE, *the* BOY, BUCKY, SCODGE *set about sweeping, rearranging the house, dragging on furniture, etc.*

The NUNS *leave* ARNOLD. *He is a mass of sores, his eyes gouged out. The* NUNS, *shrieking, leap through the house.*

BLACKOUT